LIFESTYLE MOBILITIES

Current Developments in the Geographies of Leisure and Tourism

Series Editors:

Jan Mosedale, University of Applied Sciences HTW Chur, Switzerland and **Caroline Scarles**, University of Surrey, UK and on behalf of the Geographies of Leisure and Tourism Research Group of the Royal Geographical Society (with the Institute of British Geographers)

Tourism and leisure exist within an inherently dynamic, fluid and complex world and are therefore inherently interdisciplinary. Recognising the role of tourism and leisure in advancing debates within the social sciences, this book series, is open to contributions from cognate social science disciplines that inform geographical thought about tourism and leisure. Produced in association with the Geographies of Leisure and Tourism Research Group of the Royal Geographical Society (with the Institute of British Geographers), this series highlights and promotes cutting-edge developments and research in this field. Contributions are of a high international standard and provide theoretically-informed empirical content to facilitate the development of new research agendas in the field of tourism and leisure research. In general, the series seeks to promote academic contributions that advance contemporary debates that challenge and stimulate further discussion and research both within the fields of tourism and leisure and the wider realms of the social sciences.

Other titles in the series:

Narratives of Travel and Tourism
Edited by Jacqueline Tivers and Tijana Rakić

Travel, Tourism and Art
Edited by Tijana Rakić and Jo-Anne Lester

Mediating the Tourist Experience
From Brochures to Virtual Encounters
Edited by Jo-Anne Lester and Caroline Scarles

Lifestyle Mobilities
Intersections of Travel, Leisure and Migration

Edited by

TARA DUNCAN
University of Otago, New Zealand

SCOTT A. COHEN
University of Surrey, UK

MARIA THULEMARK
Dalarna University, Sweden

Routledge
Taylor & Francis Group
LONDON AND NEW YORK

First published 2013 by Ashgate Publishing

Published 2016 by Routledge
2 Park Square, Milton Park, Abingdon, Oxfordshire OX14 4RN
711 Third Avenue, New York, NY 10017, USA

First issued in paperback 2016

Routledge is an imprint of the Taylor & Francis Group, an informa business

British Library Cataloguing in Publication Data
A catalogue record for this book is available from the British Library

The Library of Congress has cataloged the printed edition as follows:
Lifestyle mobilities: intersections of travel, leisure and migration / by Tara Duncan, Scott A. Cohen and Maria Thulemark [editors]
    pages cm
 Includes bibliographical references and index.
 ISBN 978-1-4094-5371-0 (hardback)
1. Tourism. 2. Leisure. 3. Migation, Internal. 4. Social mobility.
I. Duncan, Tara.
 G155.A1.L535 2013
 306.4'819—dc23

2013011976

ISBN 13: 978-1-138-24915-8 (pbk)
ISBN 13: 978-1-4094-5371-0 (hbk)

Contents

SECTION III   MOORINGS, MOBILITIES AND BELONGING

SECTION IV   COMPLEXITIES OF WIDER IDENTITIES

List of Figures

Notes on Contributors

Jon Anderson is a Senior Lecturer in Human Geography at the School of Planning and Geography, Cardiff University. His research interests focus on the relations between identity, culture and place, in particular the actions, practices and politics that such relations produce. He has published widely in these areas, most notably the book *Understanding Cultural Geography: Places and Traces* (2010) and *Water Worlds: Human Geographies of the Ocean* (2014, with Kimberley Peters).

Stewart Barr is Associate Professor of Geography at the University of Exeter. Stewart obtained his PhD from the University of Exeter in 2001, which focused on the attitudes and practices of householders towards sustainable waste management. After a period as a Research Fellow working on an ESRC-funded project entitled 'Environmental Action in and Around the Home' he was appointed to a Lectureship in Geography at Exeter in 2003, promoted to Senior Lecturer in 2008 and since 2012 has been Associate Professor of Geography. His current research focuses on individual 'pro-environmental' practices, particularly within the context of transport and mobility. He has recently completed a number of projects that have explored the role of climate change in framing attitudes and practices towards mobility in everyday and tourism contexts. This has raised both intellectual and pragmatic questions concerning the ways in which academics and policy makers frame and promote sustainable forms of mobility across different sites of practice.

Claudia Bell is Senior Lecturer in Sociology at the University of Auckland. She teaches in the areas of national identity and international tourism. Her published books and articles comprise work on a wide range of issues, including landscape tourism, mobilities, nation branding, small town promotion, world expos, vernacular culture, contemporary New Zealand art and artists, and global travel. Her current research is on residential tourists in Bali; international people of retirement age seeking paradise in a foreign location.

Scott A. Cohen is a Senior Lecturer in the School of Hospitality and Tourism Management and Director of Postgraduate Research Programmes for the Faculty of Business, Economics and Law at the University of Surrey, UK. Scott was a lifestyle traveller for six years before completing his PhD in the Department of Tourism at the University of Otago, New Zealand. His research interests are in lifestyle, identities, mobilities and consumer experiences across tourism and leisure contexts. He also researches the intersections between climate change and consumer behaviour, particularly tourist behavioural adaptation to climate change.

Tara Duncan is a Lecturer in the Department of Tourism at the University of Otago, New Zealand. Tara spent three years living and working in Whistler, British Columbia, Canada before completing her PhD in the Department of Geography at University College London (UCL). Her research interests focus on lifestyle mobilities, the complexities of young budget travel and, more recently, academic mobility, specifically framed within the climate change, transport and mobilities literature.

Jessica Dunkin is a Social Sciences and Humanities Research Council (SSHRC) Postdoctoral Fellow in the School of Kinesiology and Health Studies at Queen's University, Canada. The American Canoe Association encampments discussed in Chapter 11 of this volume were the focus of Jessica's doctoral dissertation, entitled 'Canoes and Canvas: The Social and Spatial Politics of Sport/Leisure in Late Nineteenth-Century North America', which she completed in the Department of History at Carleton University. Her current research explores working women's physical activity in late nineteenth-century Canada.

Kathryn Erskine is a PhD student in Human Geography at Cardiff University. Her research interests include identity, place formation and global travel and backpacking, with a specific focus on the practices and mobilities of the lifestyle traveller.

Bryan S.R. Grimwood is an Assistant Professor in the Department of Recreation and Leisure Studies at the University of Waterloo, Canada. His research explores nature–society relationships in contexts of leisure/tourism, learning and livelihoods and is informed by principles of community-based participatory research, qualitative inquiry and geographical notions of nature, ethics and mobility. The Thelon River research discussed in Chapter 11 was carried out during Bryan's doctoral studies in the Department of Geography and Environmental Studies at Carleton University, Canada, and was supported by the Social Sciences and Humanities Research Council (SSHRC) of Canada.

Katherine King is a Lecturer in Leisure Studies at Bournemouth University, UK. Her PhD explored the role of countryside spaces in the identity and lifestyles of youth mountain bikers. Her research interests include the geographies of sport and leisure, rural geographies, and youth identities and lifestyles.

Barbara A. Koth is Senior Lecturer with the School of Natural and Built Environments, University of South Australia, in Adelaide. Her research focus is in nature-based tourism and community development, behaviour change and sustainability (transport mobility, food waste, e-waste), and low-footprint tertiary education. In addition, she teaches in the areas of public engagement, sustainable development and park management. Prior to entering academia, Barbara was in the international development sector for 18 years in various positions with the World Bank (Tanzania), USAID (Ghana) and consulting firms. She is a sailor.

Garth Lean is a researcher and teacher in the School of Social Sciences and Psychology at the University of Western Sydney. He holds an interdisciplinary PhD in travel/tourism. His research interests include: travel, tourism, mobile identities, imagination, transformation, cultural heritage, visual methods, online research, the alternative presentation of travel and tourism research, multicultural education and carbon governance. He has published a variety of papers on travel, along with the edited volumes *Travel and Imagination* (Ashgate) and *Travel and Transformation* (Ashgate) with Russell Staiff and Emma Waterton. He is currently developing an edited volume titled *The Poetics of Travel* (Berghahn Books) with Russell Staiff and Emma Waterton, and the sole-authored book *Transformative Travel* (CABI). He is a member of the Geographies of Leisure and Tourism Research Group with the Royal Geographical Society.

Leslie Mabon is a post-doctoral researcher in the School of GeoSciences at the University of Edinburgh, UK. His research looks at the role mobilities play in shaping environmental values, and his doctoral work focused in particular on rally drivers in Scotland and how the rallying 'lifestyle' informs their views of environmental issues.

Norman McIntyre is Professor Emeritus at Lakehead University, Ontario, Canada. During his academic career Dr McIntyre has taught and researched in Australia, New Zealand, Europe and North America with a particular focus on multiple dwelling and tourism. Recently, his research has explored the role of tourism and amenity/lifestyle migration in rural communities in North America and more particularly along the north coast of Lake Superior in north-western Ontario, Canada.

Elia Ntaousani is a PhD candidate in humanities and cultural studies and an Associate Tutor on the BA in Arts and Humanities at Birkbeck, University of London. Born in Greece, she has also lived in France, Germany and the UK. Elia has a background in architecture and holds MA and MRes degrees in philosophy of culture, contemporary critique and cultural praxis. She was Programme Manager at the London Consortium – a collaboration between Birkbeck College, Architectural Association, Institute of Contemporary Arts, Science Museum and TATE. She had previously worked for the AHRC Artists' Moving Image Research Network as well as for the Group of Study and Research on Globalisations (GERM, Paris). Elia has co-edited *Paris – Der Architekturführer* (Berlin: Braun, 2009) with Chris van Uffelen and is now co-convener of the Mediterranean Mobilities Network. Part of her doctoral research has been recently published in the edited volume *Landscapes of (Un)belonging: Reflections on Strangeness and Self* from Inter-Disciplinary Press.

Michael O'Regan worked alongside the National Tourism Development Authority of Ireland before joining Gulliver – Ireland's Information and Reservation Service after completing his Masters at the University of Limerick. He then joined Wicklow County Tourism, Ireland as Marketing Executive in 1997 before starting a PhD programme at the School of Sport and Service Management, University of Brighton, UK which he completed in 2011. After two years as Assistant Professor at Dongbei University of Finance and Economics (DUFE), Dalian, China at its Global Institute of Management and Economics – Surrey International Institute, he is now Assistant Professor at the Institute for Tourism Studies, Macao. His research is focused on tourist, urban, historic, future, alternative, lifestyle, slow and cultural mobilities.

Jan Prillwitz is an independent travel behaviour researcher. His main research interests are in sustainable travel, mobility styles and determinants for individual travel decisions. From 2010 to 2012, Jan was an Assistant Professor at the Department of Human Geography and Planning, Utrecht University (The Netherlands). Previously, he has worked at the School of Geography, University of Exeter (UK) in a project exploring motives and barriers for adopting sustainable travel behaviour. Jan holds a PhD from the University of Leipzig (Germany); his PhD project at the Helmholtz-Centre for Environmental Research (UFZ) in Leipzig focused on interrelations between life course events and travel behaviour changes.

Jillian M. Rickly-Boyd is Visiting Assistant Professor in the Department of Geography at Indiana University. Her tourism research interests include landscape studies, the role of authenticity and alienation in travel motivation and experience, and the intersections of travel experience and identity politics.

Eleni Sideri holds a PhD in Social Anthropology from the School of Oriental and African Studies, University of London. Her research focused on the memories and practices of diaspora among the Greek-speaking communities of Georgia (South Caucasus). Currently, she teaches at the International Hellenic University, Thessaloniki, Greece. She also holds a post-doctoral fellowship at the University of Thessaly in the Department of History, Archaeology and Social Anthropology as part of the DEMUCIV project, a Research program funded by the Greek Ministry of Education and the European Union concerning the development of interactive content for the Museum of the City of Volos in central Greece.

Maria Thulemark is a PhD candidate at the School of Technology and Business Studies at Dalarna University, Sweden. Maria is currently working on her PhD thesis which focuses on the importance of tourism in rural development with a special interest in in-migration and tourism employment. Maria's research is based on both quantitative and qualitative methods including micro data analysis, in depth and focus group interviews. Maria's broader research interest lies within the field of regional development, tourism, mobility, lifestyle choices and migration.

Rodanthi Tzanelli is a Lecturer in Sociology at the University of Leeds and a member of the International Advisory Board for the Ikarian Center for Social and Political Research, Greece. She has published widely on issues of cosmopolitanism and globalization with an emphasis on identity, representations, new and old media and culture industries. She is author of six books, including *Cosmopolitan Memory in Europe's 'Backwaters': Rethinking Civility* (2011) and *Heritage in the Digital Era: Cinematic Tourism and the Activist Cause* (2013). Rodanthi is currently working on intersections of fast and slow mobilities.

Phillip Vannini is Canada Research Chair in Innovative Learning and Public Ethnography and Professor in the School of Communication & Culture at Royal Roads University in Victoria, BC, Canada. He is author/editor of nine books including *Ferry Tales: Mobility, Place, and Time on Canada's West Coast* (Routledge, 2011), *The Cultures of Alternative Mobilities: Routes Less Travelled* (Ashgate, 2009) and *Mobility and Communication Technologies in the Americas* (Peter Lang, 2011), as well as articles published in journals such as *Mobilities, Environment & Planning D, Cultural Geographies, Social and Cultural Geography* and the *Journal of Transport Geography*.

Chapter 1
Introducing Lifestyle Mobilities

Scott A. Cohen, Tara Duncan and Maria Thulemark

Introduction

Although mobility is far from a new idea (Cresswell 2010), the notion of a mobilities 'paradigm' (Sheller and Urry 2006) or 'turn' (Hannam, Sheller and Urry 2006) has gained significant traction in recent years within the social sciences. Increasingly, mobility is influenced by and through transnational ties, shifting socio-cultural outlooks and emerging technologies of communication, transport and social connectivity, all of which characterize the configuration and reconfiguration of the everyday. While these technological, societal and cultural changes continue to facilitate virtual and imaginative mobilities, physical, that is embodied movement (i.e. travel), also continues to increase. As Urry (2002: 256) emphasizes, '"being on the move" has become a "way of life" for many'.

At the same time, ideas of 'lifestyle' have also seen resurgence within the social sciences. Physical mobility has become central to many lifestyle choices as individuals use mobility options to negotiate the growing complexity of modern living (McIntyre 2006). Our lifestyles and our mobilities are more dynamic and complex than at any point in the past. Travel and mobility have become increasingly everyday practice (Edensor 2007, Hannam 2008) for many in developed countries and elites in developing countries (Hall 2005).

In this book we illustrate how the mobilities paradigm and lifestyle intersect. We engage an interdisciplinary approach to highlight mobility as an on-going lifestyle choice and we proffer the term 'lifestyle mobilities' as a theoretical lens to challenge current thinking on the intersections between travel, leisure and migration (see also Cohen, Duncan and Thulemark 2013). Our aim in this edited book is to contribute to mobilities studies by showing how voluntary on-going mobile lifestyles: 1) blur the boundaries between travel, leisure and migration; 2) are exemplary of how a binary divide between work and leisure may be destabilized; and 3) illustrate complexities of belonging, place and identity associated with sustained mobility. This analysis is important not only for foregrounding patterns of lifestyle mobility positioned at the borders of travel, leisure and migration, but also for demonstrating how these mobility choices contribute to, and are emblematic of, continuing processes of de-differentiation in contemporary social life (Bauman 2000).

In this introductory chapter, we begin by exploring the concept of lifestyle in relation to mobility, before turning to an examination of how travel, leisure and migration blur. Our analysis forms the basis for a conceptualization of lifestyle mobilities in comparison to temporary mobility and permanent migration. From here we turn to complexities of belonging, place and identity, and hence problems in distinguishing between 'home' and 'away', that are associated with lifestyle mobility. We conclude this chapter by outlining the thematic sections of the book and the individual chapter contributions contained therein.

Lifestyle choices and mobility

Definitions of lifestyle have often concentrated on identifying lifestyles through patterns of everyday tangible behaviour. Sobel (1981: 3) defined lifestyle as 'any distinctive, and therefore recognisable, mode of living' whilst Stebbins (1997) advocated that lifestyles encompass related sets of values and attitudes in addition to shared patterns of behaviour. Therefore, lifestyles can be seen to encompass on-going tangible practices and orientations constituting 'the basis for a separate, common social identity' (Stebbins 1997: 350). Thus lifestyle practices offer a distinctive sense of personal identity on the one hand, and a distinct and recognizable collective identity on the other (Cohen 2011).

The term 'lifestyle' is connected to the shifts identified with post-Fordism and post-modernism/late modernity (Giddens 1991). Identities became less based on class (Bell and Hollows 2006) and logics of production and instead were increasingly created through aesthetic consumption practices (Shields 1992). Thus consumption practices were designed together into lifestyles (Featherstone 1987) and lifestyle consumption practices became 'decisions not only about how to act but who to be' (Giddens 1991: 81).

How we choose our lifestyle has become progressively more important even as we recognize that the significance of lifestyle to a sense of identity has a longer history (Bell and Hollows 2006). Whether we are encouraged to 'play' with consumption to construct a sense of identity (Poster 1998) or make a 'project of the self' (Giddens 1991), what is inferred is that our choice of lifestyle affects our sense of self and that our sense of self affects our (mobility) consumption choices. As such, the emphasis is now on change, choice and reflexivity in and through lifestyle choices.

Yet freedom of choice is limited in that 'forces, mechanisms and institutional arrangements' limit our ability to choose (Warde and Martens 1998: 129) and so restrict our access to lifestyle choices. As Skeggs (2004: 49) argues, pursuing an individualized lifestyle 'exists for a privileged few', and Bourdieu (1984) notes when discussing class – 'some' are evidently more equal than 'others' in the decisions and freedom to make choices. Likewise, privileged citizens often see mobility as part of the everyday. Mobility is both familiar and, to some extent, taken for granted. Mobility depends on access to economic conditions, power, technology and networks that facilitate movement across borders and cultures (Cresswell 2001, 2010).

Lifestyles can be seen as mostly fashioned through the consumption of sets of goods and services as a source of meaning or identity in everyday life (Chaney 1996, Shields 1992), and, by some, are taken 'more seriously than their careers' (Binkley 2004: 72). Therefore, a particular 'assemblage of goods, clothes, practices, experiences, appearance and bodily dispositions' come together into a lifestyle (Featherstone 1987: 59), and as we suggest, can be uniquely distinguished by elements of corporeal mobility. Consequently, as corporeal mobility has become more commonplace (Urry 2002) and lifestyles have become pivotal in the constitution of self-identity (Giddens 1991), lifestyle choices and forms of mobility increasingly co-mingle in ways that can be crucial to the lives of those who are privileged enough to access them. For such individuals, lifestyle mobilities are performed as embodied everyday practice. This includes the inherent ambiguities, complexities and meanings of these movements and moorings. Thus, despite reflecting elements of travel, leisure, migration, tourism and work, such corporeal mobility, as we now discuss, is not captured by any one of these often bounded terms.

Blurring travel, leisure and migration

We argue here two main points. Firstly, Coles, Duval and Hall (2004) suggest that tourism geography's utilization of temporary mobility has provided an important point of intersection – between tourism and geography – that allowed for a broader approach to understanding the meaning behind a range of corporeal mobilities. Particularly, Hall (2005) uses time, space and distance to demonstrate how the movement of tourists throughout their life courses can blur the boundaries with other forms of temporary mobility, including migration, travel for work, return migration and diaspora. For instance, Cohen's (2011) lifestyle travellers exemplify how tourism can 'tip' into an on-going lifestyle, wherein extended episodes of tourism, or temporary mobility, blur into conceptions of geographic migration. We contend that this distinction separating tourism and migration is better grasped through a lens of lifestyle mobilities.

Secondly, Bell and Ward (2000) endeavour a comparison of temporary mobility with permanent migration, defining temporary mobility as a non-permanent move of varying duration (which assumes a circular return to a usual residence) and permanent migration as a permanent change of usual residence. We suggest that this division is too simplistic. Even factoring in Bell and Ward's (2000) further dimensions of duration, frequency and seasonality, there lacks an acknowledgement of the range of mobilities associated with both temporary and more permanent moves (see McIntyre, this volume).

Instead we expand their comparison (see Figure 1.1, Cohen et al. 2013). Alongside the questions of usual residence and return we have added the concept of belonging, and a fourth dimension of temporality. Figure 1.1 therefore illustrates, when compared to temporary mobility and permanent migration, how our conceptualization of lifestyle mobility, defined here as on-going semi-permanent moves of varying duration, offers a lens into more complex forms of corporeal mobility that may involve multiple 'homes', 'belongings' and sustained mobility throughout the life course.

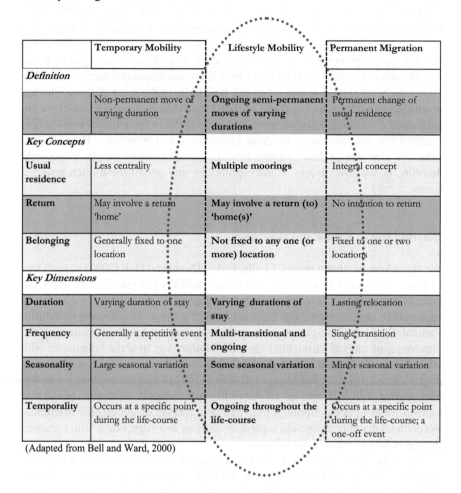

	Temporary Mobility	Lifestyle Mobility	Permanent Migration
Definition			
	Non-permanent move of varying duration	**Ongoing semi-permanent moves of varying durations**	Permanent change of usual residence
Key Concepts			
Usual residence	Less centrality	**Multiple moorings**	Integral concept
Return	May involve a return 'home'	**May involve a return (to) 'home(s)'**	No intention to return
Belonging	Generally fixed to one location	**Not fixed to any one (or more) location**	Fixed to one or two locations
Key Dimensions			
Duration	Varying duration of stay	**Varying durations of stay**	Lasting relocation
Frequency	Generally a repetitive event	**Multi-transitional and ongoing**	Single transition
Seasonality	Large seasonal variation	**Some seasonal variation**	Minor seasonal variation
Temporality	Occurs at a specific point during the life-course	**Ongoing throughout the life-course**	Occurs at a specific point during the life-course; a one-off event

(Adapted from Bell and Ward, 2000)

Figure 1.1   Comparison of lifestyle mobility to temporary mobility and permanent migration

Source: Cohen et al. 2013 (adapted from Bell and Ward 2000).

We argue that lifestyle mobility differs from temporary mobility in that it is sustained as an on-going fluid process, carrying on as everyday practice over time. The higher significance placed on physical mobility itself as a defining aspect of one's identity, is another aspect that differentiates lifestyle mobility from temporary mobility. This identification with mobility contrasts to both temporary mobility and permanent migration, as the performance of identity in these latter two has closer links to place, whether one's old or new residence.

Unlike permanent migration, lifestyle mobility does not pre-suppose that there is no intention to return. A return to point of origin, or to any other point in the on-going movement process, may be part of lifestyle mobility and so we contend that a return to any identified 'origin' cannot be presumed. Compared to temporary mobility, lifestyle mobility also differs as there is not an assumption of a return (to 'a') home. Instead, lifestyle mobility presumes the intention to move on, rather than move back. Thus over time, there may be multiple 'homes' that one can return to and/or re-visit. However, whilst someone who has permanently chosen to relocate (for example lifestyle migrants, second home owners) may also have multiple moorings and diasporic associations, we suggest the destabilization of home and away is particularly pronounced in lifestyle mobilities due to the constant intention to move on.

Therefore lifestyle mobility reiterates O'Reilly's (2003) arguments that migration and tourism (which are often considered separately) need to be brought together within research in order to better understand the interrelationships between these two types of movement. Moreover, Williams and Hall (2000) highlight that the differences between tourism and migration have often been weakly conceptualized; there has been considerable neglect of 'the grey zone of the complex forms of mobility which lie on a continuum between permanent migration and tourism' (Williams and Hall 2000: 20).

However, in the last few years, there has been a growing body of scholarship that explores the conceptual relationships between migration and tourism, with a particular focus on grasping the social-orientated aspects that may underlie migration. Benson and O'Reilly's (2009a) work on lifestyle migration is one example of approaching the relationships between migration and tourism through a social lens. Lifestyle migration (Benson and O'Reilly 2009a: 1) examines how migration may be motivated by seeking 'a route to a better and more fulfilling way of life, especially in contrast to the one left behind'. It is often preceded by one or more tourism-related visits, again illustrating how tourism might 'tip' into migration. This approach to understanding some forms of migration as lifestyle-led is based on the notion that 'lifestyle migrants are relatively affluent individuals of all ages, moving either part time or full time to places that, for various reasons, signify, for the migrant, a better quality of life' (Benson and O'Reilly 2009b: 609). Here, we maintain that to privilege any chosen way of life as 'better' is to potentially offer a romantic reading of it, and that links between romanticism and mobility have a long and critiqued history in nomadology (Cresswell 2006, Hannam 2009), embodied in the subject position of the nomad or 'neo-nomad' (for example D'Andrea 2006).

It is also worth considering McIntyre's (this volume) conception of lifestyle mobilities in relation to lifestyle migration. Both McIntyre and we understand lifestyle mobilities as a more fluid and dynamic process than lifestyle migration, yet McIntyre's approach remains enmeshed with lifestyle migration as he advocates a broader theoretical perspective through the use of the mobilities paradigm. We, however, see lifestyle mobility and lifestyle migration as distinctly separate phenomena.

Lifestyle migration differs from lifestyle mobility in that it is typically associated with a one-off lifestyle-led transition, such as choosing to move from northern Europe to rural France (for example Benson 2010), Spain (for example Casado-Díaz 2006, O'Reilly 2003) or Portugal (for example Torkington 2012), from North to Latin America such as Panama (for example Spalding 2011) or within the same country (for example Hoey 2006, Thulemark 2011). These moves are often entangled with return visits to the old or natal 'home', particularly when links are strong and distances are manageable. In contrast to lifestyle migration, lifestyle mobility is generally more fluid, on-going and multi-transitional, reflecting a 'rhizomatic' multiplicity (Deleuze and Guattari 1988), in which movement through space is both roots and routes. This, however, is not entirely the case, as even in long bouts of independent travel for example, on-going mobility is often disrupted through a need to return to the natal 'home', whether for social reasons or work (Cohen 2011, see also Erskine and Anderson, this volume). We now turn to issues of belonging and identity, and the breakdown in a distinction between 'home' and 'away', which can be associated with forms of lifestyle mobility.

Complexities of belonging, place and identity

We see lifestyle mobility, as with transnationalism and globalization more broadly, as bound up with issues of belonging in, to and with place. Increased mobility can create multiple places of belonging and aspects of transnationalism. However, to see 'home' as rooted in one place is perhaps outdated. Germann Molz's (2008) concept of a 'global abode' in her study of round-the-world travel, explores the interactions of mobility, home and belonging. Within the notion of a global abode, the 'travelers' ability to be at home in mobility allows them to be at home in the world', a veritable 'home-on-the-move' (Germann Molz 2008: 338).

The related concept of 'multiple dwelling' can also be used; not only as a device to study second homes, as has been its most common usage, but also 'how people are managing the increasing complexity of modern living' (McIntyre 2006: 14). Thus, for individuals whose mobilities have moored them in multiple places for extended periods of time, no *one* place might be 'home'. Our identities and sense of belonging to 'home', therefore, do not, by any means, have to be fixed. As Ralph and Staeheli (2011: 518) argue, the challenge 'is to conceptualize the simultaneity of home as sedentarist and as mobile'. For some, even the act of mobility in itself might be the sense of stability that a home can give (Terranova-Webb 2010).

The 'multiply-located senses of self amongst those who inhabit transnational social fields' (Conradson and McKay 2007: 168) can often lead to dilemmas in maintaining commitments to friends, family and community. Consequently, the tension between mobility, lifestyle and home (defined as a fixed place or space) remains contested. As Butcher (2010: 23) observes, 'mobility has changed the relationship between self and place including definitions of that most intimate of spaces, home, in all its manifestations: as a physical place and a metaphor for cultural belonging to a place of origin'.

Yet being mobile does not preclude a longing for (a) home. In her research on highly mobile individuals, Butcher (2010) argues there is still a 'need' for home, even if this home becomes multi-sited. She suggests that being a 'global citizen' does not negate the need to 'feel the ground beneath their feet' and to have somewhere (or many places) that can be called home (Butcher 2010: 34). Consequently, the multiple moorings that one may have with a mobile lifestyle do not imply that place has been deterritorialized and that national boundaries have fully receded. Rather as Bricknell and Datta (2011: 9) suggest, it is instead necessary to consider a grounded transnationalism which recognizes that transnational connections are 'only possible through local-local connections across national spaces'. Whilst in their work they tend to be referring to labour migrants, refugees, diaspora and asylum seekers, we believe their comments are also highly relevant when people choose to move for lifestyle reasons.

Place is hence pivotal in constructing transnational identities as individual attachment to a single place loosens, dividing attention and presence between two places or more (Hannerz 2002). The performance of identity adds another layer of complexity to lifestyle mobility as mobility choices can be subsumed into self-identities. For instance, in Nóvoa's (2012: 367) mobile ethnography of musicians on tour, he argues that 'the mobility of a musician is also one of the most relevant features in his or her life, conferring meaning to his identity as such and configuring him as a figure of mobility' (see also Bell this volume). Rather than being connected to only one place, often we now have multiple links to multiple places (and even to multiple nationalities). In this sense, the importance of familial and friendship networks (both corporeal and virtual) may take prominence (Conradson and Latham 2005) and national boundaries may recede. Individuals may therefore construct elaborate networks of on-going social relations that cover countries of origin through multiple countries of visitation or settlement (Mitchell 2009); a process further facilitated through new mobile social media and social networks.

'Home' and 'away' are therefore problematized by new technologies (Paris 2010), and so those who choose to be mobile through their lifestyle can, through emerging technologies be 'at home' while being 'away' (White and White 2007; Mascheroni 2007). White and White's (2004) discussion of the phenomenon of long-term travel by older adults highlights these possibilities. Whilst it has been suggested that these grey nomads are in transition and so are neither 'here' nor 'there' (White and White 2004), as they may be geographically distant from friends and family, they are in fact neither disengaged nor isolated (Patterson et al. 2011). Contemporary technology allows temporal and spatial aspects of long-term travel to disintegrate (Mascheroni 2007, O'Regan 2008), and affords a wealth of connections – and so possible (virtual) moorings – in and through these movements that are representative of lifestyle mobility.

A lens of lifestyle mobilities hence contributes to these quintessential questions of how we understand ourselves and relate to place in contemporary societies. By unpacking how identity constitution and notions of belonging and place attachment are affected by, and affect, mobile lifestyles, so we highlight how lifestyle and mobility choices contribute to our wider understandings of the diversity of mobilities within our social worlds. Such analyses are of growing importance as mobility become increasingly significant to various ways of life (Urry 2002).

Mobile lifestyles: travel, migration and leisure

Divided into four sections, the chapters in this book take different starting points to consider lifestyle mobilities. This in turn allows each chapter and each section to uniquely contribute to the broadening understanding of the intersections between travel, leisure and migration. As such, if lifestyle mobilities are experienced, performed, negotiated and understood through a variety of scales and temporal frames, then the different chapters in this book begin to articulate the dynamic nature of such movement.

Corporeal performance

The first section in this book focuses on lifestyle mobilities that are meaningfully performed as embodied everyday practice, including the intrinsic uncertainties and complexities within these movements and moorings. The chapters in this section accentuate the ways in which on-going voluntary movements (whether physical or virtual) can play a crucial role in the performance of corporeal lifestyle choices. These chapters highlight spatial and temporal features of mobile lifestyles and demonstrate how these mobility choices can contribute to, and are often representative of, continuing processes of de-differentiation in contemporary social life (Bauman 2000).

Claudia Bell's (Chapter 2) case study of travelling artists sees her become a mobile researcher, undertaking immersive participant observation through her experiences as part of the troupe. Her chapter highlights the necessity of mobility for these artists – for their careers but also for their art, and so their lifestyles. For many of the artists, travelling from place to place constitutes their way of life and reiterates their mobile lifestyle. Both mobility and moorings, at various scales – from a hotel room, to a sense of community within the group through to a 'mooring' of a home (perhaps) somewhere – are intrinsically important to these artists. Thus, the corporeality of these artists' experiences of place and space – and beyond this – of politics, cultures and languages, highlights what Bell terms 'mobility capital'.

Here the recognition of the global nature of the artist's life becomes evidence of particular achievements and so helps define self-identity and lifestyle.

Chapter 3 by Michael O'Regan follows on from Bell's work by suggesting that hitchhiking as a mobile lifestyle can disrupt normative notions of daily (mobile) routines and allows those who practice this type of mobility to construct an 'alternative' life trajectory. Attending hitchhiking gatherings around Europe, O'Regan (this chapter: 45) stresses that hitchhikers are 'not trapped in nostalgia for older mobilities'; rather we need to recognize, as O'Regan does, 'the necessity of seeing the mobilities of the past in the mobilities of the present and future' (Cresswell and Merriman 2011: 11). Hence, for the hitchhikers, whilst the journey is often more fragmented and less seamless than 'normal' travel, it allows them to gain an insight into contemporary society. The embodied nature of this type of travel, for both those who pick up hitchhikers and those hitchhiking, allows for a sense of self to develop. Whether this is an identity challenging the taken-for-grantedness of automobility or whether it is about exploring new peoples and cultures, O'Regan demonstrates that bodily aspects involved in hitchhiking are an essential aspect of this mobile lifestyle.

Using ethnographic methods, Jillian M. Rickly-Boyd's chapter (4) reveals some of the tensions inherent within lifestyle mobilities. In her research on 'dirtbags' (rock climbers), she suggests that whilst some may have 'given up' educational attainments and employment opportunities to pursue a specific lifestyle in specific locations, the climbers – or 'dirtbags' – see this as living in the moment and achieving pleasure from 'simple things'. Yet, they remain connected (through technology) to wider society and so whilst they embody a particular lifestyle, they also remain embedded within wider societal networks. Rickly-Boyd demonstrates the highly performative nature of identity for the 'dirtbags' and notably comments on the many facets of their mobility. It is horizontal (from place to place), vertical (ascending a cliff face for instance) and transcends both of these as the mobility of the 'journey' embodies the lifestyle itself. The physicality of the sport which in itself defines lifestyle for these 'dirtbags' also highlights their mobility and it is through this mobility that a cohesive (although often disparate) community of 'dirtbags' exists.

The final chapter (5) in this section is by Rodanthi Tzanelli. She suggests that as a tourist activity, belly dancing can lead to an embodied lifestyle that combines exercise with mobility to 'exotic' places. Her chapter utilizes a number of websites to interrogate how they move beyond historical ideas of the 'gaze' by allowing visitors (to the web pages) to see/gaze from afar something they can see/experience up close once they book their holiday or dancing experience. Tzanelli sees these websites as allowing their readers to imagine more than learning a non-Western style of movement. It allows the reader to begin to see this type of (imagined) experiential travel as highlighting how femininity and sexuality are 'style' and so, how a holiday about belly dancing can cause a transformation of identity. The mobility of the holiday therefore develops into a mobile lifestyle through the embodied (and imagined) nature of the (potential) experiences.

Applying mobile methods

The second section focuses on ways in which to research such on-going mobilities. As Büscher and Urry (2009: 112) have highlighted, it is necessary to challenge 'not just how people make knowledge of the world, but how they physically and socially make the world through the ways they move and mobilise people, objects, information and ideas'. As such, there is a need to recognize that exploring those who undertake a mobile lifestyle, whether through permanent movement or relocation(s) or through the lifestyle choices they make in their everyday lives, often involves re-thinking conventional methods (and perhaps our epistemological and ontological understandings behind them). Law and Urry (2004: 403) have suggested that existing methods deal inadequately with 'the fleeting', that methods often 'deal poorly with the non-causal, the chaotic, the complex ...' and that many 'standard social science methods are not particularly well adapted to the realities of global complexity'. As such they argue that methods need to be more 'sensitive to the complex and elusive' (Law and Urry 2004: 403). They need to be '*more mobile*' (Law and Urry 2004: 203, emphasis added).

Whilst the authors in this section may not be able to fully answer these critiques of conventional methods for researching the complexities of contemporary life, they do offer alternative lenses through which to consider and understand those who perform and live complex mobile lifestyles. As Katherine King (in Chapter 6: 94) says, her use of mobile methods was performed in conjunction with a number of other forms of qualitative inquiry and as such was 'a useful addition, rather than an all encompassing replacement for other techniques'.

King's chapter focuses on the experiences of children and their everyday leisure mobilities. Using two different case studies, her research highlights that leisure is an integral part of young people's lifestyles and influences not only their identity but also their connections to the social world. Her chapter, however, focuses on how she engaged with the young people she was involved with. She emphasizes that previous research has not sufficiently engaged with the 'mainstream' mobilities paradigm when researching young people's mobilities. Her methods are participatory with the aim of engaging and empowering the children she is working with (see Pain 2004). As she says, mobile research should be 'with' rather than 'on' those involved (see Leyshon 2002). Hence her research placed the emphasis on practice – the daily lives, performances and mobilities of those she is researching – and how this was embedded in everyday life. Her methods resonate with Büscher and Urry's (2009) conclusions that it is important to uncover how people (in this case children and young people) physically and socially make the world through the ways in which they move and interact with people, objects, information and ideas. Mobile methods therefore highlight a relevancy in young people's lives that more traditional social science methods might miss.

Garth Lean's chapter (7) takes a slightly different approach as he reflects on his experiences of using a number of different methods to understand those who have been 'transformed' through travel. His chapter is a reflective overview which offers a series of consideration for others who may be considering doing similar research. His longitudinal research, which involved developing a website and undertaking numerous rounds of email interviews as well as undertaking his own travel, highlights the ways in which researchers can participate in, inform and socially interact with a wide range of participants, some, as in Leans' case, who they may never meet. What makes Lean's chapter significant is that he highlights that mobile methods which allow the researcher to move 'with' the participant do not necessarily involve physical movement. The multi-sited nature of his research activities means that the spatial and temporal aspects of virtual spaces are equally, if not more, important and often more accessible than the physical spaces participants may (fleetingly) inhabit (see Büscher and Urry, 2009).

This section concludes with Eleni Sideri's mobile ethnographic research. Whilst Büscher and Urry (2009: 111) suggest that mobile ethnography allows the research to be 'intrinsically connected to practice', Sideri suggests (after Ingold and Lee, 2006: 68) that we should 'understand the routes and mobilities of others' as well as our own. She goes on to say that:

> We do not follow the sites, but space-time lived experiences and how our mobility takes part in or generates them. We do not study different lifestyles but we merge into them. The corporeal experience of mobility could minimise the distance of subject/object through the ethnographer's body and lifestyle ... (Sideri, this volume: 116).

Her chapter examines three specific moments of mobility and highlights how entangled our mobilities are within wider political, social and cultural contexts. Her ethnographic experiences point out the multi-sensory nature of our knowledge and understanding. They illustrate the complexities of mobile research as they create moments of shared places, moments of empathy and understanding and allow for transgressions between our many positions of researcher, 'local', tourist, commuter, traveller, student, 'expert'.

Moorings, mobilities and belonging

As we have suggested earlier, lifestyle mobility differs from more temporary forms of mobility on the one hand and more permanent forms of migration on the other (see Hall 2005, Benson and O'Reilly 2009b). Through the performances of both mobility and immobility, issues of belonging, 'home' and 'identity' are raised and the chapters in this section work to address some of these issues. Through contemporary and historical examples, these chapters highlight ways in which the complexities of our everyday lives are being negotiated and how our identities and sense(s) of belonging no longer need to remain 'fixed'. 'Home' is no longer a pre-determined location to which we 'belong' and can be, as already suggested, a 'home on the move' or we can be 'at home in the world' (Germann Molz 2008: 338). At the same time mobility can change the relationship between one's sense of self and place (Butcher 2010) and can lead to senses of self located in multiple places.

Erskine and Anderson (Chapter 9) highlight these tensions when they suggest that place strongly configures how lifestyle travellers test a sense of self, yet at the same time, place is the very thing that keeps them mobile. Their research, which involved interviews with lifestyle travellers, highlights one of the themes coming through in a number of the other chapters (for instance Rickly-Boyd, this volume), wherein the *processes* of lifestyle mobility becomes the most important aspect. Therefore, it is the mobility through, in and across place that is important rather than the mobility *between* places. Place is thus both fixed and in flux as it becomes an amalgamation of the dynamic and fluid mobilities performed by these travellers. Their sense of belonging and the periods of time they spend in various locations link to ideas of freedom and spontaneity, which is underlined through their mobility. Thus for Erskine and Anderson, they aim to understand how notions of place and mobility affect the identity of a travelling lifestyle.

Barbara A. Koth's chapter (10) follows on from Erskine and Anderson's as she discusses bluewater sailors who spend months or years navigating (parts of) the globe. Using interviews and surveys, she found that whilst these sailors were motivated by aspects of 'escape', it was escape from the quotidian rather than escape from something specific. Therefore, their mobility and moorings allowed a sense of belonging with a transient population who they met and re-met at various stages of their journeys. At the same time, through technology, they were linked, and still felt a sense of 'belonging' to wider communities of 'home' and family and friends. In some ways, Koth's bluewater sailors could be said to epitomize lifestyle mobilities through their multiple moorings, their periods of extreme mobility, and the way that many negotiate sailing with other necessary aspects of life (such as maintaining a 'home', work, and leisure).

The third chapter in this section uses two case studies to examine tensions and intersections within aspects of lifestyle mobility. The chapter takes as its case studies one historical example and a contemporary example in order to examine the micro journeys inherent in canoescapes. The historical case study considers the American Canoe Association's meeting between 1880 and 1902 whilst the contemporary example is an ethnography of an organized, guided canoe trip along the Thelon River in Canada. Dunkin and Grimwood's approach highlights the comment made earlier in O'Regan's chapter (3) by Cresswell and Merriman (2011) where they suggest that it is necessary to study the mobilities of the past to understand and value mobilities today and in the future. Whilst their discussion emphasizes the knowledge needed to participate within these canoescapes, so both examples also highlight the everyday practices of constructing camp, being mobile on the water and the interweaving lines of mobility within space and time. They conclude by suggesting that the mobile habitations of canoescapes are profoundly social and are inflected with power dynamics and routines that mark everyday life. By utilizing a lifestyle mobilities lens, they argue that their interdisciplinary case studies improve 'our understandings of movement and practice as social phenomena ...' (Dunkin and Grimwood, this volume: 173).

The final chapter (12) in this section takes the case of Isamu Noguchi (1904–1988), a Japanese-American artist who has been termed a 'global citizen'. Elia Ntaousani's chapter is a thought provoking examination of Noguchi's tensions of ideas of 'self' and 'home' to conceptualize contemporary cosmopolitanism. She cites Noguchi on three occasions to reiterate his questions – with his background and upbringing, where is his home, where are his affections and where is his identity? Ntaousani's study of Noguchi's life and art leads to the conclusion that his mobility, his moorings and his acknowledgement of the absence of a seamless identity allowed him to inherently be at 'home' everywhere. Therefore, Noguchi's constant state of foreignness was his lifestyle, implicitly and explicitly marked through, by and in his mobilities.

Complexities of wider identities

The final section in this book considers how a lens of lifestyle mobilities can contribute to questions about the growing importance of mobility as it increasingly plays a key role in various ways of life (Urry 2002) and impacts on wider communities and groups. The chapters in this section reflect broader conceptualizations of lifestyle mobilities in that they think through examples involving communities or specific lifestyle-led groups. The first two chapters in this section illustrate the intersections with discussions of lifestyle migration (Benson and O'Reilly 2009b); both also extend these discussions to consider how lifestyle mobility better fits with the communities they are discussing.

McIntyre's chapter (13) argues that lifestyle migration neglects a broad range of mobilities or flows associated with voluntary relocation and he advocates a broader-based theoretical understanding that leads to his framework of lifestyle mobilities. Using examples from Canada and Australia, McIntyre discusses notions of lifestyle mobility and imaginations, thereby illustrating the tensions with current conceptions of lifestyle migration. He suggests that quality of life markers (such as family ties, employment, climate, and so on) are key building blocks of the imagination that motivates lifestyle migrations and he uses Castell's (2000) spaces of flows and spaces of places to further problematize lifestyle migration. In utilizing Appadurai's (1996) scapes and Castell's (2000) flows, McIntyre clearly illustrates how utilizing a lifestyle mobilities lens allows for a broader account of the networks, scapes and flows involved within lifestyle migration.

Chapter 14 by Phillip Vannini examines how the cold, wet area of Clayoquot on Vancouver Island in British Columbia, Canada attracts short- and longer-term tourists and lifestyle migrants. In essence, Vannini is interested in the significance of climate and weather on lifestyle mobility. He uses examples from interviews and his own experiences in the location to highlight how storm-watching has re-framed mobility in this geographic area. His respondent's comments illustrate how weather interacts with mobility as they talk about visiting the cafés, staying in the hotels, walking, sitting and crying on the beaches. Vannini talks of storm-watching as a performance – a dance – of winds, waves, locals, tourists; their mobility, the serenity (and even stillness?) of watching the storm from inside a cosy hotel room allowing the complexities of the everyday to fade away. As such he concludes by saying that the storminess of climate allows a way to understand lifestyle mobilities as 'different constellations of practices, experiences, and representations – all with different rhythms, speeds, and feels, all for different people with different personal and collective identities' (Vannini, this volume: 221).

The final two chapters of the book begin to consider wider environmental and socio-technical aspects of lifestyle mobilities. Stewart Barr and Jan Prillwitz's chapter (15) explores the tensions between differing forms of mobility as they highlight that climate change has emerged as an influential factor in contemporary thinking about (individual) mobilities. They looked at the travel practices of a number of different groups in and around Exeter in the UK and discussed the differences between everyday mobility and tourism mobility. Most of their respondents identified with local sustainable travel options (even if they could not personally adopt these modes of travel), yet they saw tourism mobility as different to everyday mobility and their sustainable travel practices seemed to have little bearing on touristic travel. The different practices, representations and negotiations of travel illustrate an area of conflict for the respondents where tourism mobility played an important symbolic role in conveying a sense of identity through readily available air travel. Barr and Prillwitz suggest that the current ways of promoting sustainable travel are flawed and through their examples illustrate how a mobile lifestyle highlights the challenges individuals face when differentiating their daily and tourism mobilities.

The final chapter of this section considers rally driving in Scotland. Leslie Mabon argues that we need to consider groups who may currently be more cynical or resistant to environmental debates that may impinge upon their lifestyle-centred mobility choices. His research highlights that lifestyle mobilities can often be at the more local scale. As he says (this volume: 242), 'rally participants are not "migrating" as such and end up back at their homes after a very short period of time away'; but as he emphasizes, it is the context of the movement that remains important. Mabon's chapter talks about the embodied experience of rallying and expresses the sensory aspects of this type of lifestyle mobility. The chapter contends that an understanding of how mobilities fit into people's identities and lifestyles can play a pivotal role in imagining more sustainable mobility futures. This chapter thus aims to make us think differently about lifestyle mobilities and how we might consider groups such as this, who are currently resisting modifying the environmental impacts of their sport.

The book concludes with a final contribution by the editors that echoes the broader themes of the book's chapters and suggests avenues for the further study of lifestyle mobilities. In summary, the approach we have taken to lifestyle mobilities illustrates the spatial and temporal nature of much contemporary mobility. We are more interested in the mobility within, around and through place, as illustrated by lifestyle mobility, rather than mobility between places which seems limiting and short-sighted in light of the dynamic and complex lives we often lead. As such, the diversity and interdisciplinary nature of the chapters within this book invites us to re-examine our understandings of different mobilities and, as Cresswell argues (2010), encourages us to pay closer attention to mobile practices, experiences and their representation.

References

Bauman, Z. 2000. *Liquid Modernity.* Cambridge: Polity.
Bell, D. and Hollows, J. 2006. Towards a History of Lifestyle, in *Historicizing Lifestyle: Mediating Taste, Consumption and Identity from the 1900s to 1970s*, edited by D. Bell. Farnham: Ashgate, 1–19.
Bell, M. and Ward, G. 2000. Comparing temporary mobility with permanent migration. *Tourism Geographies*, 2(1), 87–107.
Benson, M. 2010. The context and trajectory of lifestyle migration – the case of the British residents in Southwest France. *European Societies*, 12(1), 45–64.
Benson, M. and O'Reilly, K. (eds) 2009a. *Lifestyle Migration – Expectations, Aspirations and Experiences.* Farnham: Ashgate.
Benson, M. and O'Reilly, K. 2009b. Migration and the search for a better way of life: a critical exploration of lifestyle migration. *The Sociological Review*, 57(3), 608–625.
Binkley, S. 2004. Everybody's life is like a spiral: narrating Post-Fordism in the Lifestyle Movement of the 1970s. *Cultural Studies <=> Critical Methodologies*, 4(1), 71–96.
Bourdieu, P. 1984. *Distinction: A Social Critique of the Judgement of Taste.* Cambridge, MA: Harvard University Press.
Bricknell, K. and Datta, A. 2011. Introduction: Translocal Geographies, in *Translocal Geographies: Spaces, Places and Connections*, edited by K. Bricknell and A. Datta. Farnham: Ashgate, 3–21.
Büscher, M. and Urry, J. 2009. Mobile methods and the empirical. *European Journal of Social Thought*, 12(1), 99–117.
Butcher, M. 2010. From 'fish out of water' to 'fitting in': the challenge of re-placing home in a mobile world. *Population, Space and Place*, 16(1), 23–36.
Casado-Díaz, M. 2006. Retiring to Spain: an analysis of difference among North European nationals. *Journal of Ethnic and Migration Studies*, 32(8), 1321–1339.
Chaney, D. 1996. *Lifestyles.* London: Routledge.
Cohen, S.A. 2011. Lifestyle travellers: backpacking as a way of life. *Annals of Tourism Research*, 38(4), 1535–1555.
Cohen, S.A., Duncan, T. and Thulemark, M. 2013. Lifestyle mobilities: The crossroads of travel, leisure and migration. *Mobilities* (in press).

Coles, T., Duval, D. and Hall, C.M. 2004. Tourism, Mobility and Global Communities: New Approaches to Theorising Tourism and Tourist Spaces, in *Global Tourism: The Next Decade*, 3rd edition, edited by W. Theobold. Oxford: Butterworth Heinemann, 463–481.

Conradson, D. and Latham, A. 2005. Friendship, networks and transnationality in a world city: Antipodean transmigrants in London. *Journal of Ethnic and Migration Studies*, 31(2), 287–305.

Conradson, D. and McKay, D. 2007. Translocal subjectivities: mobility, connection, emotion. *Mobilities*, 2(2), 167–174.

Cresswell, T. 2001. The production of mobilities. *New Formations*, 43(1), 11–25.

Cresswell, T. 2006. *On the Move: Mobility in the Modern Western World.* London: Routledge.

Cresswell, T. 2010. Towards a politics of mobility. *Environment and Planning D: Society and Space*, 28(1), 17–31.

Cresswell, T. and Merriman, P. 2011. Introduction: Geographies of Mobilities – Practices, Spaces, Subjects, in *Geographies of Mobilities – Practices, Spaces, Subjects*, edited by T. Cresswell and P. Merriman. Farnham: Ashgate, 1–19.

D'Andrea, A. 2006. Neo-nomadism: a theory of post-identitarian mobility in the global age. *Mobilities*, 1(1), 95–119.

Deleuze, G. and Guattari, F. 1988. *A Thousand Plateaus.* London: The Athlone Press.

Edensor, T. 2007. Mundane mobilities, performances and spaces of tourism. *Social and Cultural Geography*, 8(2), 199–215.

Featherstone, M. 1987. Lifestyle and consumer culture. *Theory, Culture and Society*, 4(1), 55–70.

Germann Molz, J. 2008. Global abode: home and mobility in narratives of round-the-world travel. *Space and Culture*, 11(4), 325–342.

Giddens, A. 1991. *Modernity and Self-identity: Self and Society in the Late Modern Age.* Cambridge: Polity Press.

Hall, C.M. 2005. Reconsidering the geography of tourism and contemporary mobility. *Geographical Research*, 43(2), 125–139.

Hannam, K. 2008. Tourism geographies, tourist studies and the turn towards mobilities. *Geography Compass*, 2(1), 127–139.

Hannam, K. 2009. The End of Tourism? Nomadology and the Mobilities Paradigm, in *Philosophical Issues in Tourism*, edited by J. Tribe. Bristol: Channel View, 101–113.

Hannam, K., Sheller, M. and Urry, J. 2006. Editorial: mobilities, immobilities and moorings. *Mobilities*, 1(1), 1–22.

Hannerz, U. 2002. Where We Are and Who We Want to Be, in *The Postnational Self: Belonging and Identity*, edited by U. Hedetoft and M. Hjort. Minneapolis: University of Minnesota Press, 217–232.

Hoey, A.B. 2006. Gray Suit or Brown Carhartt: Narrative Transition, Relocation, and Reorientation in the Lives of Corporate Refugees. *Journal of Anthropological Research*, 62(3), 347–371.

Ingold, T. and Lee, J. 2006. Fieldwork on Foot: Perceiving, Routing, Socializing, in *Locating the Field: Space, Place and Context in Anthropology*, edited by S. Coleman and P. Collins. Oxford: Berg, 67–85.

Law, John and Urry, John 2004. Enacting the social. *Economy and Society*, 33(3), 390–410.

Leyshon, M. 2002. On being 'in the field': practice, progress and problems in research with young people in rural areas. *Journal of Rural Studies*, 18(2), 179–181.

McIntyre, N. 2006. Introduction, in *Multiple Dwelling and Tourism Negotiating Place, Home and Identity*, edited by N. McIntyre, D. Williams and K. McHuge. Oxfordshire: CABI Publishing, 3–14.

Mascheroni, G. 2007. Global nomads' network and mobile sociality: exploring new media uses on the move. *Information, Communication and Society*, 10(4), 527–546.

Mitchell, K., 2009. Transnationalism, in *The Dictionary of Human Geography*. 5th edition, edited by R.J. Johnston, D. Gregory, G. Pratt, M.J. Watts and S. Whatmore. Oxford: Wiley-Blackwell, 772–773.

Nóvoa, A. 2012. Musicians on the move: mobilities and identities of a band on the road. *Mobilities*, 7(3), 349–368.

Nowicka, M. 2007. Mobile locations: construction of home in a group of mobile transnational professionals. *Global Networks*, 7(1), 69–86.

O'Regan, M. 2008. Hypermobility in Backpacker Lifestyles: The Emeregence of the Backpacker Café, in *Tourism and Mobilities: Local Global Connections*, edited by P.M. Burns and M. Novelli. Wallingford: CABI Publishing, 109–132.

O'Reilly, K. 2003. When is a tourist? The articulation of tourism and migration in Spain's Costa del Sol. *Tourist Studies*, 3(3), 301–317.

Pain, R. 2004. Social geography: participatory research. *Progress in Human Geography*, 28(5), 652–663.

Paris, C. 2010. The Virtualization of Backpacker Culture: Virtual Mooring, Sustained Interactions and Enhanced Mobilities, in *Beyond Backpacker Tourism: Mobilities and Experiences*, edited by K. Hannam and A. Diekmann. Bristol: Channel View Publications, 40–63.

Patterson, I., Pegg, S. and Litster, J. 2011. Grey nomads on tour: a revolution in travel and tourism for older adults. *Tourism Analysis*, 16(3), 283–294.

Poster, M. 1998. Virtual Ethnicity: Tribal Identity in an Age of Global Communications, in *Cyberspace 2.0: Revisiting Computer-mediated Communication and Community*, edited by S. Jones. London: Sage Publications, 184–211.

Ralph, D. and Staeheli, L. 2011. Home and migration: mobilities, belongings and identities. *Geography Compass*, 5(7), 517–530.

Sheller, M. and Urry, J. 2006. The new mobilities paradigm. *Environment and Planning A*, 38(2), 207–226.

Shields, R. 1992. Spaces for the Subject of Consumption, in *Lifestyle Shopping: The Subject of Consumption*, edited by R. Shields. London: Routledge, 1–20.

Skeggs, B. 2004. *Class, Self, Culture.* London: Routledge.

Sobel, M., 1981. *Lifestyle and Social Structure: Concepts, Definitions and Analyses.* New York: Academic Press.

Spalding, A.K. 2011. Remaking lives abroad: Lifestyle migration and socio-environmental change in Bocas Del Toro, Panama. Unpublished PhD Thesis. Santa Cruz: University of California.

Stebbins, R.A. 1997. Lifestyle as a generic concept in ethnographic research. *Quality and Quantity*, 31(4), 347–360.

Terranova-Webb, A. 2010. Getting Down the Road: Understanding Stable Mobility in an American Circus. Unpublished PhD Thesis, Milton Keynes: Open University.

Thulemark, M. 2011. A new life in the mountains: changing lifestyles among in-migrants in Wanaka, New Zealand. *Recreation and Society in Africa, Asia and Latin America*, 2(1), 35–50.

Torkington, K. 2012. Place and lifestyle migration: the discursive construction of 'glocal' place-identity. *Mobilities*, 7(1), 71–92.

Urry, J. 2002. Mobility and proximity. *Sociology*, 36(2), 255–274.

Warde, A. and Martens, L. 1998. Food Choice: A Sociological Approach, in *The Nation's Diet*, edited by A. Murcott. London: Longman, 129–146.

White, N.R. and White, P.B. 2004. Travel as transition: identity and place. *Annals of Tourism Research*, 31(1), 200–218.

White, N.R. and White, P.B. 2007. Home and away: tourists in a connected world. *Annals of Tourism Research*, 34(1), 88–104.

Williams, A.M. and Hall, C.M. 2000. Tourism and migration: new relationships between production and consumption. *Tourism Geographies*, 2(1), 5–27.

SECTION I
Corporeal Performance

Chapter 2

Peripatetic Artists: Creative Mobility and Resourceful Displacement

Claudia Bell

Introduction

In this chapter a group of travelling artists constitute a case study for a discussion about lifestyle mobilities. It suggests the term 'mobility capital' as a tangential refinement of the mobility paradigm, in order to identify a particular kind of lifestyle traveller, who may lack fiscal wealth, but who requires mobility for various other forms of personal and professional enrichment. This chapter also considers how the mobility of the artists is juxtaposed with the need for everyday identifiable moorings, even in foreign situations. The manner of work, and the content of a lot of the artwork produced, is also utilized as further manifestation of enacting corporeal mobility.

Nine Dragon Heads is a Korean-based organization that tours groups of international artists to various venues. Each year this includes a journey within Korea itself, to a section of the Silk Road, and to the Sarajevo Winter Festival in Bosnia Herzegovina (*Sarajevska Zima*) (Bell 2009). This initiative, led by Director Park Byoung-Uk, has been in operation for 14 years. The group, of about 12–25 per tour, varies each year, with a few regular participants. They arrive from diverse nations, including Korea, Japan, Bosnia Herzegovina, Georgia, Turkey, Switzerland, Germany, Belize, Australia and New Zealand. Indeed, they may be described as 'officially' multicultural; representatives of the artists' own embassies in countries they are visiting attend official proceedings at major events.[1] Formal welcomes and other events contribute towards creating meaning and political weight to the artist group. That hosting, and local media coverage, affirms or acknowledges a status of these visitors not experienced by everyday tourists.

Most of these artists have worked in various countries, usually as artists-in-residence or as guests during one-off exhibitions that comprise or include their own work. This is indeed a cosmopolitan group. They may meet for the first time on any tour, but they become instant international colleagues. The persistence of the organization depends on artists having both an international socio-cultural outlook, and access to funding support to enable them to travel to the designated

---

1 For example, an official welcome to the group at the Sarajevo Winter Festival includes morning tea hosted by the President of Bosnia and Herzegovina.

Nine Dragon Heads meeting point. It also depends on their individual hunger for meaningful mobility.

Their art practice is necessarily portable: most are installation,[2] video or performance[3] artists. The emphasis is always on making an extremely light or transient footprint on the planet. While there are opportunities to present prior works, at each location the artists make and perform fresh pieces for local audiences and galleries. New works, using both local materials and props from home, are contextualized within the local environment. Later, when they return home or at their next location, the artists exhibit and extend works created during this travelling workshop. To date more than 900 artists have been involved in this venture.

Boundaries between employment and leisure are blurred during Nine Dragon Heads tours. For instance, in Sarajevo a sight-seeing walk along a snowy street, or an evening in a bar, might suddenly reveal a perfect site for a spontaneous installation or performance. A crowd gathers, photographs are taken, the event is documented. Multiple juxtapositions occur: work and play, tourists and locals, art and everyday life. To the participants, this is one of the pleasures of the enterprise: that serendipity of not knowing exactly what is going to occur each day.

For the duration of each tour – generally up to three weeks – the artists perform simultaneously as professionals undertaking their own expert practices, and as tourists in a foreign space. Unlike business travellers with agendas aimed at commercial benefit, who may engage very little with local people and the physical environment, it is that engagement with both which is foundational to these artists' practice(s).

Methods and approach

My own role with this group was as an English language writer (contributing to the catalogue and website, and writing articles about the artwork), as technical assistant (making, installing and photographing works), and co-performing with a performance artist in the group. Then the academic hat goes on, and, like Crang, I am 'chasing the … mobilized topics' (Crang 2011). My methodology for this chapter is that of the mobile researcher (Vannini 2010). I draw from immersive participant observation on tours with this group within South Korea,

---

2   Installation may be a temporary or permanent arrangement of items in space, including in formal galley settings or in any environment. Materials used are generally the familiar everyday, repositioned to convey new readings, perhaps alongside video, sound and virtual reality. The works are often ephemeral, their documentation later exhibited as works in their own right.

3   Performance art: refers to conceptual art in which the physical actions of an individual or a group at a particular place and in a particular time constitute the work. Performance art can happen anywhere, in any venue or setting and for any duration.

and to Bosnia-Herzegovina. The intimacy quickly achieved by the group in an environment where everybody else is a stranger, assures safe dialogue. I have also gathered insights from informal conversations with artists who have travelled with this organization on various other tours, and from discussions over several years with the director.

Participant observation requires actual experience of the real world in order to generate analysis of social phenomena really present. My observations are firmly situated within 'personal experience and sense-making' (Atkinson Coffey and Delamont 2003, cited by Anderson 2006: 382). As Anderson prescribes, such a researcher must be 'visibly active and reflexively engaged' (Anderson 2006: 383). The visible activities – assisting the artists, talking, socializing and relaxing with them, documenting their activities and performing with them – are incorporated as ways into understanding that world I was observing. Unlike objectivist grounded theory, which is derived from positivism, the findings are not generalized across universes. Rather, the research worlds are treated as social constructions (Gubrium and Holstein 2011). This means that any generic statements are qualified according to particular temporal, social and situational conditions.

The joy of this is the facility to research idiosyncratic conditions, locations and circumstances. It is a way of giving permission to those researchers wanting to write vibrant studies that draw from their own need for a satisfying explanatory analysis of non-standard experiences. In the case of working with a group of itinerant artists, who do not all speak the same language, any other methodological proposition is unlikely to be do-able.

Mobility as lifestyle, mobility as capital

The Nine Dragon Head artist-travellers are constituent in an everyday mobility system. They are engaged in a particular range of interdependent 'mobilities' which produces social life. In this case study, we can recognize the categories of mobility identified by Busher and Urry (2009). First, their corporeal travel was organized in a time-space modality (a journey, perhaps two–three weeks with Nine Dragon Heads, away from home, to an unfamiliar environment). Second, their physical movement in spaces new to them meant a reconfiguration of understandings of place (the Bosnia-Herzegovina and North Korea experiences below are strong illustrations of this). Third, the travel, while actual, was also imaginative in pre-conceptions before the trip, and each day (the artists require some idea of what they may create and perform, in order to take at least some props with them. Hence they try to imagine works made in unimaginable settings). In addition, through their art practice, the travelling artists engage with places visited in a manner not usual for tourists. Through their global engagement they correspond to that category identified as 'mobile transnational professionals' (Nowicka 2007).

Travel is an essential component of the work. The artists must first rendezvous in the designated spot where the tour begins. This might be at an airport in Western

China, at a café or love hotel in Seoul, or perhaps at a gallery in Sarajevo. Every person's journey there will have its own story. This is very often a long and complicated tale of flight / ferry / bus / train connections, delays or cancellations, ending at last at the rendezvous. For instance, one such trip that started in Norfolk Island (near Australia) may have involved eventually arriving, exhausted, after midnight, in Ljubljana, then transferring to a bus to slowly traverse snowy night roads to Sarajevo.

Such journeys to new locations indicate the resilience of these artists. The requirement to make and exhibit work whilst on the road trains them to develop their practice independently of language, outside of familiar places and carried out minus their usual tools, materials and equipment. The artist may indeed develop an artist-persona specific to the new place in which they work, differing from their dominant art-maker persona at home. Here they do not have the authority that may go with being known locally, or the practical knowledge of where to find supplies. The journeys require that the artist be resourceful in the acquisition, in unfamiliar locations, of materials with which to build their work. Just as the artists are mobile, so are their art making concepts and praxis.

Here, far from home, they can draw with confidence on their knowledge and experience of art making: this firmly moors them in their role as visiting artist. Hunting for the material elements required to make their work, and for somewhere to create it, may indeed extend their mobility in that space – for instance, to suppliers of hardware, to technical workshops, to art school studios, in a manner not usual for tourists. Finding and using local materials grounds the work in the specific location. For the art viewers, these artists are not expected to pretend to be local; the whole point of an international event is to see new responses to and interpretations of the local. There is a semi-chaotic engagement with place, as each artist sets out on their own routes to problem solve their art making agenda, for example, seeking corrugated cardboard / electrical inspection lamps / fur fabric / white make-up ... This might be in Sarajevo, winter, snow, minus 27 degrees ... Enacting this energetic mission they demonstrate Cresswell's notion of mobility as an entanglement of movement, representation and practice. Physical movement, the shared meanings of representation of movements, and the embodied practice of movement; it is only in the analysis that these elements are disentangled (Cresswell 2010: 19).

Rerat and Lees (2011) write of 'spatial capital' with reference to the new middle classes marking out their social distinction from the suburban masses via gentrification. A new avenue to address in this chapter is 'mobility capital'. 'Mobility capital' is my response to that 'fine-tuning' of the mobility paradigm called for by Cresswell (2010: 29). In the case of these itinerant artists, whether or not they have a permanent home anywhere, their travels as artists are significant in their career progression as they enlarge their curriculum vitae. While the term 'mobility capital' obviously corresponds with Bourdieu's well-tested 'cultural capital' (Bourdieu 1984), 'mobility' has specificity. Mobility capital is irrespective of personal wealth, but required by international artists to mark them as global players. As is true in some other professions, international participation affirms status. While most tourism academics recognize the accumulation of cultural capital as one fundamental explanation for the desire to travel, in many occupations mobility capital is evidence of particular achievements. That young New Zealand travellers note their 'O.E.' [4] on their CVs as indication of having gained a particular range of skills through travel, is an additional example of mobility capital (Wilson et al. 2009, Bell 2002). For artists with limited personal financial resources, being funded to participate in events is affirmation of career achievement. This is especially true for Antipodeans, for whom long distance travel is very expensive. Such mobility indicates international recognition of their individual skills and accomplishments.

Identifying, locating and making moorings

The insistence that mobilities need moorings is clearly understood by academics addressing spatial issues (Hannam, Sheller and Urry 2006). Inherent in travel is the capacity to create a mooring, an environment of low demand and some physical comfort that is claimed as a temporary refuge within the unfamiliar. In this manner any place becomes performative, accommodating the needs of the traveller. Major catastrophes in the world vividly demonstrate the human ability and need to create some kind of comfort zone, however modest; for example, the rush to austere designated refuges, where a family gathers – is moored – on perhaps just a shared mattress; or the creation of temporary makeshift accommodation during significant earthquakes, floods and tsunamis.

For Nine Dragon Heads participants, the organization itself is the major mooring, as the artists mobilize. Their own identities are highly fluid, as they adapt to situations requiring them to be artists, tourists, colleagues, art consumers, honoured guests and event publicists. In some of these roles they become hybrids of a larger organization, for example *Sarajevska Zima* (a contingent of Nine Dragon Heads artists regularly participates in this annual winter festival in Sarajevo, Bosnia-Herzegovina). The artists' 'moorings' when they are on the road are located in their downtime with the group. At various venues they are provided with or create some kind of common space. They hang out together at airports and bus stations; they can relax in their rooms. Galleries made available to them in foreign towns or cities, or public areas designated or perceived as available for performance, are quickly and visibly occupied by the artists. Their rapid adaptability enables a quick appropriation of space. With props and personal

---

4   'O.E.' stands for 'overseas experience'. The term is in everyday usage in New Zealand, and refers to a well-established social practice by young adult New Zealanders. They undertake long term travel, usually basing themselves in Britain in order to gain international employment and travel experience.

effects deposited within the territory as work is undertaken, a process of claiming is enacted. Thus a visible anchorage is created.

For these travellers, moorings may also be identified through the opportunity to speak a shared language. The travellers are multicultural: in any Nine Dragon Heads group, there is no one common language. Hence conversations normally take place across languages, many of the participants not necessarily using their own first tongue. For those who are not bilingual or multilingual – usually true in the case of, for instance, the Australians and New Zealanders, most of whom speak only English – their chances for conversation may be less than, for instance, those Swiss and Dutch who are fluent in up to six languages. But the Europeans too may be isolated from the Asian language speakers. The art itself does not require language. Artists from assorted cultures assist one another with setting up work, and in some performances. The installations and performances are cross-cultural, accessible to diverse audiences, just as sport can be watched whatever one's language.

Yet all are identified by their nationality, however little might be known about their place of origin (Belize! Norfolk Island!). Even vague conceptions of other nations impose an order on the discrete. One's fellow travellers are psychically anchored to an officially established mooring, somewhere else. The everyday practice of asking people where they are from, whether tourists or not, demonstrates that human ability to recognize the mobile, and to satisfy a desire to identify their anchorages.

Cresswell (2010: 18) reminds us that it is tempting 'to think of a mobile world as something that replaces a world of fixities'. For the Nine Dragon Heads artists, it is often when their own individual lives' require greater fixity, perhaps through job stability or through having children that they may be unable to continue to participate. This is generally driven by the lack of mobile freedom demanded in many paid employment situations, and by the all-embracing nature of family responsibilities, which are likely to require the reprioritizing of such household resources as time and money. Their mobility curtailed, they then engage in the relative 'permanence' that global capitalism requires in order to reproduce itself (Harvey 1996 cited in Cresswell 2010). Their mooring is a contra indicator of their ability to participate; they generally disappear from the Nine Dragon Heads experience. Yet their mobility capital accrued as itinerant artists may be a useful indicator of a range of networks and skills required in their new occupation. Nine Dragon Heads is an organization that is dependent on participants' mobility.

Art is mobile, art is a mooring

'Mobility is a resource that is differentially accessed', Cresswell (2010: 21) reminds us. In the case of these artist travellers, Nine Dragon Heads is the catalyst that enables art travel. For the more experienced artists in the group, whose careers have involved a large amount of international travel, the world is perceived as an all-encompassing arena in which to make, perform and display their art practices. For the early career artists, the Nine Dragon Heads excursion reveals and opens up a world of access to the international art environment. After all, art can literally be created anywhere, attested to by, for example, artists' residency programmes in Antarctica; works by various artists in remote deserts; even sky writing artworks. Art can also be viewed from anywhere, as proven by the satellite images that show massive earthwork art pieces, which can be viewed from afar (outer space!); or readily seen on Google Earth.

Nine Dragon Heads publishes sumptuously illustrated catalogues about its shows, and maintains a very detailed website (Nine Dragon Heads 2011). These documents are distributed globally, further extending the work of these artists. Constant or frequent contact through the current range of contemporary technologies – Facebook, Bebo – enables the artists to display their work, and to view one another's. Even when the artist is anchored in one place, their work is still mobile.

Below I have provided some examples of recent Nine Dragon Heads artists' projects, illustrating that the concepts mobilities and moorings are not just a feature of the transient art-making discussed here, but also often intrinsic to the artworks. The art itself corresponds to the mobilities paradigm.

Moorings mobilized! Busan

A particular event in Busan, a south eastern sea port of South Korea, provides an intriguing reworking of the mobility / mooring dichotomy. In this huge city the Nine Dragons Heads artists stayed at a friendly but modest hotel overlooking Hyundae Beach. They happily commandeered two floors of the hotel, safely moored in decorative rooms overlooking a seashore, port and fishing village. Individual hotels rooms were quickly personalized by the emplacement of their own objects, enacting 'a space in becoming' (Nowicka 2006: 82). Home is 'not necessarily tied to a fixed location, but emerges out of the regular, localizing reiterating of social relationships with both humans and non-humans' (Ralph and Staeheli 2011: 519). As hotel guests, their blank-canvas rooms bore no permanent imprint of their own personality. Their real home (for at least some), somewhere else, provides the intimate space in which to construct an 'autobiographic narrative text' (Ceiraad 1999: 11). For travellers, the personalization of the hotel room depends on transportable trivial items such one's own toothbrush, medication and clothing. For most travellers, temporary moorings are important and necessary, but also fluid, expendable and later largely forgotten.

In their art practice the artists intended to make their work on that pebbly beach below the hotel, a wilful engagement of the physically local. They had brought props, including small tents, to undertake this long-planned venture: yet another highly mobile Nine Dragon Heads scheme. Unfortunately they could not have anticipated the extremely heavy rain.

A novel alternative was suggested. Every artist's hotel room would become a temporary gallery. In this case, those private spaces would become, for a few hours, public space. Guests, including fellow artists, would view their work, and enjoy a presentation about their work, in the bedroom. Moorings mobilized! From private sanctuary to public gallery: something perhaps akin to a real estate open home, but in a vast city where that one room is their only refuge, their one personal space. The usual boundaries were thus transgressed.

This solution was warmly welcomed. Everyone spent a day organizing their exhibitions, rearranging their bedroom furniture, or eliminating it altogether. Some set up laptops for presentations of their work. Others braved the weather to collect debris from the beach below, to install in their private spaces. Sometimes the bed itself – the ultimate personal mooring, surely! – became a surface for display.

The bedrooms become little galleries, mooring each artist's practice within a defined space. These rooms were now spaces of inclusion, not exclusion, as visitors, local art personnel, fellow hotel guests, hotel staff and passersby became the audience. The tiny bedroom foyers, where each guest deposits shoes and coats, became thresholds to a mysterious hinterland. The project demonstrated the affinity between the artistic process – imagining, creating or representing – and the idea of the threshold in its material and figurative manifestations (Mukherji 2011: xviii). The open invitation transgressed the inherent sense of the privilege of access to someone's bedroom. Instead, a spatial egalitarianism was underlined for everyone engaging with this event.

The necessarily ephemeral nature of these bedroom works is further illustration of the mobility paradigm. The artists are transients, they cannot leave their work here for long, it has to be portable or disposable. Photographic documentation preserves the work, and for some artists will be exhibited later as works in themselves. Mobility is a transient's paradigm.

Art in the caves, Jeju Island

A series of works that implicitly addressed mobilities and moorings was made in volcanic sea caves and on a beach at Jeju Island, off the southern coast of South Korea. Using the tents they had brought with them, the artists colonized the caves. The bright tents were erected in the caves, making cosy temporary abodes within the rocky enclosures. The outlook: an unwelcoming-looking grey winter sea. Park, the Nine Dragon Heads director and himself an installation and performance artist, wore a large turtle carapace on his back.

This metaphorical recapitulation of the original animal carrying its home wherever it went resonated the overall praxis of the Nine Dragon Heads enterprise.

Figure 2.1   Nine Dragon Heads' director Park Byoung Uk at Jeju Island, South Korea

Source: Claudia Bell.

Performance artists

Politics are inherent in many of the artworks. At Cheong Jui the Nine Dragon Heads artists performed at the event to mark the opening of the new Red Cross buildings. They organized their individual spaces in the outdoor car park, and set up their props. It was striking to the observers that this event took place surrounded by Red Cross trucks. A Dutch artist performed a work balanced on a wooden beam. Assisted by uniformed Red Cross volunteers, he was restating the unity required to build a good world. A Japanese artist used her tent as a portable place of refuge, resonant of Red Cross aid in disasters.

During a tour to *Sarajevo Zima*, a New Zealand artist performed a piece about an outsider's 'speechlessness' in response to the unspeakable atrocities that took place in the war in Bosnia. As an outsider to those events, what could he possibly have to say?

On another day that same artist tramped large Cartesian curves into the clean white snow, at Vogasca, an area heavily damaged during the war. This work adhered to the necessity, in the Islamic environment, of creating work that was non figurative and non-representational of any beings. In short, it inscribed the universal symbols of mathematics into a cold, pristine white space redolent of torture and genocide. This was no whimsical recapitulation of the ubiquitous 'I was here!' tagger message; obviously, in hours or days it would disappear. But while it existed, timeless but precise curves inscribed in that immaculate whiteness, it was an effective residue of corporeal transition of space. Walking, the fundamental form of mobility and 'the most humble of human acts' was used here to mobilize a complex symbolic statement (Lorimer 2011: 24). The marks – footprints – that constituted that artwork were juxtaposed with other mobile marks in the same space: the residual evidences of car and truck tyre tracks and of animal footprints in the snow, technology and animality which had traversed the same area.

In the case of the works by the performance artists, by definition they are carrying out an 'ephemeral embodied mobile practice', spatially situated (Dewsbury 2011: 210). The entangled elements Cresswell (2010) refers to that comprise mobility – movement, representation and practice – are definably present in performance art, where notions of the meanings of the embodied corporeal inhabitation of space underpin each work.

Mobility challenged in North Korea

Sheller writes of the Western core notion of mobility being one of political freedom; of not being constrained in any way, and of moving about where and when one pleases (Sheller 2008). There has been just one space where these artists experienced severe restrictions and surveillance. Events experienced by group members illustrated the stymieing of what Westerners have come to regard as a fundamental right to mobility (Cresswell 2010).

In 2007 the Nine Dragon Heads gained official permission for a one-off trip to North Korea. This expedition was naively intended as art as détente. However the Nine Dragon Heads deputation was quickly aware that they were regarded as distrusted outsiders, and were subject to strict supervision. The group's mobility beyond the DMZ was severely curtailed by officialdom. Several artists were detained and questioned by armed authorities for what was perceived as suspicious behaviour – in fact, their radical art installation practices: art that the North Korean officials associated with acts of resistance, or as too overtly symbolizing the freedom of South Korea and of the West.

This art organization, by its mobile nature, is an implicit critique of North Korea. Mobility (and immobility) are both 'productive of social relations and produced by them' (Cresswell 2010: 21). That thwarting of the artists' mobility needs to be contextualized within the tight travel restrictions permanently endured by North Korean citizens, demonstrating the 'differential mobility empowerment' noted by Tesfahuney (1998 cited in Hannam et al. 2006: 3). North Korea is indeed an example of immobility as a significant political agenda.

Mobility as postmodern nomadism?

For most of the artists the Nine Dragon Heads tours and occasional other international projects affords a satisfying experience or taste of 'postmodern nomadism as a romantic idea of total freedom' (Nowika 2007: 71). 'Neo-nomadic' parties take place on every Nine Dragon Heads tour. Participants contribute food and beverages brought from home, to provide a taste of their own culture. Small gifts might be distributed: good humoured representations of elsewhere, or the artists' own catalogues – print or CDs – from previous shows.

In Seoul in 2010 the Nine Dragon Heads exhibition *Nomadic Party* took place immediately before the group set off on its Silk Road journey. But the artists are not truly nomads (Hannam 2009). The requirements of pre-booking transport for a group, and diverse visa requirements, are counter to impetuous or random de-territorialization. Later most will geographically re-territorialize in their own countries. Wherever they eventuate, they have experienced an intellectual and artistic journey which does not have matching fixed starting and ending points.

Nine Dragon Heads provides events as venues for expanding their mobility while retaining their usual attachments to place. For most, the permanent mooring back home is secure. While they are away from home they enact some of the same rituals and habits, those quotidian practices that recreate an intimate, safe comfort zone. Some carry with them coffee, chocolate or other portable foods from home. Others travel with preferred music on their iPods, or bring their favourite perfume. These appeals to the corporeal senses help in the fortification of new moorings, however temporary. Cresswell writes that 'in the end, it is at the level of the body that human mobility is produced, reproduced, and, occasionally, transformed' (Cresswell 2010: 20). It is also at the level of the body that moorings are performed.

But some of the artists are on a life journey which does not include secure employment or long-term commitment to any one place. For the permanently mobile artists, the long-term itinerants, place, stability and dwelling are not 'steady states' (Hannam et al. 2006: 5). 'Home' is not a 'fixed, bounded and enclosed site' (Ralph and Staeheli 2011: 518). This flexibility – a mobile geography of home, as Ralph and Staeheli (2011) call it enables their participation in art opportunities as and when they arise. Their lifestyle is one of mobility across nations, negotiating spaces where they can earn an income or be supported by grants and residencies. Nine Dragon Heads may provide a few weeks each year; at other times they may find live-in residencies or artist retreats for a year or more. Hence they transport their own creativity to the widest possible experiences and audiences. Like other transnational professionals they are mobile within globally spanning networks (Nowicka 2007). Their lives and practices are peripatetic; lifestyle mobilities and corporealities are constantly formally and informally negotiated. The 'normal' identity building structures of home / job / family have been extracted or overridden. The points where past / present / future might meet have been obliterated; their works call for emphasis on the present, the future to be resolved along the way. Their wandering existence keeps them moored in the present, furthering their proficiency at creating temporary anchorages. This peripatetic mobility may eventuate as one duration of the overall life course (Hall 2005). At the same time, this study shows that there are some individuals for whom voluntary mobility truly is a long-term way of life. Their fundamental or primary mooring is their work, rather than any one geographic location.

Conclusion

Displacement has been identified as 'a vehicle towards happiness, development and emotional commitment' (Zusman et al. 2011: 339). This chapter has provided a novel example of transnational artists as workers / tourists whose portability enables them to experience diverse cultures not just for personal pleasure, but as an intrinsic component of their professional practice. That they sustain international careers as artists may be read by some as a position of privilege; but to be successful in their chosen sphere requires that they be corporeally mobile.

For these artists, their mobility expands their art and takes them and it to places literally and metaphorically well beyond the sites and ideas available had they remained moored within their own national borders. Their local knowledge of global events (such as the war in Bosnia) expands rapidly. What may have been nebulous becomes clearer as they work within the context of its physical manifestations, daily traversing, viewing or engaging with bombed buildings, street memorials and war cemeteries. Political awareness is often far greater in situ, than when mediated by television or the internet over a dispassionate distance. The shortness of the visit ladles urgency onto the drive to express ideas through art.

These artists' experiences correspond to that refocus evident in the social sciences: that mobility is now an everyday practice (Edensor 2007, Hannam 2008), and is recognized as a lifestyle choice (Hall 2005). The artists are not travelling to seek a better way of life, somewhere else (Benson and O'Reilly 2009). For them, travelling from place to place itself *constitutes* a way of life. In this case study previously assumed intersections between tourism, migration and lifestyle converge and blur.

References

Anderson, L. 2006. Analytical autoethnography. *Journal of Contemporary Ethnography*, 35(4), 373–395.

Bell, C. 2002. The big OE: young New Zealand travellers as secular pilgrims. *Tourist Studies*, 2(2), 143–158.

Bell, C. 2009. Sarajevska Zima: a festival amid war debris in Sarajevo, Bosnia-Herzegovina. *Space and Culture*, 12(1), 136–142.

Benson, M. and O'Reilly, K. 2009. Migration and the search for a better way of life: a critical exploration of lifestyle migration. *The Sociological Review*, 57(4), 608–625.

Bourdieu, P. 1984. *Distinction: A Social Critique of the Judgment of Taste*. Cambridge, MA: Harvard University Press.

Busher, M. and Urry, J. 2009. Mobile methods and the empirical. *European Journal of Social Theory*, 12(1), 99–116.

Cieraad, I. (ed.) 1999. *At Home. An Anthropology of Domestic Space*. New York: Syracuse University Press.

Crang, M. 2011. Moving Places, Becoming Tourist, Becoming Ethnographer, in *Geographies of Mobilities: Practices, Spaces, Subjects*, edited by T. Cresswell and P. Merriman. Farnham: Ashgate, 205–222.

Cresswell, T. 2010. Towards a politics of mobility. *Environment and Planning D: Society and Space*, 28(1), 17–31.

Dewsbury, J. 2011. Dancing; the Secret Slowness of the Fast, in *Geographies of Mobilities: Practices, Spaces, Subjects*, edited by T. Cresswell and P. Merriman. Farnham: Ashgate, 205–222.

Edensor, T. 2007. Mundane mobilities, performances and spaces of tourism. *Social & Cultural Geography*, 8(2), 199–215.

Gubrium, J.F. and Holstein, J.A. 2011. The Constructionist Analytics of Interpretive Practice, in *Handbook of Qualitative Research*, 4th edition, edited by N.K. Denzin and Y. Lincoln. Thousand Oaks, CA: Sage.

Hall, C.M. 2005. Reconsidering the geography of tourism and contemporary mobility. *Geographical Research*, 43(2), 125–139.

Hannam, K. 2009. The End of Tourism? Nomadology and the Mobilities Paradigm, in *Philosophic Issues in Tourism*, edited by J. Tribe. Bristol: Channel View Publications, 3–24.

Hannam, K., Sheller, M. and Urry, J. 2006. Editorial: mobilities, immobilities and moorings. *Mobilities*, 1(1), 1–22.

Lorimer, H. 2011. Walking: New Forms and Spaces for Studies of Pedestrianism, in *Geographies of Mobilities: Practices, Spaces, Subjects*, edited by T. Cresswell and P. Merriman. Farnham: Ashgate, 19–34.

Mukherji, S. 2011. *Thinking on Thresholds: The Poetics of Transitive Spaces*. London: Anthem Press.

Nine Dragon Heads 2011. Catalogue, 2007–2010 International Environmental Art Symposium, Chungnam, South Korea: Nine Dragon Heads.

Nowicka, M. 2007. Mobile locations: construction of home in a group of mobile transnational professionals. *Global Networks*, 7(1), 69–86.

Ralph, D. and Staeheli, L.A. 2011. Home and migration: mobilities, belongings and identities. *Geography Compass*, 5(7), 517–530.

Rerat, P. and Lees, L. 2011. Spatial capital: gentrification and mobility: evidence from Swiss core cities. *Transactions of the Institute of British Geographers*, 36(1), 126–142.

Sheller, M. 2008. Mobility, Freedom, and Public Space, in *The Ethics of Mobilities: Rethinking Place, Exclusion, Freedom and Environment*, edited by S. Bergmann and T. Sager. Farnham: Ashgate, 27–38.

Vannini, P. 2010. Mobile cultures: from the sociology of transportation to the study of mobilities. *Sociology Compass*, 4(2), 111–121.

Wilson, J., Fisher, D. and Moore, K. 2009. The OE goes 'home': cultural aspects of a working holiday experience. *Tourist Studies*, 9(1), 13–21.

Zusman P., Lois, C. and Castro, H. 2011. The narrative of travels. *Tourism Geographies*, 13(2), 338–342.

Chapter 3

Others Have the Clock But We Have Time: Alternative Lifestyle Mobilities and the Resurgence of Hitchhiking

Michael O'Regan

Introduction

While individuals are not simply cogs in a machine, mobility behaviours are learned early in life and performed almost unthinkingly as routine travel (and tourism) practices; performances based on an ability and willingness to habitually use established and increasingly efficient, speedier and more secure mobility systems. Movement is largely geared towards overcoming the 'friction of distance', getting from A to B conjuring up images of unfettered movement; mobility having acquired new dimensions in the late modern (postmodern) context. A constant movement of images, ideas, capital and people, the 'staggering developments in communication and transportation' (Cresswell 2006: 20) have changed 'our apprehension of space, time and subjectivity' (Simonsen 2004: 43). In the West, there has been a steady, long-term trend in mobility behaviour across generations in proportion to ascending social mobility, heightening the obligations of individuals to be mobile in order to grasp the opportunities that geographic mobility is perceived to give; whether it be in education, leisure or the labour market. Such trends are unleashing and accelerating various mobilities (Bechmann 2004) from student, staff and academic mobility to transnational elites, whose perception of time and space is ordered through modern technologies such as the airplane. However, such mobilities often eliminate older mobilities, whose rhythms are seen as outmoded or inefficient to modern societies (rickshaws, walking and often cycling), a transformation that might potentially disenfranchise groups such as the poor and the elderly. Geographic mobility, although taking place for many reasons, found at many scales and in many forms, is acceptable in Western societies if it is a means to 'get somewhere'; lifestyle mobilities are encouraged as a long as they result in 'improvement' (Cresswell 1993); creating a hierarchy of mobility that is a powerful stratifying factor. Many mobility lifestyles and travelling styles such as those of retirees, second home owners, seasonal migrants, amenity migrants and business / entrepreneurial elites (Benson and O'Reilly 2009, Moss 2006, O'Reilly 2000, Williams and Hall 2000) are often seen as the result of the indulgences of an affluent Western middle class; mobility a scarce resource that allows individuals access to amenity rich areas and private times and spaces. Such lifestyles, given innovations in technology and communications increasingly entail transnational border-crossing mobility, often from the global north to south, from urban to rural, where movement is linked with the accumulation of cultural, economic, political and social capital.

Such lifestyles are widely accepted as a consequence of globalization and have been made desirable and even normative to a minority of the world's population. However, the circulation of information, ideas, capital, goods and people through new and existing social, cultural, economic networks is also recognized as a structuring feature. It imposes its own rationale on the development of societies; transforming spaces, cities, regions, towns, coastlines and territories. Geographic movement, even if of the temporary kind can lead to socio-spatial inequalities and open up a new range of vulnerabilities; issues of 'movement, of too little movement or too much, or of the wrong sort or at the wrong time' (Sheller and Urry 2006: 208) are becoming an important tenet in lifestyle mobilities research. Institutions from universities, the World Trade Organization to car manufacturers continue to inculcate certain habits, with societies largely remaining structured by social constraints; often coerced and organized by surrounding 'successful', 'persuasive', 'seamless', 'modern' and 'friction-free' practices. Peterson (2010: 140) argues one develops 'predispositions to act in certain ways', where much consumption is undertaken in the course of achieving what people count as normal social practice, signalling membership of modern society, conforming to convention and reproducing social order. When applied to a discussion of mobility, including consumption of mobility services, movement that is without accreditation, unfamiliar, old-fashioned or apparently purposeless and aimless is often discouraged, criminalized, legislated against, demonized, monitored, curtailed and vilified. Peterson (2010: 140) argues that social life is a 'constant struggle to construct a life out of the cultural resources one's social experience offers, in the face of formidable social constraints', wherein 'friction-free' practices are often connected to signs of class, gender, age, and ability. This chapter argues, however, that individuals can be subjects and agents in their own right; movement is not simply about getting from A to B at the least cost, inconvenience, time and even social stigma. Cresswell (2006: 45) argues '[n]ot only does the world appear to be more mobile, but our ways of knowing the world have also become more fluid' which possibly might not just change the world but ways of knowing it. Growing out of living at a time 'of extraordinary complexity when systems and structures that have long organised life are changing at an unprecedented rate' (Taylor 2001: 19), innovations in transport technologies and communications during the backdrop of neo-liberal economic globalization have given rise to a much more fluid nomadic world (Attali 1990, Bauman 1996) where changes in mobility behaviour and lifestyles can both emerge to reinforce but also confront societal demands.

This chapter argues that geographic movement can produce identification and meanings beyond state-led mobility politics, family units, ethnicities, religious certainties and even nationalistic and touristic discourses; innovations in communications, transport and information technology leading to re-jigged routines, conventions and order as people enact, perform, and combine mobility and stillness in new or reimagined ways. The modern subject's search for authenticity, fleetingly satisfied by a self-induced and self-controlled mobility (Oakes 2006), is 'leading to new ways of seeing self and other, places and territories, and ultimately the social and material environment of the contemporary world' (Jensen 2009: xv). Whether it is travelling in a Recreational Vehicle (RV), parkour or urban exploration, people are 'summoning life' in an attempt 'to carve out a different kind of ethos from that which currently takes up and deadens so much of our energies' (Thrift 2004: 127). Mobility lifestyles can disrupt or even rupture the logic of daily, familiar or even seasonal routines by affirming the possibility of an alternative mode of (less habitual) practice and action (Cocker 2010). This chapter explores the practice of hitchhiking; an alternative way of practicing mobility, a bodily practice that individuals (or small groups) 'do' which is self-conscious and 'performative' (Goffman 1990), since it is largely performed through objects, people and infrastructures; the 'necessary components of many practices' (Reckwitz 2002: 252). As individuals confirm their identity claims around a mobility related practice such as hitchhiking, they are increasingly advocating subject positions where imagined collective rhythms, shared experience and temporal orderings function as social markers and ways of engaging the world, situated, collective practices such as these generating a 'communal way of seeing the world in consistent terms, sharing a host of reference points which provide the basis for shared discursive, pleasurable and practical habits' (Edensor and Millington 2010: 153).

Methodology

Unlike geographers who 'advanced a static geography … incapable of seeing movement except as pattern' (Crowe 1938: 14), the 'new mobilities paradigm' (Sheller and Urry 2006) demands mobilities be investigated from an interdisciplinary guided perspective, aiming to establish a 'movement-driven social science' (Urry 2007: 18) in which movement is conceptualized 'as constitutive of economic, social and political relations' (Urry 2007: 43). Translating how a lived, embodied, participatory performance-based practice dependent on vehicles and their drivers 'comes-together' as a kind of collective performance to engender new forms of engagement and corporeal responsibility has yet to be fully translated into the discourse of the academy. As the practice of hitchhiking (re)emerges; constituting part of a conscious and complex intellectual revolt against habitual everyday routine; it takes as its reference points many alternative ways of seeing and doing. With influences as wide-ranging as the politics of Anarchism and Environmentalism to figures such as Christopher McCandless (*Into The Wild*) and Jack London, the mobility paradigm offers a way to conceptualize the practice. It enables the researcher to explore how hitchhiking has again found value; framed, negotiated, imagined and materialized, where the intersections of the human and non-human so integral to the 'bodily movements, things, practical knowledge and routine to the centre of its vocabulary' (Reckwitz 2002: 259) combine.

While the system of 'automobility' and the privileged position of the car/ driver assemblage has become the subject of detailed analysis (Featherstone et al. 2005), it is largely an assemblage governed by, and is the consequence of, specific power regimes that that regulate it. Edensor (2004: 114) notes how Europe's roads are 'highly regulated, single-purpose ... spaces of Western highways, where conformity to rules and modes of centralized regulation endure'. Sheller and Urry (2006: 209) argue, however, that the 'sites, places, and materialities of the mobilities that are already coursing through them' should also be investigated. Since hitchhikers through encounters with objects, individuals and space seek to affect the assemblage and modify mobility behaviour, creating non-routine breaks, detours and amendments to journeys, its investigation requires a 'mobile methodology' (Fincham et al. 2010, Büscher et al. 2010). Using a mixed methodological approach, the researcher became a participant and observer in the practice of hitchhiking during 2010 and 2011. Becoming an active participant allowed the researcher to reflect upon the practice, an immersion after which the researcher 'should possess a degree of the particular know-how, appropriate conduct and common knowledge of the place and/or people ... chosen to study' (Laurier 2003: 5). The researcher participated in four hitchhiker gatherings in 2010 and 2011 as well as hitchhiking individually around Ireland during March 2010; travels that took in over 4,000 km of motorways and road. The gatherings usually require participants to hitchhike to particular destinations to camp, share activities and stories before hitchhiking away. The researcher participated in the third and fourth German 'Abgefahren' (http://race.abgefahren-ev.de/?) gatherings and the third and fourth European hitchhiking weeks (http://hitchgathering.org/). The events brought nearly 400 geographically dispersed participants from around the world together, both online and also to hitchhike and spend time together. While the former event centred on creating two-person teams in Augsburg (2010) and Freiburg im Breisgau (2011) before announcing the destination just before departure, the latter event had participants organize various pre-post gatherings across Europe, before and after the one final push towards Sines, Portugal (2010) and Kara Dere, Bulgaria (2011). The 'gatherings' make visible the social phenomena of hitchhiking, participation not only helping to focus on the practice at the level of individual practitioners but the practice itself. Twelve interviews (lasting between 25 and 60 minutes) via Skype in the days after the hitchhiking 'gatherings' were made but as in other fieldwork situations, numerous informal discussions, the researcher's own experiences, still images and observations added value to the research – a movement driven research methodology sensitive to those on the move, where 'being there', means thinking, feeling and performing their world.

(Alternative) mobility lifestyles

From increases in car ownership, private motorized transport to outbound leisure travel, individuals in post-industrial democratic societies have possibilities to relocate themselves in social and geographical space; the type, range and scope of geographic movement driving lifestyles and changes in people's lives. Most individuals will, by and large, adopt existing mobility modes upon reaching adulthood; embedded in 'historically sedimented and geographically etched patterns' (Sheller 2004: 222) of 'quotidian mobility' (Kaufman 2000) ensuring that these developments continue and intensify across generations. From buying the first car, taking the first short-break holiday or retiring to a region, societal rules, historical trends and behavioural codes mean institutionalized mobility practices have become a rite-of-passage for many. Based on norms, tradition, custom as well as promotional and regulatory discourses that generate expectations and frames of reference used to interpret the behaviour and performance of others, the expansion of mobility now seems more directly linked to institutions and industries, lifestyle practices offering the means for achieving social, political and economic inclusion. Such lifestyles require mobility systems that organize 'around the processes that circulate people, objects and information at various spatial ranges and speeds' (Urry 2007: 52), a self-perpetuating phenomenon that affects methods of communication and interaction, producing 'human relations in the service-sector style' (Baudrillard 1998: 162). Such relationships between elements that would otherwise have no connection are often founded on the circulation of money, facilitating individual independence from group interests, organic or territorially bound social relations (Aradau et al. 2010), but also facilitating the expulsion of alterity beyond new 'boundaries of the ethnically, culturally, or civilizationally "purified" homogenous enclave – at whatever level of social or geographical scale' (Morley 2004: 309).

However, this new individualism can also change the way that people conceive of themselves, assisting in the self and a 'self-recognition that one has one's own perspective on the world' (Santos and Yan 2010: 56). How we move has become 'a statement of class, identity, personality, environmental values and wealth (amongst other things), as well as a practical means of simply completing everyday tasks' (Pooley et al. 2005: 14–15). Whether it is daily, temporary or long-term movement, choice of mobility mode and ways of moving can have implications for the negotiation of identities, since mobility related practices require learning normative regulating principles, norms, expectations and socialization processes (Jensen 2009), cultural and technological achievements often necessitating the mastering of the body in a certain way. Jensen (2009) argues that such practices can become signifying practices within lifestyles, and need not be derivative of any particular nation-state, migratory network or dominant tourist culture. From freedom camping, sailing, cycling, urban-exploration to train hopping, individuals are increasingly seeking to experience different scales of mobility and dwelling – breaking with everyday life through 'marginal mobility practices' (Jensen 2009: xvii). It is an affect that 'both reveals and disrupts habitual patterns of behaviour, whilst simultaneously creating a space into which to imagine – or even produce – the experience of something new or different' (Cocker 2010: 87). While second home ownership, amenity-seeking seasonal migration or international retirement migration is generally accepted, promoted and repositioned as acceptable forms of mobility and dwelling, there often hostility towards other lifestyles, if not conforming to the standard narratives of society. Hitchhiking is one such signifying but marginal practice that is seeing some resurgence. While re-emerging in some countries because of social, economic (fuel prices) and political inequality, this chapter looks at those hitchhikers responding to hitchhiking gatherings, whose mobility is infused with cultural, social, political and environmental meaning.

Hitchhiking and hitchhikers

A very distinguishable 'way and style of acting into the world' (McCormack 2003: 501), hitchhiking is a means of transportation that requires hitchhikers to ask people, usually drivers who are strangers to them, for a free ride in their automobile or other road, sea or air vehicle to travel over distance. Over long journeys, the hitchhiker is usually required to make a variety of connections across time-space, rebelling against the sequestered spatial logic of the motorway and the car-driver assemblage to accumulate numerous 'lifts'. A relatively minor practice that emerged in the 1920s with the advent of the new technology of the car and lorry (Chesters and Smith 2001), the practice solidified, but only came to have a social, political, collective value and affect in the 1960s. Functioning as an integrative force, it knitted geographically dispersed people together in an alternative life trajectory, producing feelings of 'trust, and mutual consideration amongst a generational phenomenon we call the counterculture (1965–1975). Prior to the sixties, '[h]itchhiking did not make one a hitchhiker; practice did not lead to identity' (Packer 2008: 81). However, with the emergence of the Beats in the fifties and books like *On the Road* by Jack Kerouac (1957), the practice became central in negotiating a sense of identity. As obligations to custom and tradition broke down, the practice provided new avenues for people to be part of a generational movement unmediated by the family, traditional communities, institutions or economic trade relations. An alternative form of cultural participation associated with freedom, anti-establishment nomadism, adventure, escape and discovery established hitchhiking as normal, acceptable and even pleasurable (Chesters and Smith 2001), the practice coming 'to be associated with different ways of being and thinking, and different ethics, aesthetics and ecologies' (Cresswell and Merriman 2011: 6). According to Packer (2008: 84) the practice could have been 'integrated into an expanding regime of mobility and surveillance, but it was instead made illegal in a growing number of municipalities, on more state roads, and eventually on all federal highways' (in the United States). By the early seventies, the practice became contested and rejected as insurance company publicity, a police crackdown, widespread anti-hitchhiking legislation,[1] and a sensationalist media turned hitchhiking into a feared form of mobility and the hitchhiker into a sinister figure (Packer 2008). Reduced to a practice on the edge of a transport infrastructure, a generation of drivers and hitchhikers who regarded hitchhiking as acceptable were eroded and hitchhiking ceased to be popular, accessible or even thinkable spatial practice, its demise paralleling the demise of the counterculture as a whole.

Today, hitchhiking is undergoing resurgence as travellers engage in a practice that requires geographic mobility and corporeal engagement to perform the 'self-powered' practice, where the 'disciplined mobility of the body' (Châtelet 1993) is characterized by the upturned thumb; the hitchhiking gesture an essential, culturally celebrated indifference. While the practice again has implications for people's identities, hitchhiking's boundaries as a practice are difficult to identify. One person's mobility might be imagined as product of their own influence, while for others, it is not a choice but a necessary mode of moving, since a close relationship between hitchhiking and inequality still exists. While people (commuter, vagabond, tourist, migrant worker, refugee) will hitchhike for many reasons (rising fuel prices, the Icelandic ash cloud), larger numbers are choosing the practice to sustain and build connections and knowledge across cultural, social and geographic boundaries, demonstrating dispositions they already feel they have about themselves. Part of an alternative 'scene' (Irwin 1973) since the sixties, hitchhiking is again bringing together those who are broadly socially and political similar, once again a cultural symbol that resonates with personal identity. While individuals from different lifestyles (anarchists travelling to a demonstration, those leading a moneyless existence) may differ in many areas, the gatherings generate agreement and overlap on areas of sustainable living, more meaningful movement and hospitality but especially on the value of the practice itself. From festivals (for example the Road Junky Festival 2010), books (for example *Evasion*), documentaries (for example 'Paris 888'), films (for example 'Into the Wild'), fiction (*Norton's Ghost*), online magazines (randomroads.org), discussion groups and portals (for example hitchwiki.org), the worth of the practice is reinforced and reaffirmed. Knowledge about the practice, how and where to perform it, is built up on sites like Hitchbase.com, digihitch.com and hitchwiki.org[2] which promote the practice as a 'symbol of solidarity' (Hebdige 1976: 93), enabling hitchhikers to become active participants and creators by mapping the world in a particular

---

1   Foucault (1977: 219) argues 'discipline fixes; it arrests or regulates movements; it clears up confusion; it dissipates compact groupings of individuals wandering about the country in unpredictable ways; it establishes calculated distributions'.

2   By 16 July 2010, Hitchwiki had 1600 articles with a total of 134,583 edits and an average of 1300 visitors per day. It received 100,000 unique visitors during 2013. Another hitchhiking website, http://www.digihitch.com, had, as of April 2012, nearly 24,000 members.

way by tagging and sharing information (good hitchhiking points, how to get to the outskirts of a city, safety precautions, and so on).

The interviewed participants, a mixture of learners, samplers, dabblers and enthusiasts (Keeling 2006), were already knowledgeable of websites promoting the practice, and all had taken up or were interested in interacting 'interstitial practices' such as hospitality exchange, dumpster diving, rough camping, street performing, squatting, veganism to freeganism and political activism. Their degree of participation in an alternative life trajectory while neither agreed upon nor openly negotiated was secondary, at least for the period of travelling to and participating in the gatherings. While individuals occupied various subject positions, their shared involvement in hitchhiking was central to their sense of self and to their place with a broader alternative life trajectory. It is seen to have value in itself, allowing individuals to build a viable existence (both for episodic and longer-term travel) across time-space but also demonstrating both their embodiment of 'cosmopolitan predispositions' and a particular 'homopholy' that valued particular ways of moving, dwelling and communicating. Just as in the other 'interstitial practices', the communal principles, systems of exchange, denial of risk, trust and use of spare resources (without financial payment) inherent to hitchhiking were present. Hitchhiking, having value in itself but also as means into an alternative life trajectory also points to the overlapping attitudes, values or worldview of the participants; becoming a central cultural symbol that is discussed as a vehicle for fostering qualities such as independence and responsibility, with particular 'intellectual and aesthetic orientations towards cultural and geographical difference, and distinctive kinds of competence' (Szerszynski and Urry 2006: 114). Hitchhiking, at least under the conditions of the gatherings is a cosmopolitan practice,[3] that amongst other things allows for extensive mobility, demonstrating a curiosity about many places, peoples and cultures, a willingness to take risks by virtue of encountering the 'other', and openness to other peoples and cultures (Szerszynski and Urry 2006).

Performing motorscapes

Mobility lifestyles also need spaces in which to enact mobility – with hitchhikers utilizing the sea, roads, air to railway lines to further their mobility (O'Regan 2013). The majority of those interviewed hitch lifts on Europe's motorway network, where the acceptance of the car and the habitual performances of driving mean automobilities have entered the social and economic fabric of people's lives. These motorscapes facilitate 'practice but are also reproduced by the actions and understandings of people' (Edensor 2004: 111). Treated as one of life's constants,

---

3   While it is possible to hitchhike without cosmopolitan dispositions (since they are not universal dispositions) the practice does have performance indicators that are learned, cultivated and modified over time-space and agreeable to those who attend the gatherings.

everyday life projects are planned with the assumption that a car will be part of the environment, most presupposing its continuation as the most feasible mode of ordered mobility. A 'mode of mobility is neither socially necessary nor inevitable yet it seems almost impossible to break away from' (Urry 2008: 344). Urry (2007: 115) notes that '[c]ountry after country is developing an "automobility culture"', road space and its infrastructure and is choreographing mobility and organizing movement just like airports, railway stations and other mobility systems. While systems of automobility have produced a strong structural effect on road infrastructures and the practicing of mobility, motorscapes do not generate one specific kind of body. I argue that the roads, its drivers and supporting infrastructure help to construct a range of identity positions. Edensor (2006: 385) notes how 'performances are increasingly acted out by competing actors on the same stage', with motorways containing everyone from tourists, businessmen, truck drivers to police officers, some of whom seem appropriate to this domain, and others who have contested ideas about what practices are appropriated. The motorscapes and its amenities can become a territory in which individuals can use their (mobile) bodies and senses in 'doing' movement differently, the practice of hitchhiking requiring them to leave their homes and occupy a highly visible space on the world's motorways and roads. More than just a bodily practice, the individual is also carrying the ideas, reasons, and objects that make the practice work, their very performance of hitchhiking making motorscapes a fluid space, an assemblage of signified features evolving in function according to the activities they need to perform. Objects, amenities, other bodies and infrastructure are positioned according to their ability to meet the requirements of the practice. Service stations become a place where hitchhikers can replenish their bodies, interact with drivers and sleep overnight, the maintenance of sprawling transportation networks, criticized for social affects (that come with being so spread out and disconnected from one's friends and family) becoming a place of movement relations and exchange with other hitchhikers, drivers and service station employees. These motorways and roads constitute the hitchhikers' territory, its drivers, cars, petrol stations and trucks enabling them to orchestrate in complex and heterogeneous ways their mobilities and socialities, and therefore their identities across very significant distances.

In order to be able to stay mobile, it is necessary for hitchhikers to develop ties with drivers, landowners and service station workers (and sometimes police) at varying times, in different places, a practice that demands human interaction, intimate engagement, connectivity and exchange. This is not a one-sided exchange, since those who pick up hitchhikers usually have excess capacity and providing a ride has advantages, providing both driver and hitchhiker with a 'comparative advantage' (Ricardo 1817) in trade. Nevertheless, driving (especially on motorways) is based on an ensemble of institutionally defined and socially recognized behaviours based on prescribed ways and rules (traffic systems, speeds, tolls). Any practice that lies outside the range of prescribed ways, irrespective of its potential value is defined as inappropriate by some drivers (many of whom have considerable physical, financial and social resources) who seek to defend their personal space. They often regard hitchhikers as unsettled, transitional and non-integrated, their mobility deviant, suspect and potentially dangerous. For other drivers, their 'quasi-private' mobility is associated with sexual desire and masculinity (Urry 2000) with hitchhiking bodies perceived to be exploitable or weak and easily harassed. However, for many others who allow the hitchhiker into their private space by overcoming perceptions of 'risky strangers' (Furedi 1997), the hitchhiker may enliven their mobility experience, the encounter creating a very unique atmosphere. Many of the drivers have a sense of obligation, while others have a sense of reciprocity. Others come from countries where hitchhiking is more socially acceptable or had grown up during a period when it was acceptable. The scale, range and scope of Europe's motorway system are increasing each year, creating greater possibilities for seamless mobility but also extreme disconnection. Drivers recognize the mobility capital in this form of circulation, their willingness to trust outweighing any perception of risk. Just as with the hospitality exchange host, the exchange requires a sense of solidarity, a willingness to share and co-operate and an active acceptance of difference. Requiring intimate engagement, they engender moments; 'those instants that we would each, according to our own personal criteria, categorise as "authentic" moments that break through the dulling monotony of the "taken for granted"' (Shields 1999: 58, citing Harvey 1991: 429), providing insight into drivers' lives that are tangible and memorable. These encounters potentially affect the individual's notion of self, and for the interviewees reciting their mobility biographies, the moments, incidents, learning, new knowledge and hospitality encountered are of uppermost importance. These moments are related to the construction and validation of their alternative lifestyles, however temporary or episodic they may be.

The world of difference

Compared with the 'seamlessness' of car journeys (since you do not have to change modes of travel), hitchhiking as a mode of self-directed mobility is largely fragmented, inconvenient and less seamless, bringing turbulence, friction, slower speeds and intensities of encounter. Without a shield, it involves a space of performance that can be acutely open and sensitive to the affects outside the self, where sensations and physical efforts are acutely felt. The practice is both constructive and unsettling; each journey associated with complex feelings, unexpected moments, instant decisions, gratitude, fear, excitement, boredom, marginalization and risk. Considering the turbulence and friction inherent in the practice (waiting for lifts, sleeping at motorway service stations, harassment, exposure to the automobile gaze, weather), participants talk about their journeys (encounters, experiences) as something valuable, with the potential to affect and develop the self, the practice 'reproduced by the views and understandings of people' (Edensor 2004: 111). Imagining themselves as creators of their own life and authors of their own environment, they feel the practice helps them to recover 'the world of difference – the natural, the sensory/sensual, sexuality and pleasure' (Lefebvre 1991: 50). The world, they believe, is navigated and browsed more efficiently with their bodies, their movements more 'real' than those that could be accomplished by the passive and risk-adverse tourists, who do not have the time, stamina or bodily/physical competences or skills.

As a practice, it is essentially a product of bodily mobility, performed into being, a performance that requires competence and knowledge (to recognize and make use of access) and appropriation (involving all behavioural components) of particular choices (Kaufman 2002). Kesserling and Volg (2008: 167) suggest that 'mobility' can be defined 'as an actor's competence to realise specific projects and plans while being on the move', the practice of hitchhiking unrealizable without mobility and regular displays of skill, patience, risk and courage. The hitchhiking gatherings are based on the premise that the more hitchhikers on the roads, the more likely parents, educators, authorities, the media and drivers can overcome potential psychological barriers and social distrust, since fear once visited on the practice is difficult to eliminate. Enabling first time hitchhikers to share risk by hitchhiking with experienced others, attempts are made to challenge perceptions and fear amongst drivers and first time hitchhikers. At the gatherings, sharing information, hitchhiking tutorials, social activities, playing games, sharing books/food whilst telling stories, networking and identifying areas of agreement become central, moments later recounted on hitchhiking websites. Experiences are decoded during informal and group discussion, providing a platform for recognition, validation and socialization, the experiences used as a resource to assert oneself and demonstrate belonging. The (re)emergence of hitchhiking should not be read for or against the role of mobility in modern life, or mobility as a cultural, economic, political and social imperative. Alternatively, rather than see their mobility as counter-hegemonic resistance, hitchhikers are not trapped in nostalgia for older mobilities, although it does alert us 'to the necessity of seeing the mobilities of the past in the mobilities of the present and future' (Cresswell and Merriman 2011: 11). The issue is 'not so much the activity per se, but rather what the activity stood for, for what purpose was it used, who was in charge of it, and what economic forms it operated within' (Packer 2008: 105). Hitchhiking for its adherents attests to the sociality of the 'stranger' experience, the car representing a concentrated space of emotions (Sheller 2004) that allows the hitchhiker to cross cultural, social and physical boundaries by relying on 'communication ... non-verbal clues or signals ... a sense from the body beside you ... [the ability to] anticipate and negotiate expression and variation' (Morton 2005: 672).

Hitchhikers see the value of the globalizing system of automobility (Urry 2007) but understand the fragilities on which this mobility is based, since you must set aside personal ambitions and often go with someone else's flow, travelling on someone else's time. Looking beyond comfort, make, speed or any other benefit inherent in vehicles themselves, hitchhiking for its participants means holding 'onto something real as everything melts' (Bermann 1988: 14).

It is 'to make oneself somehow at home in the maelstrom, to make its rhythms one's own, to move within its currents in search of the forms of reality, of beauty, of freedom, of justice, that its fervid and perilous flow allows' (Bermann 1993: 345–346). Hitchhiking has again become central to many people's worldview, emerging through particular conjunctions of flows of people, objects, money, information and knowledge, creating border-crossing geographies of circulation and multi-locationality. It embroils hitchhikers in multiple relationships, potential encounters, emotional connections as well as intensities of risk, fear, atmosphere, excitement; proving 'living, breathing, corporeal human beings arrayed in various creatively improvised networks of relation still exist as something more than machine fodder' (Thrift 1996: 1466). Getting lost as a passenger in the labyrinth of Europe's road networks is one method of gaining insight into modern society as individuals 'repeatedly couple and uncouple their paths with other people's paths, institutions, technologies and physical surroundings' (Mels 2004: 16).

Conclusion

Worldwide communications, trade and technologies have given a new impetus to human mobility, contemporary societies increasingly organized around movement, where innovations in transportation and communications form the backbone of a more accelerating and more interconnected world. Machine-based fast movement and automobility in particular is dominating in an era of globalization, becoming a seamless and feasible mode of everyday life transport for many, sustaining networked patterns of social and economic life. Lifestyle mobilities when self-controlled can enable new possibilities and openings for individuals, taking possession of what is possible in the domain of mobility potentials, building on particular practices congruent with self-identity to sustain life-projects. Often derided as being minor, episodic and occasional, this chapter instead argued that mobility lifestyles allow people to explore different aspects of their personalities and values; people enacting and performing mobility (and stillness) in new ways. Driven to the surface because of environmental, political, social, technological and economic changes, (alternative) mobility lifestyles can transgress societal pressures and habitual social norms, as much as second homes and lifestyle gated communities can also affirm self-hood.

This chapter took a fresh look at hitchhiking, an alternative mode of (less habitual) practice and action which has again risen in importance by individuals searching for and/or demonstrating an alternative life trajectory, affirming self-hood by breaking with traditional ethnic, class, religious and Western tourist boundaries. Frequently overlooked, caricatured and stereotyped as outmoded or anachronistic, the cultural value of the practice and the social, political and environmental values of the participants who coalesce around it are easily disregarded. While few are willing to break with societal conventions or habit and 'learn bodily', putting their body on the line when more convenient modes of dwelling and moving are available, participants rather than feeling disempowered or powerless because of the disrupted mobilities feel their mobile bodies have agency. Participation demands a corporeal engagement and mastering of the body to endure hardships according to the situation, their voluntary displacement in time-space giving the body and mind a taste of something they feel is often lacking in everyday life. The practice is a social, political and cultural achievement, enabling those who practice it to live, even temporally, outside of the expectations, behavioural codes, familiar routines and corporate control of linear time that accompany modern societies.

This chapter argued that the practice has become ideologically and physically constituted across nations, drawing those with enough overlapping affinities to hitchhiking books, websites and gatherings and therein enabling individuals to forage their way into or demonstrate an alternative life trajectory. In an enlarged and largely borderless Europe, a shared practice and sharing stories of practice, both at gatherings and online, contribute to the construction and development of identities. As other practices from skateboarding, yoga, urban cycling to graffiti are incorporated or 'fused' within the tense and routine rhythms and rhetoric of modern-mobility and reduced to a socio-economic practice (insofar as if they are perceived as agents, who, by spending their money can promote the circulation of capital, goods, services, ideas and bodies as a prerequisite for social and economic growth), hitchhiking remains outside, intervening in established social and technical systems to create social relations unstructured by past histories and institutions.

References

Aradau, C., Huysmans, J. and Squire, V. 2010. Acts of European Citizenship: A Political Sociology of Mobility. *JCMS: Journal of Common Market Studies*, 48(4), 945–965.

Attali, J. 1990. *Millennium: Winners and Losers in the Coming World Order*. New York: Times Books.

Baudrillard, J. 1998. *The Consumer Society: Myths and Structures*. London: Sage Publications.

Bauman, Z. 1996. From Pilgrim to Tourist – or a Short History of Identity, in *Questions of Cultural Identity*, edited by S. Hall and P. du Gay. London: Sage Publications, 18–36.

Bechmann, J. 2004. Ambivalent Spaces of Restlessness: Ordering (Im)mobilities at Airports, in *Space Odysseys: Spatiality and Social Relations in the 21st Century*, edited by J.O. Bærenholdt and K. Simonsen. Farnham: Ashgate, 27–42.

Benson, M. and O'Reilly, K. (eds) 2009. *Lifestyle Migration – Expectations, Aspirations and Experiences*. Farnham: Ashgate.

Berman, M. 1988. *All That Is Solid Melts Into Air*. New York: Penguin Books.

Büscher, M., Urry, J. and Witchger, K. (eds) 2010. *Mobile Methods*. London: Routledge.

Châtelet, G. 1993. *Les enjeux du mobile*. Paris: Seuil (Engl. transl., by R. Shore and M. Zagha).

Chesters, G. and Smith, D. 2001. The neglected art of hitch-hiking: risk, trust and sustainability. *Sociological Research Online*, 6(3). Available at: http://www.socresonline.org.uk/6/3/chesters.html [accessed: 8 August 2011].

Cocker, E. 2010. Performing Stillness: Community in Waiting, in *Stillness in a Mobile World*, edited by D. Bissell and G. Fuller. London: Routledge, 87–106.

Cresswell, T. 1993. Mobility as resistance: a geographical reading of Kerouac's 'On the Road'. *Transactions, Institute of British Geographers*, 18(2), 249–262.

Cresswell, T. 2006. *On the Move: Mobility in the Modern Western World*. London: Routledge.

Cresswell, T. and Merriman, P. 2011. Introduction: Geographies of Mobilities – Practices, Spaces, Subjects, in *Geographies of Mobilities – Practices, Spaces, Subjects*, edited by T. Cresswell and P. Merriman. Farnham: Ashgate, 1–19.

Crowe, P.R. 1938. On progress in geography. *Scottish Geographical Magazine*, 54(1), 1–18.

Edensor, T. 2004. Automobility and national identity: representation, geography and driving practice. *Theory, Culture & Society*, 21(4–5), 101–120.

Edensor, T. 2006. Performing Rurality, in *Handbook of Rural Studies*, edited by P. Cloke et al. London: Sage Publications, 484–495.

Edensor, T. and Millington, S. 2010. Going to the Match: the Transformation of the Match-day Routine in English Premier League Football, in *Stadium Worlds: Football, Space and Built Environment*, edited by S. Frank and S. Steets. London: Routledge, 146–162.

Featherstone, M., Thrift, N. and Urry, J. (eds) 2005. *Automobilities*. London: Sage Publications.

Fincham, B., McGuinness, M. and Murray, L. (eds) 2010. *Mobile Methodologies*. Basingstoke: Palgrave Macmillan.

Foucault, M. 1977. *Discipline and Punish*. London: Tavistock.

Furedi, F. 1997. *Culture of Fear: Risk-Taking and the Morality of Low Expectation*. London: Cassell.

Goffman, E. 1990. *The Presentation of Self in Everyday Life*. London: Penguin.

Hebdige, D. 1976. *Subculture: The Meaning of Style*. London: Methuen.

Irwin, J. 1973. Surfing: The Natural History of an Urban Scene. *Urban Life and Culture*, 2(2), 31–60.

Jensen, O.B. 2009. Foreword: Mobilities as Culture, in *The Cultures of Alternative Mobilities: Routes Less Traveled*, edited by P. Vannini. Farnham: Ashgate, xv–xix.

Kaufman, V. 2000. *Mobilité quotidienne et dynamiques urbaines: la question du report modal*. Lausanne: Presses Polytechniques et Universitaires Romandes.

Kaufman, V. 2002. *Re-thinking Mobility: Contemporary Sociology*. Farnham: Ashgate.

Keeling, A. 2006. Understanding the outdoor activity tourism market. *Countryside Recreation*, 14(2), 3–6.

Kesselring, S. and Volg, G. 2008. Networks, Scapes and Flows – Mobility Pioneers between First and Second Modernity, in *Tracing Mobilities*, edited by W. Canzler et al. Farnham: Ashgate, 163–180.

Laurier, E. 2010. Participant Observation, in *Key Methods in Geography*, 2nd edition, edited by N. Clifford and G. Valentine. London: Sage Publications, 116–130.

Lefebvre, H. 1991. *The Production of Space*. Oxford: Blackwell.

McCormack, D. 2003. An event of geographical ethics in spaces of affect. *Transactions of the Institute of British Geographers*, 28(4), 488–507.

Mels, T. 2004. Introduction: Lineages of a Geography of Rhythms, in *Re-animating Place: A Geography of Rhythms*, edited by T. Mels. Aldershot: Ashgate, 3–44.

Morley, D. 2004. At Home with Television, in *Television After TV: Essays on a Medium in Transition*, edited by L. Spigel and J. Olsson. Durham, NC: Duke University Press, 303–323.

Morton, F. 2005. Performing ethnography: Irish traditional music sessions and new methodological spaces. *Social and Cultural Geography*, 6(5), 661–676.

Moss, L.A.G. (ed.) 2006. *The Amenity Migrants: Seeking and Sustaining Mountains and Their Cultures*. Wallingford, Oxfordshire: CAPI Publishing.

O'Regan, M. 2013. Independent travel: creative tactics in the margins. *E-Review Tourism Research (eRTR)*, 10(5/6). Available at: http://ertr.tamu.edu/volume-10-issue-56-may-2013-special-issue-3/ [accessed 30 August 2013].

O' Reilly, K. 2000. *The British on the Costa del Sol: Transnational Identities and Local Communities*. London: Routledge.

Oakes, T. 2006. Tourism and the Modern Subject: Placing the Encounter between Tourist and Other, in *Seductions of Place: Geographical Perspectives on Globalization and Touristed Landscapes*, edited by C. Cartier and A. Lew. London: Routledge, 36–55.

Packer, J. 2008. *Mobility without Mayhem: Safety, Cars, Citizenship*. Durham, NC: Duke University Press.

Peterson, M.A. 2010. 'But It Is My Habit to Read the Times': Metaculture and Practice in the Reading of Indian Newspapers, in *Theorising Media and Practice*, edited by B. Bräuchler and J. Postill. Oxford and New York: Berghahn, 127–146.

Pooley, C., Turnbull, J. and Adams, M. 2005. *A Mobile Century? Changes in Everyday Mobility in Britain in the Twentieth Century*. Farnham: Ashgate.

Reckwitz, A. 2002. Toward a theory of social practices: a development in culturalist theorizing. *European Journal of Social Theory*, 5(2), 243–263.

Ricardo, D. 1817. *On the Principles of Political Economy and Taxation*. London: John Murray.

Santos, C.A. and Yan, G. 2010. Genealogical tourism: a phenomenological examination. *Journal of Travel Research*, 49(1), 56–67.

Sheller, M. 2004. Automotive emotions: feeling the car. *Theory, Culture and Society*, 21(4–5), 221–242.

Sheller, M. and Urry, J. 2006. The new mobilities paradigm. *Environment and Planning A*, 38(2), 207–226.

Shields, R. 1999. *Lefebvre, Love & Struggle*. London: Routledge.

Simonsen, K. 2004. Spatiality, Temporality and the Construction of the City, in *Space Odysseys: Spatiality and Social Relation in the 21st Century*, edited by J.O. Bærenholdt and K. Simonsen. Farnham: Ashgate, 43–61.

Szerszynski. B. and Urry, J. 2006. Visuality, mobility, and the cosmopolitan: inhabiting the world from afar. *British Journal of Sociology*, 57(1), 113–131.

Taylor, M.C. 2001. *The Moment of Complexity: Emerging Network Culture*. Chicago: University of Chicago Press.

Thrift, N. 1996. New urban eras and old technological fears: reconfiguring the goodwill of electronic things. *Urban Studies*, 33(8), 1463–1493.

Thrift, N. 2004. Performance and performativity: a geography of unknown lands, in *A Companion to Cultural Geography*, edited by J.S. Duncan et al. Oxford: Blackwell, 121–136.

Urry, J. 2000. *Sociology Beyond Societies*. London: Routledge.

Urry, J. 2007. *Mobilities*. Cambridge: Polity Press.

Urry, J. 2008. Governance, flows, and the end of the car system? *Global Environmental Change*, 18(3), 343–349.

Williams, A.M. and Hall, C.M. 2000. Tourism and migration: new relationships between production and consumption. *Tourism Geographies*, 2(1), 5–27.

Chapter 4

'Dirtbags': Mobility, Community and Rock Climbing as Performative of Identity

Jillian M. Rickly-Boyd

Introduction

Alternative sports, such as rock climbing, surfing or mountain biking, tend to be more participant-oriented than institutionalized, spectator sports such as basketball, soccer/football, or baseball. Among a number of alternative sports, also known as 'lifestyle' sports by participants (Wheaton 2004) or 'extreme' sports in popular media discourse (Wheaton 2007, Robinson 2008), can be found highly dedicated, full-time participants. Because many alternative sports have a strong seasonality, frequent and continuous travel in pursuit of the activity results. While some of these athletes gain sponsorships that support their full-time participation, others support themselves, thus (for most) necessitating a minimalist lifestyle. Among these latter devotees, a strong sense of identity and community develops. While such recreational pursuits are underexplored in the literature, these mobile communities have been identified among surfers and rock climbers in particular, as 'surf rats', surf/climbing 'bums', or 'dirtbags' (see Chouinard 2006, Waeschle 2009, Taylor 2010). The rock climbers, self-identified as 'dirtbags', are the focus of this chapter.

In Craig Stevens' (2010: 46, emphasis added) 'Confessions of a Dirtbag', the author writes of the lifestyle of this social group:

> A funny thing happens to a person when they find themselves stuck in the elements with no food, no water, and no cash. Whether it's natural instinct that takes over, progressive de-evolution, or a mixture of both, something inside all of us emerges in times of desperation and proves that no matter how long and dark the tunnel may be, there's always a light at the end. Sometimes the end just happens to be tucked away beneath stale bread and moldy oranges. *This is the point at which everyday climbing bums transcend into a new social ranking altogether. Dirtbags.*

Despite his melodramatic tone, the author goes on to explain how one can manage to feed oneself on only a few dollars a week, the inessential daily or even hot showers and other modern creature comforts, and the fruits of undertaking such a minimalist lifestyle. But what remains unspoken in his confessions is the voluntary nature of this very self-induced poverty. The majority of 'dirtbags' come from backgrounds of relative affluence, and many have given up significant educational and employment opportunities to explore this recreational and existential pursuit, supporting Urry's (1990, 2002) claims that the new leisure class of postmodern tourism is characterized by a descending social mobility.

Moreover, Stevens (2010: 49) notes that the number of 'individuals taking favor to the idea of calling home wherever you decide to lay your head is growing', as 'dirtbagging', he asserts, 'is not based on a need to alienate oneself from society, but instead a passion to seek out new experiences that force us to live completely in the moment, and through that, achieve an entirely new level of appreciation for the simplest pleasures'. In fact, while earlier generations of 'dirtbags' in the 1960s, 70s and 80s did experience a degree of isolation, or even alienation, as a result of continuous travel in pursuit of climbing, the increasing prevalence of global communications technology now helps to keep many in touch with family and friends, particularly as for a growing number of 'dirtbags' a minimalist lifestyle includes a laptop or smartphone.

The existential motivations, travel patterns and social networks of 'dirtbags' suggest similarities to several travel phenomena, including pilgrimage, drifting and backpacking. As 'pilgrims of the vertical' (Taylor 2010), they seek out the existential and even spiritual experiences of rock climbing. Yet, their frequent travel along 'circuits' of climbing destinations, characterized by highly flexible itineraries, sociality and community networks suggest the backpacker as the closest travel phenomena to this group.

This chapter presents the findings of research focused on these itinerant rock climbers known as 'dirtbags', in particular addressing the implications of this lifestyle on individual and collective identities. Investigations of the online community forums at Rockclimbing.com, the most popular website dedicated to the sport, uncover first person narratives of the 'dirtbag' identity and lifestyle. The application of ethnographic methodologies to the Internet enables the 'investigation of cross-cultural, multi-levelled, and multi-sited phenomena; emerging constructions of individual and collective identity; and the culturally embedded nature of emerging communicative and social practices' (Wilson and Peterson 2002: 450). Analysis of this community resource reveals discursive aspects of 'dirtbag' as an identity within the larger, diverse community of rock climbers, as well as the motivations, goals, and reflective experiences of this temporary lifestyle, and suggests this identity, as an extension of rock climbing, is highly performative.

It begins with a review of the literature regarding identity as a construction as well as a performance, particularly as it is related to tourism, travel and mobility. This is followed by a brief description of the methodology and its application to the online forums of Rockclimbing.com. Next, the 'dirtbag' as an identity is examined with specific focus on the significance of rock climbing, society, self-discovery and community. Finally, some conclusions as to motivations and goals of this hypermobile pursuit are offered.

Identity and mobility

Identity is constructed on the distinctions between the self and the other (Anderson 1983, Hall 1996, Smith 1991). While many have also suggested it is also rooted in place (Paasi 1997, Sewell 1999, Graham et al. 2000), others contend place is not necessary for identity construction, particularly in referencing diasporic and migratory communities (Hall 1995, Massey 1994). Since the act of touring juxtaposes the self and the other in places away from our everyday, tourism, as a type of mobility, is an exercise in identity construction (McCabe and Stokoe 2004, Morgan and Pritchard 2005, Oakes 2006). Because of the structural break from the everyday, Wang (1999) suggests that tourism also offers the potential for existential authenticity, the realization of the authentic self. Through the performance of tourism, Wang (1999) argues, authenticity of the self, as well as relationships with others can be achieved. Cohen (2010, 2011a, 2011b) observes among lifestyle travellers, however, a de-differentiation of touristic experiences and everyday; as such, travel becomes a way of life and mobility a means of identity construction and performance.

Identity is a product not only of metanarratives, such as gender and class, 'but also a number of governing narratives by which we continuously (re)locate ourselves in the world' addressing questions 'of who we are, of where we as individuals are located, and where and how we locate ourselves' (Morgan and Pritchard 2005: 32, see also Ricoeur 1991, McCabe and Stokoe 2004). Thus, Desforges (2000: 927) suggests, 'touristic stories are used to present new self-identities'. Tourism places, according to Baerenholdt et al. (2004: 10), 'are not only or even primarily visited for their immanent attributes but also and more centrally to be woven into the webs of stories and narratives people produce when they sustain and construct their social identities'. Accordingly, Noy's (2004a, 2004b) examinations of Israeli youth backpackers' experiences illustrate how 'self-change narratives' result from adventurous undertakings, reflect on internal changes, and express realizations of existential authenticity. The performance of these tours amounts to a rite of passage and narrative retelling subsequently utilizes this cultural capital as performative of identity (Noy 2004a, 2004b, Shaffer 2004).

Shaffer (2004: 139) argues that the backpacker's journey, in particular, 'is a carefully choreographed performance of a self' complete with scripts, costumes and props. This focus on performance emphasizes agency – the being, doing, touching and seeing of tourism (Coleman and Crang 2002, Baerenholdt et al. 2004, Larsen 2008). Noy's (2004a: 82, see also Shaffer 2004) study of backpackers finds that participation in such a touristic practice 'grants the youths cultural capital (in the form of narrative capital), which actually serves as an admittance right to a subculture, thereby giving them a valid claim for a collective identity'. This cultural capital is gained through the performance of tourism then expressed as narrative. Personal narratives are performed through their telling (McAdams 1993, Eakin 1999). Such a performance, however, requires an audience; as Holstein and Gubrium (2000: 101) assert, 'we talk ourselves into being'. Likewise, Noy (2004a: 84) contends, 'it is precisely the interpersonal communication of personal narratives that grants the individual self-reflection, on simultaneously psychological and social levels'. Thus tourist narratives, as a type of autobiographical narrative, are more than just a story about a place and time, but they shift across these dimensions, highlighting certain events and eliminating others (Bruner 1991, Somers 1994, Cary 2004, Chronis 2005, Rickly-Boyd 2010).

For those involved in long-term travel, including tramps, drifters, backpackers, lifestyle travellers and some pilgrims, it is argued that their narratives extend beyond the retelling of events to the wider scope of the journey. Whereas tourism studies have tended to focus on the destination, it is the study of pilgrimage that has shed more light on the performance of the journey. Morinis (1992: ix) contends, 'a true typology of pilgrimages focuses on the pilgrims' journey and motivations, not on the destination shrines'. '[T]he essence of the journey is movement' (Morinis 1992: 12); and thus, he argues, pilgrimage as a term can be applied 'whenever journeying and some embodiment of an ideal intersect' (1992: 3).

This emphasis on the journey and movement, as opposed to the destination and sightseeing, suggests *mobility* as a more appropriate, overarching context for the investigation of tourism and pilgrimage (Hannam 2009). Mobility, argues Hannam (2009: 102), is 'a kind of displacement – the act of moving between locations' and thus involves space *and* time, more specifically – the spatialization of time and the temporalization of space (see also Cresswell 2006). Considering a mobilities perspective, we can draw a distinction between lifestyle travel, such as 'dirtbags', and lifestyle migrants. Common to the motivations, expectations and experiences of these mobilities are notions of lifestyle and self-identity (see Benson 2011, Cohen, 2010, Benson and O'Reilly 2009). Distinguishing them, however, are perceptions of mobility. While lifestyle migration is made possible by individuals' mobility, socially, economically and spatially, they value the potential of future immobility; that is, finding a place to settle down (Benson 2011, Benson and O'Reilly 2009, Cresswell 2006). Lifestyle travellers, on the other hand, regard their mobility as more essential to their identities, as it frames their lives.

Methodology

In an age of increasing globalization, accompanied by the growing popularity of social media and networks, communities are being established that span vast distances (Massey 1994, Hall 1995). In fact, Hall (1995) questions the very nature of place in community formation. The communicative functions of websites like Rockclimbing.com support such claims. While climbers do meet and perform group identities on the ground, in specific places, the website's forums facilitate community development and maintenance. Many climbers keep in touch and even plan trips via the website; meanwhile one can develop friendships that may never materialize outside of cyberspace.

Rockclimbing.com is the largest and most encompassing website dedicated to the sport. The website provides information for more than 100,000 climbing routes around the world, articles and media sources pertaining to the sport, gear reviews and ratings, climbing videos, a partner board, and over 30 different forums regarding topics from regional U.S. climbing areas and techniques to memorials and gender dynamics. Forum members create profiles that contain personal information, but are particularly focused on climbing information such as style, skill level, favourite destinations and travel experience, and routes climbed. Thus, their Forum identity is centred on the sport. While one must become a member to participate in forum discussions, they are open to public reading. Therefore, the more than 100,000 registered users of the site do not fully capture the readership of this climbing community resource.

D'Andrea (2006) advocates ethnographic methods in the study of hypermobile phenomena. Moreover, Altheide et al. (2008: 135) suggest 'an ethnographic perspective can be brought to bear on symbolic communication in other than "physical spaces", including information bases and cyberspace' (see also Wilson and Peterson 2002, Hine 2008). In fact, Mautner (2005: 813) argues, 'if it was not for the internet, many representations of reality and social relationships would not be articulated at all'. While the rock climbing community is based in physical locations, performed through real world actions and relationships, Rockclimbing. com does add elements of community cohesion and extends its social relationships worldwide. Accordingly, analysis of the website's forums provides insight into the social and discursive relationships that characterize this sport, particularly the 'dirtbags'.

While some forms of textual analysis, such as content analysis, semiology and iconology, analyse the text itself as a transparent vehicle of expression, discourse analysis prioritizes 'the *effects* of a particular cultural text on what an individual may do or think by unravelling its production, social context, and intended audience' (Waitt 2005: 166). It is a way to examine the outcomes of discourse in terms of perceptions, attitudes and actions, to identify frameworks through which social knowledge is produced, circulated and communicated, and to uncover the mechanisms that maintain such social knowledge as 'natural' (Waitt 2005, Phillips and Jorgensen 2002, Fairclough 2003). Therefore, discourse analysis tends to proceed with a particular focus on intertextuality – 'the way in which meanings are sustained through mutually related verbal, written, and visual texts' (Waitt 2005: 168).

Investigation of the Forum at Rockclimbing.com began with a search for the word 'dirtbag'. The first step of analysis identified forum conversational threads which pertained directly to 'dirtbag', revealing 52 threads and 1450 individual posts. The next steps included coding and the identification of themes and sub-themes among the forum discussions, which further reduced the number of viable posts to just 535. This resulted in nine themes – travel patterns, philosophical arguments, spiritual experiences, lifeways, identity, appearance, gender dynamics, community dynamics and forum dynamics. The forum discussions of 'dirtbag' as it relates to identity are the focus of this chapter (for further reference see Rickly-Boyd 2012). Those posts relating to 'identity' were further analysed to reveal five sub-themes – self and society, to be a 'dirtbag', attitude, transitional life phase and finding self – each of which will be explored in the following section.

Because individuals post their own comments to forum discussion threads, quotes from these posts used in this chapter are kept as is, including any spelling or grammatical errors. References to individual's comments are cited in terms of the thread number and post number, for example T3P56 represents post number 56 within conversation thread three.

'Dirtbag' as identity

When Rockclimbing.com users post about the motivations for a lifestyle of 'dirtbagging', whether it lasts weeks to months to years, many reveal societal push and pull factors. Although one declares, 'you can take the dirtbag out of the climber, but you can't take the climber out of the dirtbag' (T14P29), the desire for more focused and frequent rock climbing is unspoken as a motivation for the most part. The fact that rock climbing is less frequently elaborated upon as a motivating factor is not surprising as it is individuals' interest in the sport that brings them to this online community and establishes a common bond among members.

Individuals' relationships to societal norms and demands are a primary push into the lifestyle as well as noted reasons not to pursue it. Several climbers condemned the lifestyle as 'over romanticized' (T9P8, T20P11, T51P3), as they argue that 'dirtbags' do not fulfil their societal obligations (T2P20, T2P45, T3P14), particularly as they are not viewed as 'productive members of society' (T2P1) and in terms of not upholding their 'personal responsibility' (T2P38, T2P47). Some even go so far as to equate a 'dirtbag' with a 'parasite' (T2P20, T3P25, T34P11). As described by one climber:

> Your "total freedom" is contingent upon living parasitically on the peripheries of the most exploitative, destructive, and selfish culture in the history of humanity. (T2P47)

Others long for the opportunity to be 'dirtbags', but they note financial constraints (T6P10, T6P28, T32P3) and family responsibilities (T6P5, T6P32, T6P53) that keep them at home and only climbing for leisure:

> I'd do it if I didn't have children. Without hesitating. (T6P3)

> I wish I could drop all the financial responsibilities and just travel and climb. (T6P8)

Yet, it is such societal 'norms' that arouse others' daydreams, as well as fuel their continued pursuit, as many do not find satisfaction in their current endeavours (T2P12, T8P1, T29P1, T29P13, T31P17):

> I admire those of us who can remove themselves from the daily grind and commit to climbing full time while not being a pro or be sponsored by anyone ... those who are dirtbags. (T32P1)

> Anyone can go get a job and 'contribute to society'; it takes a real man/woman to embrace the ideals of freedom and sacrifice the comforts of financial gain. (T2P16)

> Every day that I continue to work the 40–40 plan (40 hours a week for 40 years), the draw of the dirtbag gets stronger and stronger. (T6P21)

> I am feeling pretty much like I'm missing out on the best travelling years of my life to work. (T8P24)

In fact, several identify distinct events that were catalysts to taking this new approach to life, including a serious car accident (T32P6), divorce (T6P15, T6P45) and 'painful family changes' (T6P22). Thus, in writing about their motivations many also began narratives of life transitions and self-discovery on the road, 'You can find out alot about yourself on the road, you just have to go and look' (T6P33) writes one former 'dirtbag'. Another aspiring 'dirtbag' regularly posted on a thread as she came to a decision to quit her job to travel and climb, noting her preparation, both financial and emotional:

> I'm so looking forward to a simpler life. I'm only 26, but I feel 40. There is so much that I need to leave behind right now, so that I can focus on me. It's my time to be selfish, and I will relish this selfish period for as long as I can. I feel so fortunate to have had this "awakening" at a young age ... I can only imagine the basketcase I would be if I kept being miserable for 10 more years. I need to get to know myself, cause I've nearly forgotten who I am. I have been groomed into a corporate lemming, and nearly lost site of what is TRULY important to me. (T8P32)

However, a few make note of the difficulty of returning to a more settled life after this extended period of travel, and turn to this forum for advice (T10P1, T43P1, T46P3). Thus, the decision to return to a 'normal' life seems to be much more difficult than was the decision to take up this lifestyle. Their apprehension for return suggests fears of falling back into old patterns of daily life and a potential loss of a sense of self; 'Maybe there is a proverbial crossroads every dirtbag must face: To join the rest of society or remain at large' (T10P14). Another 'dirtbag' writes a lengthy narrative of his transition out of a Silicon Valley lifestyle through two years of 'dirtbagging' and to his current situation at such a crossroads:

> But funds got alarmingly low, and sitting out in the desert around J-Tree [Joshua Tree, California] just a couple of weeks ago I realized that I needed to go back. … I need to get a job and return to whatever it is most people consider normal. … The goal stopped being just to climb a lot. I wanted to avoid getting sucked into the whole consumer yuppie fucking lifestyle again. … The thought of sitting in an office all day terrifies me. The thought of having actual responsibilities is mortifying. (T29P1)

Consequently, there is a theme among these discussions – such a lifestyle should occur at a certain time in one's life. 'Do it while you're young' (T31P7) advises one former 'dirtbag', and others agree this is best pursued in the transitions of youth (T10P42, T20P22, T37P13). Accordingly, many younger climbers assert plans to take such a trip after high school/before college (T6P43, T6P55, T6P70, T8P23) or after university (T6P46, T31P5, T43P1, T10P21):

> Do yourself a favor and go. Defer for a year or go after college but make sure you carve out some purely selfish road time for yourselves. (T6P35)

For those in the midst of this travel, there is a sense of freedom (T6P50, T16P27, T31P11) to their narratives. They describe 'living in the moment' (T2P44) and the 'rush' (T8P33) and 'adventure' (T46P1) of not knowing what lies ahead. According to one:

> I have nothing to escape from, just activities and places to enjoy. … Carpe diem-sieze [sic] the day. Live for today, don't let the past bug you, don't worry about the future. Make every day worthwhile. (T6P46)

Those who proclaim the identity of 'dirtbag', speak of the title with pride. A 'dirtbag' 'is someone who lives a very frugal existence to maintain their rockclimbing lifestyle, keeping the sport pure and from being corrupted by money'. (T3P28) Therefore, to be a 'dirtbag', for however short or long a time, takes a certain attitude or mind-set, argue those who take up the lifestyle (T3P24, T16P27, T43P9):

> Part of being a 'dirtbag' is the ability to figure your way through your adventure. (T26P3)

> If money and material possessions are important to you, this life is not for you. (T6P46)

Truth is, there is a huge difference between what is *needed* and what is *desired*. We often confuse these things. (T2P44)

life = short, time = limited, climbing = freedom ... frightening how many lives are lived without risking things for freeing experiences. climbing is in my world freeing. but sacrifices must be made – money, material wealth. (T2P105)

Moreover, it is a 'way of life' (T2P93, T11P28, T18P10) accompanied by strong community bonds (T2P24, T20P25, T21P11):

... there are communities of like minded people to hang out with. ... if you stick to "the circuit" of "destination" sites it isn't too hard to find partners. (T6P45)

they reject loyalty to the needs of a larger society in the name of loyalty to the much smaller society that holds an obvious place for them. (T2P109)

Those reflecting on this lifestyle speak of it fondly, particularly as a time of happiness (T6P61, T10P36, T53P2). Moreover, they describe this period as transitional and life changing. Similar to the 'self-change' narratives of backpackers recorded by Noy (2004a, 2004b), these 'dirtbags' gain a new perspective on life which they attribute to this time. In particular, they describe realizations of their adaptability (T2P62, T46P1), and others note they have come away with a better sense of balance in their lives (T10P37, T46P3, T46P4). It is a way to gain life experience (T6P45, T8P24, T31P12, T29P3) as they consider their future reflections on lives lived and possible regrets.

I've learned one very important thing on this trip ... and I think this is fundamentally what I sought out to prove to myself ... I don't need any of these luxuries. (T29P15)

I was dirt poor then, but happy. Hindsight is 20/20. (T8P32)

When I'm old and on my deathbed reflecting back on my life and any regrets, I know that I will not say, 'I just wish I had spent more time at the office'. (T6P18)

Shaffer's (2004) auto-ethnography of backpacking suggests a sense of authenticity is created in performative ways, as well as in the narrative moments that claim unique and original experience. Overall, reflections and ambitions of the 'dirtbag' lifestyle indicate the significance of this identity as constructive and performative. While for some it is but a short-term 'strategy' to maximize engagement with the sport of rock climbing and is thus one component of their social identity, for many others it is performative of their values of rebellion against societal norms. For these more dedicated 'dirtbags', who spend years of their lives in pursuit of this lifestyle, there are expressions of frustration with what they see as consumerism and a lack of appreciation for the moments of life, all of which motivates them to action. They perform the antithesis of what they see as problematic societal norms by taking to the road, dedicating themselves to rock climbing, and thereby living minimalist lifestyles with strong community bonds and the potential for authentic experiences.

In the space *and* time of the road, there is the discovery and construction of a sense of self which had been unrealized in everyday life, thus suggesting, similar to Noy's (2004a, 2004b) and Shaffer's (2004) studies of backpackers, this becomes more about the journey than the destinations and as such functions as a transitional life phase or rite of passage. Their journeys illustrate 'spatialized time and temporalized space' (Hannam, 2009: 102), emphasizing movement – horizontally, like nomads use 'points and locations to define paths' (Cresswell 2006: 49, Deleuze and Guattari 1988), but also vertically, as the points that define their paths are determined by the quality of rock climbing a destination offers and thereby designated by moments of ascent. Their narrative retelling of these journeys continues to utilize this cultural capital as performative of ever-evolving social identities.

Conclusion

Taylor (2010: 133) argues the 'dirtbag' evolved out of a generation of Beatnik climbers who had 'developed a novel philosophy, one that simultaneously honored tradition and championed a countercultural quest for authentic experience'. As the original 'climbing bums', they pursued a 'vagabond life of cross-country climbing and partying' (Taylor 2010: 134). Yet, the 'dirtbags', who began to show up on the scene in 1960s, he argues, were characterized by a 'lack of any philosophical agenda. ... It was recreation, pure and simple' (2010: 197). This research suggests, however, it is not that 'simple', particularly when considered within a wider context of mobilities.

These itinerant rock climbers do exhibit a philosophical agenda, as they rebel against what many see as consumerism and materialism. In particular, many believe a minimalist lifestyle focused on climbing and framed by continuous travel, as opposed to broader societal norms and constraints, offers the potential for authentic experiences and self-discovery. This may be why so many who choose this strategy describe points of transition, personal conflict or trauma in their lives as impetus, such as after schooling or divorce. It provides a way for these individuals to connect with a sense of self, to discover who they believe they are and their place in this world. But to do this, they must find a time and space away from their everyday lives, and the road and constant mobility offers this. Moreover, a dispersed mobile community also exists, with which they have a common bond – rock climbing.

Analysis of community forums at Rockclimbing.com reveal complex and layered constructions of 'dirtbagging' as performative of identities characterized by individuals' perspectives on society, existential motivations, moments of self-discovery, community bonds, as well as some negative perspectives on this lifestyle from fellow climbers who are outside of this sub-culture. However, as with all cultures, this community is ever-changing. The use of technology and social media seem to be creating a divide between those who have lived this lifestyle for years, and even decades, and the newer members who engage 'dirtbagging' as a more temporary, transitional strategy. These younger generations are seen as having less of a dedication to the sport and lifestyle and more of a social dependence.

This suggests the cultural capital of the 'dirtbag' as an identity may be changing among the rock climbing community. Whereas this was once an individual and highly exclusive identity, characterized by a strong dedication to both rock climbing and a self-sufficient life on the road, it is now growing in popularity, signifying a collective, highly social community that maintains close connections despite its mobility. Increasing global communications technology facilitates these changes, which are also illustrated by the growing presence of self-identified 'dirtbags' on online community forums, such as Rockclimbing.com, as well as an increase in the number of personal weblogs. Further ethnographic research with this subculture may help to determine if the mobility that characterizes this lifestyle remains central to individual and collective identities as global connectivity increases and social isolation decreases. Nevertheless, 'dirtbags' are a form of lifestyle mobility intricately woven into the history of the rock climbing community. Despite its cultural contestation and changing performative expression, for those who are passionate about this sport it will remain an aspiration.

References

Altheide, D., Coyle, M., DeVriese, K. and Schneider, C. 2008. Emergent Qualitative Document Analysis, in *Handbook of Emergent Methods*, edited by S.N. Hesse-Biber and P. Leavy. New York: The Guilford Press, 127–151.

Anderson, B. 1983. *Imagined Communities: Reflections on the Origin and Spread of Nationalism*. London, Verso.

Baerenholdt, J.O., Haldrip, M., Larsen, J. and Urry, J. 2004. *Performing Tourist Places*. Burlington: Ashgate.

Benson, M. 2011. The movement beyond (lifestyle) migration: mobile practices and the constitution of a better way of life. *Mobilities*, 6(2), 221–235.

Benson, M. and O'Reilly, K. 2009. Migration and the search for a better way of life: a critical exploration of lifestyle migration. *The Sociological Review*, 57(4), 608–625.

Bruner, J. 1991. The narrative construction of reality. *Critical Inquiry*, 18(1), 1–21.

Cary, S.H. 2004. The tourist moment. *Annals of Tourism Research*, 31(1), 61–77.

Chouinard, Y. 2006. *Let My People Go Surfing: The Education of a Reluctant Businessman*. New York: Penguin.

Chronis, A. 2005. Coconstructing heritage at the Gettysburg storyscape. *Annals of Tourism Research*, 32(2), 386–406.

Cohen, S.A. 2010a. Chasing a myth? Searching for 'self' through lifestyle travel. *Tourist Studies*, 10(2), 117–133.

Cohen, S.A. 2010b. Personal identity (de)formation among lifestyle travellers: a double-edged sword. *Leisure Studies*, 29(3), 289–301.

Cohen, S.A. 2011. Lifestyle travellers: backpacking as a way of life. *Annals of Tourism Research*, 38(4), 1535–1555.

Coleman, S. and Crang, M. (eds) 2002. *Tourism: Between Place and Performance*. New York: Beghahn Books.

Cresswell, T. 2006. *On the Move: Mobility in the Modern Western World.* London: Routledge.

D'andrea, A. 2006. Neo-nomadism: a theory of post-identitarian mobility in the global age. *Mobilities*, 1(1), 95–120.

Deleuze, G. and Guattari, F. 1988. *A Thousand Plateaus.* London: The Athlone Press.

Desforges, L. 2000. Travelling the world: identity and travel biography. *Annals of Tourism Research*, 27(4), 926–945.

Eakin, P. 1999. *How Our Lives Become Stories: Making Selves.* Ithaca: Cornell University Press.

Fairclough, N. 2003. *Analysing Discourse: Textual Analysis for Social Science Research.* New York: Routledge.

Graham, B., Ashworth, G.J. and Tunbridge, J.E. 2000. *A Geography of Heritage: Power, Culture and Economy.* London: Oxford University Press.

Hall, S. 1995. New Cultures for Old?, in *A Place in the World? Places, Cultures and Globalization*, edited by D. Massey and P. Jess. Oxford: Oxford University Press, 175–213.

Hall, S. 1996. Introduction: Who needs 'Identity', in *Questions of Cultural Identity*, edited by S. Hall and P. du Gay. London: Sage, 1–17.

Hannam, K. 2009. The End of Tourism? Nomadology and the Mobilities Paradigm, in *Philosophical Issues in Tourism*, edited by J. Tribe. Bristol: Channel View Publications, 101–113.

Hine, C. 2008. Internet Research as Emergent Practice, in *Handbook of Emergent Methods*, edited by S.N. Hesse-Biber and P. Leavy. New York: The Guilford Press, 525–541.

Holstein, J.A. and Gubrium, J.F. 2000. *The Self We Live By: Narrative Identity in a Postmodern World.* Oxford: Oxford University Press.

Larsen, J. 2008. De-exoticizing tourist travel: everyday life and sociality on the move. *Leisure Studies*, 27(1), 21–34.

McAdams, D. 1993. *The Stories We Live By: Personal Myths and the Making of Self.* New York: The Guilford Press.

McCabe, S. and Stokoe, E.H. 2004. Place and identity in tourists' accounts. *Annals of Tourism Research*, 31(3), 601–622.

Massey, D. 1994. *Space, Place, and Gender.* Minneapolis: Blackwell.

Mautner, G. 2005. Time to get wired: using web-based corpora in critical discourse analysis. *Discourse & Society*, 6(6), 809–828.

Morgan, N. and Pritchard, A. 2005. On souvenirs and metonymy: narratives of memory, metaphor and materiality. *Tourist Studies*, 5(1), 29–53.

Morinis, E.A. 1992. *Sacred Journeys: The Anthropology of Pilgrimage*. Westport, CT: Greenwood Press.

Noy, C. 2004a. This trip really changed me: backpackers' narratives of self-change. *Annals of Tourism Research*, 31(1), 78–102.

Noy, C. 2004b. Performing identity: touristic narratives of self-change. *Text and Performance Quartery*, 24(2), 115–138.

Oakes, T. 2006. Get Real! On Being Yourself and Being a Tourist, in *Travels in Paradox: Remapping Tourism*, edited by C. Minca and T. Oakes. Lanham: Rowman & Littlefield Publishers, 229–250.

Paasi, A. 1997. Geographical perspectives on Finnish national identity. *GeoJournal*, 43(1), 41–50.

Phillips, L. and Jorgensen, M.W. 2002. *Discourse Analysis as Theory and Method*. London: Sage Publications.

Rickly-Boyd, J.M. 2010. The tourist narrative. *Tourist Studies*, 9(3), 259–280.

Rickly-Boyd, J.M. 2012, in press. Lifestyle climbers: towards existential authenticity. *Journal of Sport & Tourism*.

Ricoeur, P. 1991. Narrative Identity, in *On Paul Ricoeur: Narrative and Interpretation*, edited by D. Wood. London: Routledge, 20–33.

Robinson, V. 2008. *Everyday Masculinities and Extreme Sport: Male Identity and Rock Climbing*. Oxford: Berg.

Sewell, J.W. 1999. The Concept(s) of Culture, in *Beyond the Cultural Turn: New Directions in the Study of Society and Culture*, edited by V.E. Bonnell and L. Hunt. Berkeley: University of California Press, 35–61.

Shaffer, T.S. 2004. Performing backpacking: constructing 'Authenticity' every step of the way. *Text and Performance Quarterly*, 24(2), 139–160.

Smith, A.D. 1991. *National Identity*. Reno: University of Nevada Press.

Somers, M.R. 1994. The narrative constitution of self: a relational and network approach. *Theory and Society*, 23(4), 605–649.

Stevens, C. 2010. Confessions of a Dirtbag. *Dead Point Magazine*. Fayetteville, WV: Matt Stark, 46–49.

Taylor, J.E. 2010. *Pilgrims of the Vertical: Yosemite Rock Climbers & Nature at Risk*. Cambridge: Harvard University Press.

Urry, J. 1990. *The Tourist Gaze*. London: Sage Publications, Inc.

Urry, J. 2002. *The Tourist Gaze*, 2nd edition. London: Sage Publications, Inc.

Waeschle, A. 2009. *Chasing Waves*. Seattle: The Mountaineers Books.

Waitt, G. 2005. Doing Discourse Analysis, in *Qualitative Research Methods in Human Geography*, 2nd edition, edited by I. Hay. Oxford, UK: Oxford University Press, 163–191.

Wang, N. 1999. Rethinking authenticity in tourism experience. *Annals of Tourism Research*, 26(2), 349–370.

Wheaton, B. 2004. Introduction: Mapping the Lifestyle Sport-Scape, in *Understanding Lifestyle Sports: Consumption, Identity and Difference*, edited by B. Wheaton. London: Routledge, 1–28.

Wheaton, B. 2007. After sport culture: rethinking sport and post-subcultural theory. *Journal of Sport and Social Issues*, 22(2), 283–307.

Wilson, S.M. and Peterson, L.C. 2002. The anthropology of online communities. *Annual Review of Anthropology*, 31(4), 449–467.

Chapter 5

From (Dis)Embodied Journeys to 'Artscapes': Belly Dancing as a Digital 'Travelling Culture'

Rodanthi Tzanelli

Introduction

In this chapter I connect travel experience, embodied consumption of place and electronic perceptions of the social world (Prideaux 2002: 319). More specifically, I consider how belly dancing transformed into lifestyle travel with reference to its inclusion in holiday packages advertised online. As an embodied style, dance produces 'artscapes' – that is, flows of art, ideas, humans and products as well as the virtual and imaginative environments in which these develop (Appadurai 1990, Hannam, Sheller and Urry 2006, Sheller and Urry 2006, Urry 2007, Tzanelli 2013). The fluidity of belly dancing was not acknowledged from the outset: originally it was ascribed an ambivalent status as a traditional 'craft' performed on a 'know-how' basis mainly by 'disreputable' women and eunuchs (de la Fuente 2007: 413). However, during the twentieth century it evolved into a hybrid subcultural genre difficult to attribute to one national tradition. Its virtual marketing today stresses individual experiential authenticity in tradition's stead (Hebdige 1979).

One may also argue that today belly dancing mimics travel to construct the embodied self in public through regularized repetition of moves, twists and turns (Butler 1993: 225). As a tourist activity it is a form of leisurely education leading into embodied lifestyles that involve regular exercise combined with aesthetic consumption of exotic places (Rojek 1995, Chaney 1996, Lanfant 2009). Western individualism, which presupposes the public presentation of a unified self, is a common characteristic of contemporary dance performance and its electronic transpositions as experience on relevant professional websites (Becker 1999, Pink 2007: 144). Sennett's (1976) suggestion that modernity connects the individual development of personality to the development of shopping and department stores finds continuation in late modernity's shopping for belly dancing holidays on the web.

66 *Lifestyle Mobilities*

Epistemology, methodology and methods

As a digital tourist or virtual flâneuse of foreign cultures, I understand that the ethics of interaction evade immediate translatability, as do the identities of virtual tourists who may also be male, non-white, homosexual or bisexual – but always privileged world citizens who can afford an Internet connection (Lax 2004). Instead I focus on the ways the image-making techniques professional dancers employ corroborate with, or are functionally analogous to, those used by cultural industries (media, tourism) and reflect or contradict intersectionalities of gender, class, race and ethnicity. Of course, Internet consumers of belly dancing holidays are diverse but less easily traceable than the profiles of on-site tourists (Urry and Larsen 2011, Shields 1991, Taylor 2001). The point is ultimately methodological: the technology of the camera and the Internet become potential 'universal translators' of culturally specific ideas through multiple hermeneutic chains – by internet businesses, viewers, photographers and scholars (Giddens 1987, Friedberg 1995). However, mobility research into the deterritorialized domains of the Internet does not entail methodological erasures of space and culture (Büscher and Urry 2009). On the contrary, cultural hybridizations sharpen the geographical coordinates of human movements for work and consumption that relate to belly dancing.

I cite 19 websites marketing belly dancing holidays open to the public (Cavanaugh 1999). They are produced by multiple, predominantly Western, agents and commercially maintained in a variety of urban centres of the West (for example London or Leeds), East (for example Egypt, Tunisia) or the European periphery (Greece, Cyprus). Yet, the intertextual presence of hyperlinks within their structure (Mitra and Cohen 1999) does not prevent them from constructing a hegemonic gaze. I am not just their reader but also their secondary author, as my searches map a distinctive trajectory in cyberspace (Ingold 2000). As a virtual mobile subject I do not challenge the multiplicity of experiences of belly dancing students, but focus instead on the prevalent norms and practices consolidated in their staging as mass tourism by networks of international tourist providers (MacCannell 1973).

I begin by explaining how belly dancing became enmeshed in visual narratives of gendered embodiment in blogospheres and websites. Thereafter I explore commercial uses of the styles' associations with Eastern cultures through the introduction of new framing practices for the visited places that commercially depend on what happens to be practiced within them instead of 'fixed' Orientalist scripts (Sheller and Urry 2004: 5). Understanding belly dancing as a travel genre is therefore constitutive of the new mobilities paradigm: it highlights the budding relationship between the electronic and terrestrial commerce of tourism, while obscuring the ethics of mobility that thrive on hegemonic discourses of race, gender, class and travel.

Proximity and distance in dance travel

Online advertising of belly dancing modifies the original Grand Tourist narratives: on the one hand it privileges the gaze over other senses. The travel exploits of artists, students and colonial administrators to places Western empires recognized as Europe's civilizational birthplace (Rome, Greece and the Holy Lands) privileged detached gazing of visited lands as an ego-enhancing rite for the better off, predominantly male, travellers (Dann 1977, Tzanelli 2007). The shift from aristocratic leisure to middle-class conspicuous consumption during the eighteenth and nineteenth centuries dictated the accruement of symbolic capital abroad to display at home – a practice that continues to inform Western travel (Desforges 2000). The idea that artistic travellers would travel between cultures to position the other 'as irremediably different (and, often inferior) to the self' (Shilton 2008: 437, Said 1978) must be updated to encapsulate the ways websites today invite consumers to move from virtual to embodied dance-related travel.

The movement of the dance is literally and figuratively embedded in websites and blogospheres, allowing web surfers to taste from afar what they are subsequently invited to experience proximately. Internet 'map-reading' produces and reinforces the language of abstract mobilities and comparison, an expression of an abstract mode of being-in-the-world and colonizing 'from above' (Tzanelli 2010, Tzanelli 2013: 76). Through this mode places get transformed into a collection of abstract characteristics, ever easier to be visited, appreciated and compared from above, but not really known 'from within' (Szerszynski and Urry 2006). The shift from map-reading to finding the way on site through interactions with the place's colour, taste and people invite consumers to become investigators and commercial tourist-pilgrims of alien custom (Graburn 1983, Moutafi-Galani 2000). But professionals involved in this commerce are predominantly women who, knowing tourist sites from within, endeavour to communicate their autobiographical narratives to potential customers, constructing thus their own version of a distant tourist gaze (Kien 2008). Their professional oscillation between different worlds allows them to process immediate encounters to reflections (Peirce 1998).

Travel genre: gendered and sexualized mobilities

The population of websites by female images produces a 'genre', a style that allowed belly dancing to transform in industrialized environments into a form of reputable artwork with a pool of standardized features. Such audiovisual flows enabled human flows from East to West: belly dancing entered Hollywood through the image of the *femme fatale*, a transgressive heroine that destroys men and defies family commitment (Doane 1991: 2, Rich 1995: 8). The slippage from the specificity of style (*femme fatale* as a sort of Eve) to visual-artistic genre standardizes experiential authenticity as in a Hollywood movie (Huggan 2011: 122). Adhering to systemic conventions through narrative formulas, genres helped artists to market their work, propelling the establishment of connections between creative industries such as Hollywood, lived lives and their public narration (Langford 2005: 9). The visual display of dancing women on all relevant websites – professionals or amateur – capitalizes on these early spectacular associations. This propelled representational changes across time and space, as the belly dancers' acquisition of a digital 'public face' enabled the transposition of a private, Eastern act (belly dancing as domestic entertainment exclusively amongst women) to the public domain of Western fandom (Rojek 2001: 11).

The feminization of the gaze at both ends (production and consumption) might silence the custom of male dancers in the East but might also include them in queer glamorizations of the dance in Western domains (Connell 1987, Stavrou Karayanni 2004: 71, Deagon n.d.). Thus, on the fringes of this gendered discourse develops one on 'sexual(ized) exposure' which might enmesh belly-dancing into the contemporary pornographic discourses and categories in lifestyle consumption: the obscure category of 'sex' is used today to sell everything, especially in media consumption spheres (Ang and Hermes 1991, Attwood 2002: 95, 98). Take for example Farida Adventures' (2011) new 'Sex in the City' pamper break in Marrakech, which promises *women* to 'live the dream' of sexual emancipation, reproducing Western taste in Oriental settings. But the staff at Farida Adventures who operate from Eastern belly dancing centres such as Cairo, are multicultural in profile. The programme promises small master classes with 'good English speaking teachers' that prioritize 'your individual development'. The website's presentation shares in resonance with other media centres of dance in the East that figure in similar package holidays. A post on Moroccan TV 2M's website (7 March 2011) presents belly dancing as 'a glorious way to lose [one's] inhibitions' resorting to images of 'lithe women' dancing like natives. The site is an example of media and ideas convergence in one digital space: it debates American tribal belly dance as a Hollywood style that demonstrates maturity but also 'rare dignity' (TV 2M 2011.). A version of belly dancing, tribal dancing prioritizes personal expression and defiance of male desire (Buonaventura 2010: 198) but as it involves public performance and bodily adornment it is symmetrical to hegemonic narratives of masculinity some national centres use(d) to fix ethnic – especially Islamic – and gendered identities even in global consumption spaces (Herzfeld 1985; Cresswell 2001). If indeed politically Islamic 'hyperveiling' developed as a response to the Western colonial gaze, Western unveiling of the Orient developed as a tourist gaze (MacMaster and Lewis 1998: 123, 126).

Jasmine Journeys (n.d.) is a website maintained by Christina Hatt, an educated British woman with knowledge of Eastern medicine and healing that promises customers will improve their physique and well-being. Her packages make space for men for whom a number of activities are available during their partners' training (golf, scuba-diving, paragliding, horse-riding). The fusion of Eastern complementary therapy with belly dancing produces a mobility complex that ennobles Oriental knowledge as Western science. Yoga and meditation sessions are recurring themes in tourist websites that combine belly dancing free afternoons 'to sunbathe, swim, enjoy spa treatments or even do some sightseeing in the Medina of Marrakech' (Lanzarote Information 14 March 2011; Mia Serra Belly Dance 2010; Aurora Bellydance n.d.). Such holiday kits include multiple cosmetic offers, including transport, English-speaking guides, professional hair, makeup, photo and video shoot on a final performance day and recording on DVD, insurance, body sugaring (a Moroccan alternative to waxing) and sunbathing (Farida Adventures 2011, Aurora Bellydance n.d.). The pedagogical and performative aspects of learning to move in non-Western styles while on holiday become accessories to a more general cosmetic experience that trains and beautifies the female body. This pedagogy marks the shift from relational to recreational models of highly sexualized behaviour, allowing women 'to enjoy the dubious consumption equality in the marketplace' (Featherstone 1991: 179, Attwood 2006: 80). Dance 'styles' in which students can practice are matched with Eastern grooming and therapeutic styles. Here 'style' is a psychosocial complex of attributes with embodied dimensions that facilitates secular audiovisual genres (Bourdieu 1977, Herzfeld 2009). Stripped of their original religious meaning, some of these advertised leisure practices repackage the exposed belly-dancing body in erotic leisure-wear to maximize consumption incentives: looking glamorous is equated with feeling self-confident and beautiful (Turner 1982, Featherstone 1991: 182, Plummer 1995: 124–125).

The introductory visual narrative in Jasmine Journeys dissolves geographical specificity into a generic experience of being in an Eastern domain – addressed to women who nevertheless head for specific destinations in the East (Massey 1994). Belly dancing is 'about women loving their bodies no matter what their shape or size and who love to dance' states The Oriental Belly Dance (2010). The site assumes its customers will be women and advertises the spirit of a generic category of 'middle eastern dance' which is 'sexy, erotic and great fun to learn'. For other holiday providers the combination of diverse activities, such as snorkeling shows and boat trips with belly dancing, resembles other conventional tourist or leisure forms (see Hilary's Bazaar n.d.). The overall imaginative travel proffered in these websites feminizes discourses of civility through rituals of looking after the body in order to heal the soul. Good climate and healthy food also stand for cultural capital – a common theme in tourism-related migration to the sunny countries by working-class groups from the Northern hemisphere (Bott 2004, Haug et al. 2007) and backpack tourism (Cohen 2011). Replacing dietary management as such with supervised, regularized exercise while on holidays detaches the disciplined body from old tropes of asceticism (focusing on religious salvation), stressing instead appearance enhancement and a 'more marketable [feminine] self' (Featherstone 1991: 171, Attwood 2006: 83). Notably, in belly dance holidays men are pushed in the background, performing leisure as *accessories* to female travel.

Mobility and frameworks of belonging

The guarantee that students will collect experiential signs for display at home is provided by the dance professionals' and tourist entrepreneurs' semi-ethnographic involvement with the hosting cultures in which they act as guides. Reliability of service is constructed in two different ways: by blood affiliation (when the dancer-entrepreneur was born in tourist sites or married into a local family) or acculturation in the customs of the place. This kinship agenda assists in symbolizations of authenticity as an embodied artistic endeavour with tacit dimensions that are acquired upon migration to the Orient (Polanyi 1966, Herzfeld 2009). Farida Adventures (2011) offers an intimate account of the enterprise's history, focusing by turns on the initial travel exploits of its founder (Kay Taylor) and her acquaintance with the culture and language in Cairo and Luxor, costumier Bella's artisanship, Nibal's cooking sessions and passion to become a professional guide and teach travellers about her country, and Claire, Anne and Yasmina's belly dancing. These entrepreneurs are examples of the ways new knowledge economies revise traditional frameworks of belonging along geospatial movement for work (Freudental-Pedersen 2009). Where nation-states seek to homogenize symbol creators under the banner of a community rooted in national 'land', tourist-like artistic groups create alternative networks and new industrial communities that commercialize abstract 'landscapes' (Urry 2004, Hesmondhalgh and Baker 2010: 29). Websites such as those based in Leeds or London function as such industrial-artistic nodes, bringing together different sites, groups and artists under the umbrella of belly 'dancing holidays'. Mobilities and fixities coexist in this schema by necessity to better sell artwork to global audiences.

Yasmina of Cairo (n.d.), who combines family commitments with global professional networking, recommends Farida Adventures (in which she features) on her own website. Her self-narration exemplifies more subtle shifts from kinship to commodification of 'active female sexuality' and liberation in consumption domains (Attwood 2006: 83): married to an Egyptian and residing in Egypt but originally from the UK, she spent years travelling in the Middle East before settling in Cairo in 1995. Her website notes that she can convey 'the essence of Egyptian dance' to British belly dancers like no-one else 'with the clarity of a native English speaker'. This is succeeded by the claim that 'the core' of Yasmina's teaching remains 'Modern Cairo style' – hence she applies a degree of authentic innovation to her labour as a (para-)linguistic translator of foreign styles. She is a student and close colleague of Raqia Hassan, the leading choreographer in Cairo and 'arguably the creator of the Modern Cairo style of dancing'.

Yasmina's narrative blends technology and embodied experience (Headland et al. 1990, Banks 2001: 115, Walkowitz 2003: 34). Her website advertises her *Journey of Desire*, a full-length feature film exploring the relationship between Cairo and foreign dancers, further contributing to the commodification of sexualized leisure. Whereas conceptions of desire are already embedded in Orientalist histories of belly dancing that valorize the subjection of female performers to the male gaze (Chua 2008: 1184), Yasmina's 'desire' is performative in its own right.

Desire here is connected to embodied and emotional labour in borderline societies (for example in Greece and Turkey) in which versions of belly dancing flourished as travelling styles. In these contexts *meráki* (= desire but also curiosity) and *kéfi* (= joy) are stereotyped conceptions of the good life in the tourist trade that thrives on dance styles as practices of self-presentation (Loizos and Papataxiarchis 1991: 226). As a feeling that propels action, desire communicates imaginative and real movement, tying reflexivity to ways of being in the world through consumption narratives and actions.

Yasmina's website explains that she has worked as a photo-journalist in Cairo and abroad and a publicity photographer 'helping other performers look glamorous'. Her autobiography (a variation of a CV most belly dancers include on their websites) communicates a form of 'subcultural camaraderie' (Moore 2007: 451) with Egyptian and other foreign networks, enhancing her transnational status. Her spectacular profession feminizes image-making, once reserved only for male performers, especially outside Western cultural domains (for example Geertz 1973). The production of feminized imagery to stimulate sales through digital photography matches the contemporary culture of individualism (Sontag 1978). Yasmina's home beside the Giza pyramids co-hosts several international dance tours each year, and acts as a retreat for adventure travellers in Egypt. Populated by her images in cabaret-style costumes performing belly dancing, the website provides holiday packages tailored as a form of experiential adventure in which femininities and sexualities are understood as style (Attwood 2006: 86). Keft-Kennedy (2010: 292) notes that belly dancers enter the public domain not just with performance but also the artifice of femininity: the cabaret costume, the veil, the cymbals and body jewels activate an audiovisual complex that is spectacular and excessive. In fact, some holiday packages connect place to such half-fetishistic dance props, as is the case with Jameela Bellydancer (2008) that promises customers to 'learn Egyptian rhythms and [work] with a live drummer ... veil and finger cymbals'. Yasmina ties her dancing to ideal travel places (the Pyramids) to capitalize on the value of Oriental markers: objects and embodied action are placed in a continuum to foreground the digital experience of 'being in the Orient'.

Just like Yasmina, Jameela, a British performer that lives, teaches and performs in Dalyan, Turkey, presents her travel as symbolic capital. But in the location's stead the website promotes luxuries familiar to potential Western customers, including the Beyaz villas in which they are promised to stay. Coupling luxury with intensive workshops *distances* dancing from common labour, even though belly dancing holidays involve 'irregular work' away from home (Urry 1996: 120). Blogs, Facebook and Twitter links advertise customer satisfaction, granting holiday organizers and belly dancers with a public face but also generating virtual 'neotribes', global mobile groups bound by travel or performative experience (Maffesoli 1996, Vannini 2010: 111). Yet, to reiterate Büscher's and Urry's (2009) methodological point, the marketization of belly dancing also depends to some degree on the cultural backgrounds in which it was first *constructed* as gendered custom.

Phantasmagoric complexes and 'Oriental' cities

The websites embed a memory complex into cities with alleged historical connections to belly dancing, which include Eastern and ancient Greek elements. This connection between cultural roots and tourist routes defines the global tourist trade of historical 'fixities' that in reality were never stable (Clifford 1997). Thus in our case Renaissance and Enlightenment interpretations of ancient Greek antiquity that partly defined belly dancing archaeologies in the West survived the postcolonial diffusion of capitalist centres to networks and became hegemonic cultural tropes (Eagleton 2006). The Euro-American genre *dance Orientale* pioneered by Isadora Duncan at the start of the twentieth century was a hybrid interpretation of surviving depictions of Hellenic rituals and the living cultures of the Middle East (Buonaventura 2010: 114–117). Duncan's choreographies challenged gender hegemonies by emphasizing the movement of the upper torso and the head (stereotyped as male domains of reason) at the expense of midriff display and hip movement (stereotyped as female regions of reproduction) (Bakhtin 1968: 26). But contemporary media discourses utilized such tropes to reconcile exotic 'vulgarity' with European artistic refinement, eventually embedding both in the commercial milieus of tourism as fluid and easily manipulated signs (Spooner 1986: 222–223). Empires of capital sprang up in the urban centres of yesteryear's colonial domains, transforming global cities into phantasmagoric centres, sites inviting embodied and virtual visits (Patke 2000). Today individual agents insert themselves in such neo-capitalist networks through the collection, *interpretation* and commercial display of signs from the anthropological cabinets of the past.

On such memories (that are reinvented while claimed to be fixed in time) thrive multiple mobilities of airports, motorways, media representations and tourism (Featherstone et al. 2004). Farida Adventures offers a selection of packages to Cairo that appeal to different types of tourists. The 'discovering' package refers to a combination of culinary, dance, musical and cultural explorations (for example visiting the Egyptian museum, Saquarra and the Pyramids), whereas the 'customized' package emphasizes urban rambles and shopping activities and the 'independent' stresses adventure tourism. 'Cultural Cairo' promotes cultural urban tourism – from lunch in Egyptian restaurants to visits to the Pyramids and Giza, Cairo's Museum and big markets, shopping and evening entertainment by the Nile, camel rides and folklore shows. Just as other websites do, Farida Adventures maintains its own award-winning festival (*Farha*) – featuring in company-produced DVDs, music and dance fiestas. Other world destinations and tours include the Greek island of Hydra (with its Theatre and Arts Centre as the venue), Marrakech and Istanbul ('a city of two continents', with a hotel close to the sites of Topkapi, Agia Sophia and the Grand Bazaar). These tours draw upon stereotypical tourist images of place which are also photographically displayed as generic Oriental signs. Sites generate networks of tourist activities, for example, in Oriental Belly Dance (2010) Australian Carolyn Evanoff teaches the 'ancient art of belly dance' in connection with explorations of Dahab, a place allegedly fusing images of Arabia and Egypt.

Another such example is Suzan French, a professional dancer that operates from London. Her website (with a start page figuring an Oriental carpet on which she sits), blends shots from her performance in tourist resorts, hotels and beach images with major national sites such as Agia Sofia, a Byzantine temple that was turned into a mosque by the Ottoman Turks. Snuggling amongst a series of rootless tourist-like performances, Agia Sofia becomes a mobile site of memory adhering to belly dancing moments and tourist sojourns (Crang 1997). Susan's website is one of those that figure male performers in ethnic costumes. Yet the holiday packages themselves, which focus on Turkish and Greek resorts, are mostly addressed to female travellers who wish to combine fun with pedagogical-performative pursuits. 'Suzi' promises 'shows with Arabic musicians, belly dancers [and] tarot card readers' – an unusual combination of activities that connects her celebrity status to imaginary Oriental travel. Her art of dancing appeals to tarot traditions invented in European cultural centres such as France and Italy that also travelled to American sites hosting events (expos) influenced by European Orientalist flows.

Advertising *tsifteteli* holidays on Cyprus, World Belly Dancer stresses how archaeologists have located the dance in ancient Greece as a religious ceremony for Aphrodite. However, it also explains that the 'Mediterranean island' of Cyprus has a blend of European-Greek and Oriental-Turkish influences (8 February 2011). The website invites web surfers to visit the Saturday Layali Café in Nicosia and see women 'shaking their stuff – and if you are feeling adventurous (or you've had one too many) you can get involved and the dancers are always happy to share some techniques and tricks of the trade' (World Belly Dancer 2011). But while engaging in such sexual innuendos, it also constructs a complex archaeology and taxonomy of belly dancing (at least four popular styles are mentioned, including zambra mora, khaleeji, American Tribal and Gothic). In a similar fashion the site attaches belly dancing to musical fusions that appeal to a generic Oriental authenticity to produce symbolic meeting grounds and shifting interdependencies for multiple cultural industries such as film, music and tourism (Castells 1996: 151–168, Tzanelli 2007: 9–10). For example, Worldbellydancer.com recommends 'authentic Arabian music' which can be purchased on Amazon but also in major UK cities such as London and Birmingham (8 February 2011).

Orientalism, Mediterraneanism and migrations

Some websites infuse the Orientalization of belly dancing into a form of practical Mediterraneanism, another philosophy of the margins. The trope of invasion of the European Mediterranean by alien artistic forms is omnipresent in debates upon the origins of belly dancing as an Egyptian style. Its genealogical attribution to gypsies or 'untouchables' (Hinduist-Greek *athínganos*) forged connections between migration, gender, race and civilization. An unwanted type of stranger traffic (Simmel 1923), the female (*dance du ventre* or *hootchie-coochie*) performers of such mobile, working-class and ethnic enclaves became initially associated with prostitution. Turning in recent decades from 'strangers' into tourist guides and hosts, belly dancers transcended traditional social dichotomies through their professionalized labour. The genre remains populated by genealogies of strangerhood, either because they sell well or because structures of thought sustain them in specific countries (Larsen et al. 2006). For example, the dancing *athínganoi*, the *ghawazee* (original Egyptian dancers) and the flamenco dancers (originally Arab women) often denote the 'invaders' or 'outsiders' (Buonaventura 2010: 40–42).

Incidentally today *ghaziyeh* dancers such as Kharriya Mazzin ('a local cabaret dancer, a Cruise ship dancer, a village girl and a housewife' (Belly Dancing Holidays in Luxor n.d.)) adopt tropes of household intimacy and sex mobility as self-marketing techniques. In some Islamic countries belly dancing is persecuted as an act that publically humiliates the state and the family, prompting *ghawazee* dancers such as those of the Mazin family to advertise their art in Anglophone websites as a form of activism (Nearing, n.d., Cere 2002). Likewise the Greek *tsifteteli* (çifteteli = two strings) originally communicated the politics of purified collective self-presentation. Commonly attributed to migrations of Greek artistic communities and styles from Turkey (1920s), it became for Greek authoritarian regimes another way to discuss phenotypal extensions of moral pollution (Stavrou Karayanni 2004). The dialectics of 'open' (suspect) and 'closed' (safe) memoryscapes, which have always been overdetermined by gendered ideas of propriety (Herzfeld 2006: 54–55), are now negotiated in discourses of gendered tourism. Therefore my reference to 'practical' Mediterraneanism corresponds to professional belly dancers' alignment with practical ways of acting upon historical representations of marginality through processed experience.

Such tourist industries sustain mobility matrixes with audiovisual and culinary extensions, adapting the consumption of cultural variations of humanity to new commercial needs (Carlton 1994: 13–15). The cosmopolitan hybridity of visited places is used by holiday providers as a status symbol, as is the case with The Lures of Dubai Holidays that presents Dubai as the 'city of merchants', a place recommended for retail therapy and camel safaris 'complete with belly dancing and gourmet meals' (8 March 2011). As a package 'Cultural Cairo' promotes the exoticism of Eastern urban cultures. Such travel itineraries invite visitors to commune in exotic custom by visiting the local market (souk), spending evenings by the Nile, riding a camel and partaking in belly dancing nights while tasting special delicacies. 'The opportunity to take in the colours and scents of the Souk in Marrakech's ancient medina, where you can browse an array of goods including leather shoes, jewellery, spices and belly dance accessories' (Jasmine Journeys n.d.) amounts to a digital simulation of experience. The move from artistic urbanity to rustic rurality provides the reverse image of belly dancing in the Oriental city, sustaining functional interdependencies between centre and periphery. Jameela's holiday in Dalyan (2008) discusses the place as a small fishing village in the South

Western Mediterranean, 'one of the surviving corners of paradise still un-spoilt by tourism [with] outstanding natural beauty [and] much historical interest'. Historical connections between sites unspoilt by the advent of mass tourism and European culture are also promoted by Hammamet Plus which discusses a popular holiday resort in the Cap Bon region of Tunisia. Originally a fishing village, Dalyan later transformed into a recuperative retreat for European royal families and today hosts an Art Deco Villa (Hammamet Plus, n.d.). Such alternative travel trails follow the Grand Tourist script of pedagogical performativity: thus Belly Dancing Holidays in Luxor (n.d.) promises that dance lessons aside, tourists will visit classical sites in and around Luxor, including Luxor Temple, Luxor Museum, Karnak Temple, the Valley of Kings and Hatshepsut. At the same time, tourists can 'go on a felucca boat trip at sunset to Banana Island, a horse and carriage ride, and will be guided around the souk' (Belly Dancing Holidays in Luxor n.d.). Even though most of these holiday packages take place in the urban centres of an ever-expanding Orient (Andalusia to Turkey, Lanzarote and Dubai), they tend to purify the visited culture as a form of 'Arcadia', a site constructed on the logic of metaphysical sedentarism as 'paradise on earth' for commercial purposes (see also Cresswell 2006). Thus diverse mobilities are brought together, including virtual representations of place, imaginary staging of Edenic-like worlds for consumption and also the materialities of telecommunication and teleportation networks (Featherstone et al. 2004).

Conclusion

This brief tour indicates that belly dancing has evolved into a form of mobile good endorsing the consumption of blended activities in a variety of tourist sites. These sites reconstruct yesteryear's Orient, an always-undefined geo-temporal concept that encourages the production of exotic imaginaries virtually and terrestrially. The gendered and racialized histories of belly dancing are placed at the service of such commercial routes, today inviting primarily (but not exclusively) Western women to market (as belly dancers, or website managers) or construct (as consumers) a new form of tourist gaze. This gaze allows them to tour electronically the material (for example culinary or architectural sites and beaches) and intangible (for example histories, sounds and music) aspects of culture before or even after experiencing an embodied journey. Belly dancing has come a long way to become the site of personal travel memory through successive industrial manipulations of landscape, embodied movement and individual style. The symbol creators involved in this process of manipulation are the belly dancers I introduced. The hermeneutics of such agents borrow from practices of 'image-making' that may involve different types of audiovisual performance (in DVDs, CDs or even YouTube clips) for tourists. Embodied interpretations of style transmute into textual diaries that blogospheres and electronic travel agencies disseminate in every part of the world as memoryscapes and artscapes, flows of creativity that is legitimated as art due to its reinvention as a form of gendered pedagogy.

References

Ang, I. and Hermes, J. 1991. Gender and/in media consumption, in *Mass Media and Society*, edited by J. Curran and M. Gurevitch. London: Arnold, 325–347.

Appadurai, A. 1990. Disjuncture and difference in the global cultural economy. *Public Culture*, 2(2), 1–24.

Attwood, F. 2002. Reading porn: the paradigm shift in pornography research. *Sexualities*, 5(1), 91–105.

Attwood. F. 2006. Sexed up: theorizing the sexualisation of culture. *Sexualities*, 9(1), 77–94.

Aurora Bellydance (London) n.d. Available at: http://www.aurorabellydance.com/ [accessed: March 2011].

Bakhtin, M.M. 1968. *Rabelais and His World*. Cambridge: MIT Press.

Banat Eshorouk Arabian Dance Group (Leeds) n.d. Available at: http://www.banateshorouk.co.uk/ [accessed: March 2011].

Banks, M. 2001. *Visual Methods in Social Research*. London: Sage.

Becker, H. 1999. Visual sociology, documentary photography and photojournalism, in *Image-Based Research*, edited by J. Prosser. London: Falmer, 84–96.

Belly Dancing Holidays in Luxor, Egypt n.d. Available at: http://www.everythingegyptian.co.uk/pages/bellydancing_holidays.htm [accessed: March 2011].

Bellydance Holidays – Jameela Bellydancer (Dalyan, Turkey) 2008. Available at: http://www.jameelabellydancer.co.uk/bellydanceholidays.htm [accessed: March 2011].

Bott, E. 2004. Working on a working class utopia: marking young Britons in Tenerife on the new map of European migration. *Journal for Contemporary European Studies*, 12(1), 57–70.

Bourdieu, P. 1977. *Outline of a Theory of Practice*. Cambridge: Cambridge University Press.

Buonaventura, W. 2010. *Serpent of the Nile*. London: Saqi.

Büscher, M. and J. Urry. 2009. Mobile methods and the empirical. *European Journal of Social Theory*, 12(1), 99–117.

Butler, J. 1993. *Bodies that Matter*. London: Routledge.

Carlton, D. 1994. *Looking for Little Egypt*. Bloomington, Indiana: IDD Books.

Castells, M. 1996. *The Rise of the Network Society*. Oxford: Blackwell.

Cavanaugh, A. 1999. Behaviour in public? Ethics in online ethnography, *Cybersociology*, 6. Available at: http://www.cybersociology.com/files/6_2_ethicsinonlineethnog.html [accessed: October 2012].

Cere, R. 2002. Digital counter-cultures and the nature of electronic social and political movements, in *Dot.cons: Crime, Deviance and Identity on the Internet*, edited by Y. Jewkes. Tavinstock: Willan, 147–163.

Chaney, D. 1996. *Lifestyles*. London: Routledge.

Chua, P. 2008. Orientalism as cultural practice and the production of sociological knowledge. *Sociology Compass*, 2(4), 1179–1191.

Clifford, J. 1997. *Routes*. Cambridge, MA: Harvard University Press.

Cohen, S.A. 2011. Lifestyle travellers: backpacking as a way of life. *Annals of Tourism Research*, 38(4), 117–133.

Connell, R.W. 1987. *Gender and Power*. Stanford: Stanford University Press.

Crang, M. 1997. Picturing practices: research through the tourist gaze. *Progress in Human Geography*, 21(3), 359–373.

Cresswell, T. 2001. The production of mobilities. *New Formations*, 43(1), 11–25.

Cresswell, T. 2006. *On the Move*. New York: Routledge.

Dann, G.M.S. 1977. Anomie, ego-enhancement and tourism. *Annals of Tourism Research*, 4(4), 184–194.

De la Fuente, E. 2007. The 'new sociology of art'. *Cultural Sociology*, 1(3), 409–425.

Deagon, A. n.d. *Feminism and belly dance*. Available at: http://www.tribalbelly dance.org/articles/feminism.html [accessed: February 2011].

Desforges, L. 2000. Travelling the world: identity and travel biography. *Annals of Tourism Research*, 27(4), 926–945.

Doane, M.A. 1991. *Femmes Fatales*. New York: Routledge.

Eagleton, T. 2006. *The Idea of Culture*. Oxford: Blackwell.

Farida Adventures. 2011. Available at: http://www.faridaadventures.com/ [accessed: March 2011].

Featherstone, M. 1991. The body in consumer culture, in *The Body*, edited by M. Featherstone et al. London: Sage, 170–196.

Featherstone M., N. Thrift and J. Urry (eds) 2004. Cultures of automobility. Special Issue of *Theory, Culture & Society*, 21(4), 1–284.

Freudental-Pedersen, M. 2009. *Mobility in Daily Life*. Aldershot: Ashgate.

Friedberg, A. 1995. Cinema and the postmodern condition, in *Viewing Positions*, edited by L. Williams. New Jersey: Rutgers University Press, 59–86.

Galani-Moutafi, V. 2000. The self and the other: traveler, ethnographer, tourist. *Annals of Tourism Research*, 27(1), 203–224.

Geertz, C. 1973. *The Interpretation of Cultures*. New York: Basic Books.

Giddens A. 1987. *Social Theory and Modern Sociology*. Cambridge: Polity Press.

Graburn, N.N.H. 1983. *To Pray, Pay and Play*. Aix en-Provence: Centre des Hautes Etudes Touristiques.

Hannam, K., M. Sheller and J. Urry 2006. Mobilities, immobilities, and moorings. *Mobilities*, 1(1), 1–22

Haug B., G.M.S. Dann and M. Mehmetoglu 2007. Little Norway in Spain: from tourism to migration. *Annals of Tourism Research*, 34(1), 202–222.

Headland, T.N., K.L. Pike and M. Harris. 1990. *Emics and Etics*. Newbury Park: Sage.

Hebdige, D. 1979. *Subculture*. London: Routledge.

Herzfeld, M. 1985. *The Poetics of Manhood*. Princeton: Princeton University Press.

Herzfeld, M. 2006. Practical Mediterraneanism, in *Rethinking the Mediterranean*, edited by W.V. Harris. Oxford: Oxford University Press, 45–64.

Herzfeld, M. 2009. The cultural politics of gesture. *Ethnography*, 10(2), 131–152.

Hesmondhalgh, D. and S. Baker. 2010. *Creative Labour*. London: Routledge.

Hilary's Bazaar (UK) n.d. Available at: http://www.hilarysbazaar.com/ [accessed: March 2011].

Huggan, G. 2011. The Postcolonial Exotic: Marketing the Margins, in *Feminist Literary Theory*, edited by M. Eagleton. Oxford: John Wiley & Sons, 119–122.

Ingold, T. 2000. *The Perception of the Environment*. London: Routledge.

Jasmine Journeys (Cairo) n.d. Available at: http://www.jasminejourneys.com/ belly.htm [accessed: March 2011].

Kien, G. 2008 Technography=technology+ethnography: an introduction. *Qualitative Inquiry*, 14(7), 1101–1109.

Lanfant, F.M. 2009. Roots of the sociology of tourism in France, in *The Sociology of Tourism*, edited by G.M.S. Dann and G. Liebmann Parrinello. Bingley: Emerald, 95–129.

Langford, B. 2005. *Film Genre*. Edinburgh: Edinburgh University Press.

Lanzarote Information 14 March 2011. Available at: http://www.lanzaroteinfor mation.com/content/dance-lessons-lanzarote [accessed: March 2011].

Larsen, J., Urry, J. and Axhausen, K. 2006. *Mobilities, Networks, Geographies*. Farnham: Ashgate.

Lax, S. 2004. The Internet and Democracy, in *Web Studies 2*, edited by D. Gauntlett and R. Horsley, 2nd edition. New York: Oxford University Press, 217–220.

Loizos, P. and E. Papataxiarchis 1991. Gender, Sexuality, and the Person in Greek Culture, in *Contested Identities: Gender and Kinship in Modern Greece*, edited by P. Loizos and E. Papataxiarchis. Princeton: Princeton University Press, 221–235.

MacCannell, D. 1973. Staged authenticity. *American Journal of Sociology*, 79(3), 589–603.

Macmaster, N. and T. Lewis 1998. Orientalism: from unveiling to hyperveiling. *Journal of European Studies*, 28, 121–135.

Maffesoli, M. 1996. *The Time of the Tribes*. London: Sage.

Massey, D. 1994. *Space, Place and Gender*. Cambridge: Polity.

Mia Serra Belly Dance 2010. Available at: http://www.miaserra.com/pages/ Morocco%20holidays.php [accessed: March 2011].

Mitra, A. and Cohen, E. 1999. Analyzing the Web: Directions and Challenges, in *Doing Internet Research*, edited by S. Jones. London: Sage, 179–202.

Moore, R. 2007. Friends don't let friends listen to corporate rock: Punk as a field of cultural production. *Journal of Contemporary Ethnography*, 36(4), 438–474.

Nearing, E. n.d. *Khairiyya Mazin struggles to preserve authentic Ghawazi dance tradition*, Guilded Serpent [book]. Available at: http://www.gildedserpent. com/articles25/edwinakhairiyyastruggles.htm [accessed: March 2011].

Patke, R.S. 2000. Benjamin's arcades project and the postcolonial city. *Diacritics*, 30(4), 2–14.

Peirce, C.M. 1998. Harvard lectures on pragmaticism, in *Essential Peirce*, volume I, edited by N. Houser and C. Kloesel. Bloomington: Indiana University Press, 1867–1893.

Pink, S. 2007. *Doing Visual Ethnography*. London: Sage.

Plummer, K. 1995. *Telling Sexual Stories*. London: Routledge.

Polanyi, M. 1966. *The Tacit Dimension*. New York: Doubleday.

Prideaux, B. 2002. The Cybertourist, in *The Tourist as a Metaphor of the Social World*, edited by G.M.S. Dann. Wallingford: CAB International, 317–339.

Rich, R.B. 1995. Dumb lugs and femme fatales. *Sight and Sound*, 5(11), 6–11.

Rojek, C. 1995. *Decentering Leisure*. London: Sage.

Rojek, C. 2001. *Celebrity*. London: Reaktion.

Said, E. 1978. *Orientalism*. London: Penguin.

Sennett, R. 1976. *The Fall of Public Man*. Cambridge: Cambridge University Press.

Sheller, M. and J. Urry 2004. Places to Play, Places in Play, in *Tourism Mobilities: Places to Play, Places in Play*, edited by M. Sheller and J. Urry. London: Routledge, 1–10.

Sheller, M. and J. Urry 2006. The new mobilities paradigm. *Environment and Planning A*, 38(2), 207–226.

Shields, R. 1991. *Places on the Margin*. London: Routledge.

Shilton, S. 2008. Belly dancing to the *Marseillaise*: Zoulikha Bouabdellah's *Dansons*. *Contemporary French and Francophone Studies*, 12(4), 437–444.

Simmel, G. 1923. *Exkurs über den Fremden, Soziologie*, 3rd edition. Berlin: Dunker and Humblot.

Sontag, S. 1978. *On Photography*. New York: Doubleday.

Spooner, B. 1986. Weavers and Dealers: Authenticity and Oriental Carpets, in *The Social Life of Things*, edited by A. Appadurai. Cambridge: Cambridge University Press, 195–235.

Stavrou Karayanni, S. 2004. *Dancing Fear and Desire*. Canada: Wilfrid Laurier University Press.

Suzan French's Belly Dancing Holidays n.d. Available at: http://www.bellydancingholidays.co.uk/ [accessed: April 2011].

Szerszynski, B. and Urry, J. 2006. Visuality, mobility and the cosmopolitan. *British Journal of Sociology*, 57(1), 113–131.

Taylor, J.P. 2001. Authenticity and sincerity in tourism. *Annals of Tourism Research*, 28(1), 7–26.

The Lures of Dubai Holidays 8 March 2011. Available at: http://awayholidays.blogspot.com/2011/03/lures-of-dubai-holidays.html [accessed: March 2011].

The Oriental Belly Dance 2010. Available at: http://sheikhsalemhouse.com/BellyDanceHolidayInfo [accessed: March 2011].

Turner, B.S. 1982. The discourse of the diet. *Theory, Culture & Society*, 1(1), 23–32.

TV2M.com 7 March 2011. Available at: http://tv2m.com/belly-dancing-is-a-glorious-way-to-lose-your-inhibitions-9802 [accessed: March 2011].

Tzanelli, R. 2007. *The Cinematic Tourist*. London: Routledge.

Tzanelli, R. 2010. The Da Vinci node: networks of neo-pilgrimage in the European cosmopolis. *International Journal of Humanities*, 8(3), 113–128.

Tzanelli, R. 2013. *Heritage in the Digital Era.* London: Routledge.
Urry, J. 2007. *Mobilities.* Cambridge: Polity.
Urry, J. and J. Larsen. 2011. *The Tourist Gaze 3.0,* 3rd edition. London: Sage.
Vannini, P. 2010. Mobile cultures: from the sociology of transportation to the study of mobilities. *Sociology Compass,* 4(2), 111–121.
Veijola, S. and Jokinen, E. 1994. The body in tourism. *Theory, Culture and Society,* 11(3), 125–151.
Walkowitz, J.R. 2003. The 'vision of Salome': cosmopolitanism and erotic dancing in central London, 1908–1918. *American Historical Review,* 108(2), 337–376.
Worldbellydancer.org 8 February 2011. Available at: http://www.worldbellydan cer.org/2011/02/places-to-see-and-learn-belly-dancing.html [accessed: March 2011].
YasminaofCairo.com n.d. Available at: http://www.yasminaofcairo.com/biogra phy.htm [accessed: March 2011].

SECTION II
Applying Mobile Methods

Chapter 6

Choosing Their Own Paths:
Mobile Methodologies for Understanding
Youth Lifestyles

Katherine King

Introduction

It is argued that through their lifestyles, young people exhibit a continued 'tiedness' to the local spaces in which they live out their everyday lives (Bennett 2000) and geographical writings have focused attention to the processes and politics of identity, space and place in the study of youth. Within social sciences more broadly, understandings of the experience of space have been given a further dimension through theoretical concerns with the ways in which meaning is affected, changed, altered, or enhanced by mobilities (Urry 2007, Fincham et al. 2009). There is, however, criticism that the movements of children and young people have not sufficiently informed this new mobilities paradigm (Barker et al. 2009). This chapter presents findings from two separate case studies; the first involving young people in a multi faith urban context and the second conducted with young people who visit the countryside for leisure; and which employed mobile methods to explore the ways in which these different groups of young people locate their lifestyles in particular spaces. The mobile element of both research methodologies was influenced by participatory approaches to research which acknowledge young people's own capabilities to self-represent (Pain 2004). This chapter will draw upon examples from each of these case studies to demonstrate how observing individuals chosen mobilities can address power imbalances in research with young people, provide important insights into their social worlds, and capture dynamic, embodied and meaningful relationships with space.

Youth lifestyles

As 'lived cultures in which individuals actively express their identities' (Miles 2000: 26), lifestyles offer an important conceptual tool for exploring the complexities of everyday interpretation and negotiation of cultural resources in the experience of contemporary youth. Whilst lifestyles are mediated in relation to social categories such as gender, occupation, class and so on, the construction of lifestyles is an interactive process created through an assemblage of symbolic materials, practices and values. Leisure practice is an integral feature of youth lifestyles, influencing individual identities and providing a connection to their own social worlds. Research that advances understandings of youth lifestyles has explored the patterns, choices, and cultural meanings of a wide variety of leisure activities, and of recent geographical concern are the physical, social and symbolic dimensions of space. Young people attach meaning to the practices, values and experiences which inform their lifestyles, but also to the spaces within which they locate these experiences.

Identity formation is a spatially situated process achieved through identification with others as well as through performative repertoires that are expressive and symbolic (Hetherington 1998). Research has examined the 'spatialities' of leisure activities such as nightclubbing (for example Chatterton and Hollands 2002, MacRae 2004), shopping (for example Matthews et al. 2000, Thomas 2005), skateboarding (for example Owens 2001, Borden 2001) 'hanging around' in public spaces (for example Hendry et al. 2002, Valentine 2004, Macdonald and Shildrick 2007, Robinson 2009) and the implications for identity and lifestyle in youth. Exploring the spatial and social contexts of young people's lives gives important consideration of the materials available for the construction of self-identity and the expression of lifestyle in particular locales. Adopting a 'lifestyle' approach therefore takes account of these important elements of identity formation by offering what Miles (2000) refers to as a constructive and reflexive conceptualization of the roles of leisure and space.

Mobilities and mobile methods

Within social sciences more broadly, understandings of the spatial have benefitted from a shift to explore the ways in which meaning is affected, changed, altered, or enhanced by mobilities (Urry 2007, Fincham et al. 2009). By moving beyond the 'static' in social science, the mobility turn challenges the ontological distinction between people and place reproducing boundaries as fluid and unfixed, whilst also acknowledging patterns of connection and disconnection made and unmade through performance and practice in space (Sheller and Urry 2006). These theoretical concerns with the making of space (and social relations) through movement have been accompanied by a methodological interest in the influence of place and the experience of mobility on the knowledge produced during the research process. In essence, a focus on tools which get us closer to the embodied experience of movement allow us to interrogate the social relations formed here (Fincham et al. 2009) which are rooted in the 'new mobilities paradigm' (Sheller and Urry 2006). As Kincheloe and McLaren (2005: 320) have argued:

... as parts of complex systems and intricate processes, objects of inquiry are far too mercurial to be viewed by a single way of seeing or as a snapshot of a particular phenomenon at a specific moment in time.

Attempts to capture the experience of movement through mobile methods often position mobilities as transport, such as through train travel (for example Bissell 2010) car journeys (for example Sheller 2004), or travelling as work (for example Fincham 2007). Yet there has also been a growing interest in developing mobile methods to investigate the leisure experience, focusing attention on the relationship between the body, the leisure activity and the landscape within which it is performed (for example Edensor 2000, Wylie 2005, Macpherson 2010). Within the geographies of childhood and youth, the emphasis has remained upon transport, and mobile methods have been most commonly employed to explore the way in which young people engage with their environments whilst travelling to school (for example Ross 2007, Walker et al. 2009, Porter et al. 2010). The role mobilities take as part of the youth leisure experience, and the use of mobile methods as part of youth leisure research is largely underexplored.

There is particular criticism that the mobilities of children and young people have not sufficiently informed the mainstream mobilities paradigm despite a burgeoning interest in these experiences within new social scientific studies of childhood and youth, and the clear co-relations between the two (Barker et al. 2009). Mobile methods can make an important contribution to research regarding mobility, childhood and youth by embodying the concerns of new social scientific studies of childhood and youth to acknowledge children and young people as active agents in their own right (see Valentine et al. 2001, Panelli 2002) and through their potential to increase our understanding of the variety and complexity of their everyday lives.

The mobile research methodologies reviewed within this chapter reflect the central tenets of new social scientific studies of childhood and youth, privileging inclusivity of young people who are considered 'hard to reach', and listening to the multiple voices of young people through research methods which are participatory, empowering and engaging (Pain 2004, Holt 2004). Importantly, respondent led mobile research reflects calls for research conducted 'with' rather than 'on' young people (Leyshon 2002). This chapter offers a contribution to the emerging youth mobilities paradigm by demonstrating how mobile methods offer a creative and participatory approach to research that is youth centred and can enhance our understanding of the social and spatial contexts which within which they situate their lifestyles.

Case study one: a mobile 'minibus' methodology

The first case study draws upon research conducted as part of the Youth On Religion (YOR) project[1] established to augment contemporary knowledge on the role of religion for young people growing up in British multi-faith contexts. The main study blended large scale quantitative surveys with qualitative methods conducted with secondary school pupils in the London Boroughs of Newham and Hillingdon, and in Bradford, to explore young people's negotiation of religious identity, their attitudes towards religion in society and the role of religion as part of the discourse of social cohesion. To increase the spread of participation, young people from Hillingdon who attended an alternative education programme following permanent exclusion from mainstream schooling were invited to take part in a mobile and visual methods exercise to explore their experiences of everyday life within a multi-faith community.

Ten young people aged between 11 and 14 years attended a briefing about the Youth on Religion project and were invited to take part in a mobile photography activity which answered the brief 'tell us about where you live'. Eight young people initially volunteered to take part which subsequently reduced to six. The participants identified as either Christian or having no religion, and as either black, mixed race or white ethnicity.

Before the journey took place a discussion group was held at the educational centre to consider the role of religion and culture in the local area, as well the places that participants chose to visit (or avoid) as part of their own leisure lifestyles, culminating in the formulation of a provisional route for a photography minibus tour. Participants were responsible for choosing the destinations to visit, designing a route for us to follow and for taking the photographs accompanied by a researcher and three youth workers. The minibus tour lasted approximately two hours during which around 13 different locations were photographed. On completion of the mobile research activity the researcher conducted short interviews with each of the participants in a classroom at the alternative education centre to discuss the photographs they had taken.

Empowering young people

The mobile element of the research methodology was largely influenced by a participatory approach to research through which young people could self-represent, rather than be represented by those with authority (Pain 2004). Young people who have been excluded from mainstream education may have complex needs or exhibit challenging communication or behaviour, and task based

---

1   This case study is based on research carried out for the Youth On Religion project under Grant AH/GO14086/1 from the AHRC/ESRC Religion & Society programme held by Professor Nicola Madge at Brunel University.

activities are considered a practical way of promoting these young people's active involvement in research (Conolly 2008).

This research employed visual methods whilst 'on the move' to encourage participants to communicate their lifestyles in creative and participatory ways. Moving between places engaged young people's attention and taking photographs was a skill which could be easily learnt and which participants appeared to enjoy. During preparatory meetings and observations at the alternative education project it became clear that young people's daily activities were heavily structured and directed by the youth worker team. In order to shift the conventional power differential and achieve a more autonomous engagement in the research, young people were responsible for leading the activity in the sense that they were able to choose the route taken, the places visited and the photographs that were taken. Whilst travelling on the minibus young people were actively involved in shaping the research encounter, for example by verbally dictating the route to the driver, by choosing the radio station we listened to, and by sitting with their friends rather than in their 'working groups'.[2] Whilst the youth workers sat in the front or at the very back of the minibus, I chose a seat in the middle of the bus. Whilst this was not an intentional decision I found I was well placed to engage in conversation with the participants in a way that felt 'natural' and unrehearsed. The shared experience of mobility helped in developing a rapport and avoided uncomfortable silences, both of which were particularly useful for research with young people that was complicated by a strong imbalance of power relations (also see Porter et al. 2010).

Whilst the research encounter aimed to encourage autonomy wherever possible, it would be misleading to imply the activity was entirely participant led. The young people were always accompanied by adults in places usually accessed independently with their friends and sometimes participants became embarrassed to be seen with the youth workers where other young people might be watching. Participants experienced more autonomy than that of the classroom context, yet were still expected to follow the rules and authority of the youth working team. For example one participant was split from his friend for part of the minibus journey because of poor behaviour. This research made no attempt to emulate their natural encounters, or to observe their lifestyles in the making, instead the research intended to capture a snapshot of the everyday spaces which young people considered important to them as part of their experiences within a multi-cultural and multi-faith urban setting. Mobile methods gave young people more opportunity to dictate the nature of the research encounter than conventional 'static' or school based methods and by showing the researcher the spaces which informed their lifestyles, situated the enquiry within the context of the phenomena in question.

---

2   Young people who attended the alternative education project were assigned working groups according to their ages, abilities, and behavioural characteristics.

Generating data on the move

The minibus journey was originally intended as a 'vehicle' for data collection via the photography exercise and subsequent photo elicitation interviews, yet travelling with young people, and the documentation of this journey through my research diary, revealed some important relationships with local spaces in itself. Whilst the photography activity enabled individuals to visually represent their lifestyles and provided some important insights into the importance of particular settings (Morrow 2001), it was travelling through the locale and the unsolicited observations, narrations and conversations participants held that gave a more embedded account of their everyday experiences.

Brown and Durrheim (2009) argue that mobile interviewing produces a different kind of conversation that is both more interactive and more spontaneous; in part because it is directed by the movements in space. For example in taking responsibility for navigation, participants were actively engaging with and responding to the locations we passed through. This activity in itself was deeply revealing of the way in which young people constructed the environment around them. For example, by using local landmarks to identify the route one of the participants commented on the prevalence of pubs and bars in an area with a large minority ethnic population. Further discussion led to a debate over the relative absence of a visual representation of British culture in the local area and the problematics of identifying 'Britishness'.

In several instances, participants chose to take photographs at local transport hubs, either at train stations, bus stops, or even of the minibus we were travelling in, the opportunities for mobility itself emerging as particularly significant in these young people's lives. Three participants chose to photograph one particular train station, expressing its importance for providing access (for themselves and others) to places beyond their own neighbourhoods, but also because of its location next to a canal where they would hang around with their friends. On leaving this area one participant, who chose not to photograph this location, spoke about the role of train stations as gang territories in this area. As I enquired further he explained the way in which some tensions between young people of different ethnic and religious backgrounds played out in local public space, and its effect on feelings of safety for young people who visit these areas. As we continued our journey, other participants interjected to build a more complete picture of the nature of these tensions, the spaces beyond the minibus providing the raw materials for them to construct their narratives.

In a second example, whilst the minibus was parked in a residential street waiting for one participant to photograph a church that he had once visited with his family, the remaining participants began to question why we had stopped in this particular road. Two of the participants commented that this area was full of 'posh houses' (NADINE: 12 years) 'for posh people, with their tea and biscuits' (DANTE: 11 years). This particular locale did not resonate with their own lifestyles and their discussions provided important insights into the construction of local spaces in relation to feelings of belonging or exclusion.

In each of these examples, none of the participants who spoke about these issues took photographs to capture these experiences, perhaps because these (perceivably) less remarkable aspects of their local neighbourhoods did not warrant the special focus a camera imposed. It became a real difficulty at times to reassure young people, and accompanying youth workers, that the photographs they were taking were 'significant enough'. Instead it was the interactive, informal and situated nature of the mobile research encounter that facilitated these kinds of accounts. In mobile interviews, conversations are inevitably informed by the visual and aural stimuli of the surrounding environment acting as what Brown and Durrheim (2009: 920) term 'situated talk'. Not only was this useful for contextualizing the conversation, these distractions may have also acted to dilute the intensity of questioning and ease the process of exploring affective experiences. During the interviews which followed this activity, which were performed at the alternative education project, participants were far less willing to discuss these clearly sensitive issues and it is unlikely these issues would have emerged freely during a static interview as they did whilst we travelled through the gang territories or affluent neighbourhoods as they were being discussed.

The findings generated from mobile methods in this setting complemented the use of more conventional qualitative and quantitative methods performed in school contexts that informed the main study of the Youth On Religion Project. Mobile methods helped to contextualize accounts around social cohesion and religion in society, for example whilst issues around gang culture emerged through some of the other qualitative methods, the minibus activity showed how these activities were linked to local environments. In addition being mobile contributed to a lively research encounter which enabled participation of young people who attended alternative forms of schooling to contribute new perspectives to the research.

Case study two: a mobile 'mountain biking' methodology

The second case study adopted a mobile methodology to explore the relationship between countryside leisure space and lifestyle and identity formation in youth. The research employed an assemblage of qualitative methods, including a mobile element with 40 mountain bikers aged between 13 and 25 years old who participated in mountain biking in a rural forest location in South East England. Recruitment of the participants was achieved primarily through direct contact within the local mountain biking community and snowballing. In addition, participants were recruited at cycle club events, through local advertisements, and via a local online forum.

In keeping with debates in cycling research and with youth centred approaches to research, it was a central methodological concern 'to keep the socialities of cycling in the context of their inherent mobility as far as possible' (Spinney

2006: 716) whilst ensuring the youth voice was heard (Holt 2004, Leyshon 2002, Pain 2004). Consequently the methodology was formed evoking Wolcott's (1999: 46) 'ethnographic mindset' which privileges 'experiencing, enquiring and examining' processes of research and was conducted within contexts which retained a relevance to young people's own identities and lifestyles. A mix of mobile interviews, participant observation and 'static' semi structured interviews was employed in different combinations according to participants' levels of skill, previous experience, and choice of mountain biking discipline. For the purposes of these discussions, the chapter will focus on the contributions of mobile methods (interviews and participant observation) to understandings of leisure, lifestyle and identity formation in countryside spaces.

Mobile interviews took the form of a recorded cycle ride with the researcher and between one and three young people on a route participants had chosen within the forest. During these rides, each participant and the researcher wore a 'bike mic': small microphones attached by a lapel to clothing and recorded using a small digital recording device, to record their opinions, observations and discussions. Recorded rides followed Kusenbach's (2003: 463) ethnographic principles of go-alongs, where fieldworkers join individual informants on their 'natural' outings, exploring their stream of experiences and practices as they move through, and interact with, their physical and social environment. In one case three participants chose to cycle without the researcher and in this instance recordings took the form of unsolicited mobile diaries which documented self-reflective participant narratives and captured interactions between mountain bikers as they travelled.

The second element, mobile observation sessions, were designed for young people who chose to perform dirt-jump, downhill or freeride versions of mountain biking in a designated 'freeride area'. Participation in these sub-disciplines was characterized by high speed, or highly skilled forms of mobility using artificial or naturally occurring obstacles to perform tricks and stunts, interspersed with periods of rest where participants would congregate to watch others, swap techniques and socialize in a sequence of events referred to by participants as 'sessioning'. Recording the movements involved in this through mobile interviewing was considered an unnecessary distraction during an already high risk activity and the researcher visited the space alongside the participant but did not always move with them. This did not restrict the respondents from movement, nor preclude the researcher from being involved in the 'session'.

Understanding relations with space and landscape

For Adams et al. (2001) place experience is based upon a set of ideologies related to particular types of mobility. Mountain biking is an embodied practice, through which space is constructed kinaesthetically and in one sense, employment of a mobile methodology allowed for the recognition of certain dimensions of mobility that contribute to place experience. Following Spinney (2006), whilst these feelings cannot be entirely captured, sharing the experiences of moving within these spaces with participants lends itself towards an embodied rather than disembodied account of the relations mountain bikers develop with space and landscape. Cycling with participants revealed the different ways in which participants would construct the spatialities of landscapes as they were engaged in mobile practice.

Participants sought to experience a variety of different terrains and routes as part of mountain biking, often making alternative routes through the forest, finding new ways of using original routes, by building their own jumps, or by digging new trails to follow. Insights into these playful behaviours emerged most prominently through cycling with participants in the spaces which captured their imaginations. During a mobile interview with two participants a discussion ensued about their landscape preferences and on enquiring further, participants cycled to a particular section of forest to situate their ideas:

> James (15 years): First of all we look for a slope.
>
> Joner (15 years): Cos downhill's fun.
>
> James (15 years): It's like say we were building there [points to forest section ahead] we have a quick look around it for any natural trails that we can either build on or avoid depending on what it's like and then we have a look for any trees, or any natural obstacles we can use, like this one here [points to different forest section ahead]. It's got no natural routes through so we'd just be looking at where we could go, where there's a fallen tree say or loads of mud that's fallen down the hill in rain or something to make like a natural ramp.

Whilst this example documents a largely visual encounter with space and landscape, other extracts show how mobile methods were used to capture a personal, multisensory account of how mountain bikers developed place attachments and experienced space kinaesthetically. The participant below chose to use mobile interviews as an opportunity to reflect on his individual experiences whilst the researcher was out of earshot.

> Jimmy (18 years): Even though I'm out of breath that's pretty relaxing … so you can get a certain momentum going and just carry it the whole way through without breaking too much on the corners, and when you just don't have to think about pedalling and you can just flow through the landscape, that's the real thrill of mountain biking for me.

The embodied and embedded nature of mobile methods facilitated the articulation and expression of the experience of space and landscape as part of mountain biking lifestyles. Performed as part of practice, mobile interviews provided participants with the means to animate their responses, by visualizing and modelling scenarios, by interacting with material objects, or by reflecting on the feelings they experienced as they happened, enriching understandings of the embodied experience of space. By moving with participants researchers can begin to appreciate the personal significance of certain spatial attributes bringing new insights into the construction of countryside leisure space for young people.

Capturing the (spatial) socialities of cycling

The employment of a mobile methodology additionally offers scope for recognizing the changing social relations which occur through mobilities. For Anderson (2004), social identity is tied to particular places. Activities are sometimes so embedded in their local contexts that to dismiss this removes the relationship between interviews and the emotional and social space being discussed. In this sense observing, interviewing, and at times experiencing movement with participants in context privileged the participant-place relationship, providing new layers of understanding and interpretation surrounding the socialities of mountain biking and the construction of identity and lifestyle in youth.

Mountain biking lifestyles were mediated through belonging and involved a strong community ethic that was expressed and maintained by sharing the experience of mountain biking at particular locations through the social practice of 'sessioning':

> Sarah (19 years): So sessioning you kind of stop and you've got a ledge or something to jump or to test your skill on so you need to spend a couple of times doing a jump going back and forth doing the same thing and it's also with your mates as well so you've got people around you so you see them jump and they see me jump.

By attending these sessions I was able to witness the subtle negotiation of community rules, values and norms which were inherently linked to the way in which participants conducted themselves in space. During sessions participants asserted particular identities as 'insiders', 'outsiders', 'novices', or 'locals' by demonstrating their knowledge of techniques, equipment, and local cycle spaces and by negotiating other community norms and values referred to as 'trail etiquette', and described below:

> Joner (15 years): ... when people come along and ride it, break it and then don't repair it or just come down and destroy it when they can't ride.

> Pete (22 years): ... they like to buy their way in to the sport rather than starting where everybody else starts with a rubbish bike, breaking it, upgrading it and getting in that way and they don't know the etiquette of being there.

> Sharpshooter (21 years): nobody has got any right to dig or change anyone else's jumps, I think I'd be very angry if anyone modified my stuff. I would always ask someone very nicely if I wanted to do x,y,z ... it's like etiquette.

Trail etiquette was an attitude or approach to mountain biking that was intangible, embodied and fluid in meaning, making it difficult for individuals to define. Whilst participants described a range of behaviours that contributed towards trail etiquette, it was observing their personal conduct and treatment of space which gave a more nuanced impression of trail etiquette. The interactions between mountain bikers, for example, revealed subtle participant hierarchies within the community as individuals negotiated the complex unwritten rules for demonstrating trail etiquette. Observing how participants chose to demonstrate their skill, took part in trail maintenance or jump building, and liaised with forest managers was deeply revealing of the power dynamics operating as part of mountain biking lifestyles and which governed the shared experience of space. Their performances more generally highlighted the importance of a sense of ownership, belonging and control as part of the youth leisure experience in externally managed countryside space (see King 2012).

Social relations are embedded in local contexts and being mobile offered an opportunity to witness the dynamics of these socio-spatial processes as they were enacted, reflecting the call for more holistic research methods which capture the 'other' factors which affect people's experiences of space (Scott 2009). Observing and moving with mountain bikers within the forest revealed a more complex picture than could be articulated via conversation alone, illustrating how community norms, expectations, rules and etiquettes played out as part of the lived experience of mountain biking in rural spaces.

Conclusion: mobile methods in practice

The findings from these case studies demonstrate the different ways in which data generated by mobile methods can enrich our understanding of space and lifestyle in youth.

In part, observing and experiencing movement with young people provides a means to explore the dynamic experience of space, facilitating the development of knowledge that is spatially determined (Brown and Durrheim 2009). For leisure activities such as mountain biking, mobile methods are particularly useful where meaning is deeply embedded in practice and where practice is inherently linked to the experience of space. In a different form, travelling with young people through the spaces in which they locate their everyday lives can give important insights into their perceptions of their local communities and neighbourhoods. However, the spatial experience is subjective, largely subconcious and at times may appear inconsequential to either participants or researchers. Mobile methods result in data that is spatially specific and we cannot assume that simply by being present in these places we understand their connection to them. Yet for young people who are actively engaged in the practice of identity making, observing the practices that inform their identities, in the spaces within which these experiences are located has contributed to a more holistic understanding of young people's lifestyles.

In another sense mobile methods represent a way of harnessing the changing socio-spatial relations which can occur through mobility. Transcripts from mobile interviews provided valuable insights into the social worlds of young people and the dynamics of their social interactions which inform and are informed by the environments in which they are played out. Sharing the experience of movement disrupts the fixity of interviewer – interviewee relations that dominate the qualitative paradigm and results in the development of knowledge that is more intersubjective. Mobility, from the remarkable to the most mundane, makes for a very different kind of research encounter that, in some senses, shares the natural encumbrances of the everyday. Mobile methods are therefore often unpredictable and perform best when they are loosely planned. In each of these cases mobile methods were performed in combination with other forms of qualitative inquiry as a useful addition, rather than an all encompassing replacement for other techniques.

Lastly, incorporating mobility into the generation of data responds to the calls for a more flexible, creative and youth-centred approaches to research recognizing the importance of participant led research and the employment of empowering research relations (Holt 2004). Inviting young people to choose the routes of the research for themselves offered important insights into young people's experience of space that other more conventional methods may have overlooked. By directing attention towards an emphasis on practice and the way in which this is embedded in the fabric of everyday life, mobile methods retain a relevance to young people's lives, and provide the opportunity for individuals to choose the direction of the research.

Conducting mobile methods with young people is not without its difficulties and opens the research encounter to distractions which may or may not befit the path of inquiry. Yet mobile methods get us closer to solving what Leyshon (2002) has termed the researcher's biggest problem: understanding young people's lives from their perspective and transferring this from one field to another. Despite their limitations, mobile methodologies have significant potential to increase our understanding of young people's experience of place and environment as mobility, in its myriad forms, becomes an increasingly pervasive feature in the experience and expression of youth lifestyles.

References

Adams, P.C., Hoelscher, S.D. and Till, K.E. 2001. *Textures of Place: Exploring Humanist Geographies*. Minneapolis: University of Minnesota Press.
Anderson, J. 2004. Talking whilst walking: a geographical archaeology of knowledge. *Area*, 36(3), 254–261.
Barker, J., Kraftl, P., Horton, J. and Tucker, F. 2009. The road less travelled – new directions in children's and young people's mobility. *Mobilities*, 4(1), 1–10.

Bennett, A. 2000. *Popular Music and Youth Culture: Music, Identity and Place.* Basingstoke: Macmillan.

Bissell, D. 2010. Passenger mobilities: affective atmospheres and the sociality of public transport. *Environment and Planning D: Society and Space*, 28(2), 270–289.

Borden, I. 2001. *Skateboarding, Space and the City: Architecture and the Body.* Oxford: Berg.

Brown, L. and Durrheim, K. 2009. Different kinds of knowing: generating qualitative data through mobile interviewing. *Qualitative Inquiry*, 15(5), 911–930.

Chatterton, P. and Hollands, R. 2002. Theorising urban playscapes: producing, regulating and consuming youthful nightlife city spaces. *Urban Studies*, 39(1), 95–116.

Conolly, A. 2008. The challenges of generating qualitative data with socially excluded young people. *International Journal of Social Research Methodology*, 11(3), 201–214.

Edensor, T. 2000. Walking in the British countryside: reflexivity, embodied practices and ways to escape. *Body and Society*, 6(3–4), 81–106.

Fincham, B. 2007. Bicycle Messengers: Image, Identity and Culture, in *Cycling and Society*, edited by D. Horton, P. Rosen and P. Cox. Farnham: Ashgate, 179–196.

Fincham, B., McGuinness, M. and Murray, L. 2009. *Mobile Methodologies.* Basingstoke: Palgrave Macmillan.

Hendry, L.B., Kloep, M. and Wood, S. 2002. Young people talking about adolescent rural crowds and social settings. *Journal of Youth Studies*, 5(4), 357–374.

Hetherington, K. 1998. *Expressions of Identity: Space, Performance, Politics.* London: Sage.

Holt, L. 2004. The 'voices' of children: de-centering empowering research relations. *Children's Geographies*, 2(1), 13–27.

Kincheloe, J.L. and McLaren, P. 2005. Rethinking critical theory and qualitative research, in *Handbook of Qualitative Research*, edited by N.K. Denzin and Y.S. Lincoln. London: Sage, 303–342.

King, K. 2012. Encouraging active lifestyles: the spatialities of youth mountain biking, in *International Sport Events: Impacts, Experiences and Identities*, edited by R. Shipway and A. Fyall. London: Routledge, 181–194.

Kusenbach, M. 2003. Street phenomenology: the go-along as ethnographic research tool. *Ethnography*, 4(3), 455–485.

Leyshon, M. 2002. On being 'in the field': practice, progress and problems in research with young people in rural areas. *Journal of Rural Studies*, 18(2), 179–181.

Macdonald, R. and Shildrick, T. 2007. Street corner society: leisure careers, youth (sub)culture and social exclusion. *Leisure Studies*, 26(3), 339–355.

Macpherson, H. 2010. Non-representational approaches to body-landscape relations. *Geography Compass*, 4(1), 1–13.

MacRae, R. 2004. Notions of 'us and them': markers of stratification in clubbing lifestyles. *Journal of Youth Studies*, 7(1), 55–71.

Matthews, H., Taylor, M., Sherwood, K., Tucker, F. and Limb, M. 2000. Growing-up in the countryside: children and the rural idyll. *Journal of Rural Studies*, 16(2), 141–153.

Miles, S. 2000. *Youth Lifestyles in a Changing World*. Buckingham: Open University Press.

Morrow, V. 2001. Using qualitative methods to elicit young people's perspectives on their environments: some ideas for community health initiatives. *Health Education Research*, 16(3), 255–268.

Owens, P.E. 2001. Recreation and restrictions: community skateboard parks in the United States. *Urban Geography*, 22(8), 782–797.

Pain, R. 2004. Social geography: participatory research. *Progress in Human Geography*, 28(5), 652–663.

Panelli, R. 2002. Young rural lives: strategies beyond diversity. *Journal of Rural Studies*, 18(2), 113–122.

Porter, G., Hampshire, K., Abane, A., Munthali, A., Robson, E., Mashiri, M. and Maponya, G. 2010. Where dogs, ghosts and lions roam: learning from mobile ethnographies on the journey to school. *Children's Geographies*, 8(2), 91–105.

Robinson, C. 2009. Nightscapes and leisure spaces: an ethnographic study of young people's use of free space. *Journal of Youth Studies*, 12(5), 501–514.

Ross, N. 2007. 'My journey to school': foregrounding the meaning of school journeys and children's engagements and interactions in their everyday localities. *Children's Geographies*, 5(4), 373–391.

Scott, A., Carter, C., Brown, K. and White, V. 2009. 'Seeing is not everything': exploring the landscape experiences of different publics. *Landscape Research*, 34(4), 397–424.

Sheller, M. 2004. Automotive emotions: feeling the car. *Theory, Culture and Society*, 21(4–5), 221–242.

Sheller, M. and Urry, J. 2006. The new mobilities paradigm. *Environment and Planning A*, 38(2), 207–226.

Spinney, J. 2006. A place of sense: a kinaesthetic ethnography of cyclists on Mont Ventoux. *Environment and Planning D*, 24(5), 709–732.

Thomas, M. 2005. Girls, consumption space and the contradictions of hanging out in the city. *Social and Cultural Geography*, 6(4), 587–605.

Urry, J. 2007. *Mobilities*. Cambridge: Polity Press.

Valentine, G. 2004. *Public Space and the Culture of Childhood*. Farnham: Ashgate.

Valentine, G., Butler, R. and Skelton, T. 2001. The ethical and methodological complexities of doing research with 'vulnerable' young people. *Ethics, Place and Environment*, 4(2), 119–125.

Walker, M., Whyatt, J.D., Pooley, C., Davies, G., Coulton, P. and Bamford, W. 2009. Talk, technologies and teenagers: understanding the school journey using a mixed-methods approach. *Children's Geographies*, 7(2), 107–122.

Wolcott, H.F. 1999. *Ethnography: A Way of Seeing*. London: Sage.

Wylie, J. 2005. A single day's walking: narrating self and landscape on the South West Coast Path. *Transactions of the Institute of British Geographers*, 30(2), 234–247.

Chapter 7

Investigating Perpetual Travel: Email Interviews and Longitudinal Methods in Travel, Tourism and Mobilities Research

Garth Lean

Introduction

Corporeal travel is deeply entwined in daily experiences, performances, sensualities, imaginings, memories, communications and mobilities (Leed 1991, Rojek and Urry 1997, Urry 2007). As such, in a liquid modern world, it becomes increasingly difficult to distinguish between notions such as home, away, departure, arrival, return, before, during and after – travel is a perpetual state of being (Bauman 2000, Urry 2007). In this context, researchers such as Urry (2007), Hannam (2009) and Mavrič and Urry (2009) argue that physical travel should not be separated from other forms of mobility; courtesy of historic and contemporary mobilities, they are entangled. Corporeal travel is informed by (and informs) all other mobilities, whether they be physical, virtual, communicative and/or imaginative (Urry 2007); albeit to varying degrees, an individual is travelling before, during and after any given physical travel experience. In addition, physical travel does not end upon one's 'return' home – it is continued in a variety of ways, including through photographs, objects, social relationships, roles, routines and performance and through inhabiting a fluid place (Lean 2012a).

Given the growing acknowledgement of the perpetual nature of travel and its intersection with mobile lifestyles (as evidenced in this volume), there is a need for a concomitant shift in the methods used for investigating this phenomenon (Urry 2007, Büscher, Urry and Witchger 2011). Methods that can observe lived experience over an extended period need to be employed. The following chapter reflects upon methods used in an ongoing exploration of transformation through travel. Commencing in 2005, the study utilizes email interviews, in a longitudinal design, to investigate the accounts of individuals who believe they have been 'transformed' by physical travel. It explores how these corporeal travel experiences and transformations intersect with other mobilities and experiences over the respondent's life course. Drawing upon participant feedback and literature on email interviews and longitudinal research, I reflect upon my experiences using this method and provide a series of considerations for other researchers who may want to employ a similar methodological design in their own projects.

Investigating transformative travel

Throughout history, physical travel has been viewed as both an agent of individual and social transformation (Leed 1991). Despite this, research on the topic is somewhat limited (see Lean 2009 for a review of the literature). It has drawn upon what has been conceptualized as an old paradigm in tourism theory, focused upon groups/niches, motivations, destinations, origins, nationalities/nation states and attempting to build typologies (Lean 2012b). These approaches have come under considerable criticism over the past decade, influenced by shifts within social and cultural studies (see, for example, Franklin and Crang 2001, Minca and Oakes 2006, Ateljevic, Pritchard and Morgan 2007, Franklin 2007, Mavrič and Urry 2009, Robinson and Jamal 2009, Tribe 2009). In relation to tourism, but equally applicable to travel research, Robinson and Jamal (2009) argue that the notion of discrete research boundaries fails to capture the dynamic(s) of tourism. This is something more substantive than the elaboration of trends and the extrapolation of data and scenarios, and refers to the ways in which tourism – in the ways that it is organized, structured and practised – moves through societies in the context of wider systems of being (Robinson and Jamal 2009: 696).

Within this paradigm, physical travel is seen as removed from one's everyday existence and is framed as its antithesis (Mavrič and Urry 2009). Travel and tourism become processes through which an individual can 'escape' regular roles and routines and view, and/or engage with, the 'extraordinary' (Franklin and Crang 2001, Franklin 2004). From this perspective, physical travel has been singled out for its potential to transform individual travellers with little regard for its inherent complexity or the influence of other mobilities. An understanding of this complexity is critical to an exploration of transformation through travel, as those aspects of an individual that may be transformed – thinking, knowledge, behaviours, reality, identity – are not static, but under the continual influence of mobile lifestyles before, during and after travel. Given this assessment, it was determined that a new approach to researching this topic that could allow for the intersection of these various mobilities should be developed.

The study

In early 2005 I faced a challenge. I wanted to conduct a holistic investigation of transformation through travel that could capture the richness of the topic and not be confined to the 'old' paradigm of tourism research detailed above. The challenge was amplified given I only had a few months in which to conduct such a study. It seemed improbable that this exploration could be achieved by investigating a particular tour group or a given site or destination. It would require a methodology that could allow access to a diverse group of individuals who had been transformed by travel.

At the time of developing a methodology I happened to be working in the eBusiness unit of a state tourism organization, managing industry updating of a consumer tourism website and database. It was in this environment that the idea of developing a website and marketing it around the world was conceived. While I had never created a website and had no experience with online research, with the help of my brother and colleagues I constructed a site – www.transformativetravel. com – within two weeks. The website was subsequently promoted through travel message boards and forums, and among personal and industry contacts, with some scepticism on my part as to whether it would actually work. Along with information about the project, the website contained a simple form asking participants to indicate their country of residence, age group, transformative travel experience/s and consequential transformation. The form also asked respondents to indicate whether they would be willing to participate in future aspects of the study, providing space to supply an email address if they were willing to do so.

Sixty-one individuals from 17 different countries, and representing a diverse range of ages and physical travel experiences, submitted a form on the website; 22 of these respondents participated in follow-up interviews. The interviews collected basic demographic information and asked a series of open ended questions based on various hypotheses made within previous studies across a range of disciplines. Transformation through travel was found to be a complex area of investigation. The research confirmed that seeking to develop a typology of a 'transformative traveller' was problematic and that the identification of particular aspects that could bring about transformation was flawed. Findings showed that, while there appear to be factors that influence the probability of transformation, one can never make any overarching claims about what conditions lead to an alteration as transformation is dependent on the individual traveller and their unique makeup and experiences before, during and after travel. The study also argued against looking at any transformation as static. In the retrospective accounts of participants it could be seen that, for many, transformation was a progression of earlier changes (physical travel playing a dramatic role within these) and that upon 'returning' one's thinking and behaviours were in a continual state of flux (see Lean 2009 for further details on the findings of this initial study).

Having only scratched the surface, in 2006 I decided to pursue the topic as a PhD. This gave me the unique opportunity to re-interview my initial participants and to seek new respondents using a revamped website. Through doing so, the study could go beyond looking at a snapshot in time and begin to explore how reality continues to alter, along with how physical travel experiences intersect with other mobilities. Follow-up interviews were conducted in 2007 and, again, in 2009/2010.[1] At the completion of the last round of interviews, 78 participants from 17 different countries, and a variety of age groups, had reported their experiences through the website since 2005. This encapsulated a diverse range of experiences, spanning from a few days to five years, including physical travel for pleasure, study, work, volunteering, migration and even military service.

---

1   At the time of writing the author was embarking upon his fourth round of interviews, seeing the study enter its seventh year of data collection.

In addition to internet based methods, I conducted six months of my own travels – moving, sensing, observing, conversing, photographing, writing and performing – as a way of exploring the embodied and sensual nature of the travel experiences and those elements, which may, or may not, influence one's thinking and behaviour while travelling. This included four weeks in East Timor, two months in Cambodia and Laos and two months in West Africa (Niger, Benin, Togo, Burkina Faso, Mali and Cote d'Ivoire). I was also able to incorporate other trips conducted for business and pleasure over the study's timeframe (see Lean 2012b for details on the findings of this study).

While these methods were somewhat organic in their design, the use of longitudinal email interviews, in combination with an exploration of my own experiences, became a useful way of unpacking how transformation through travel takes place in a mobilities landscape. These techniques deserve careful consideration in determining methods for exploring the perpetual nature of physical travel, its relationship to other mobilities and mobile lifestyles.

Longitudinal and email research

The use of longitudinal methods within tourism and travel research is quite limited (Ritchie 2005). What is more, there is a dearth of longitudinal studies looking at the effects of travel upon the traveller (Lean 2009). In a review of the use of longitudinal methods in tourism research conducted by Ritchie (2005), no examples of longitudinal studies looking at the visitor experience and its enduring impact were provided. The use of longitudinal methods, however, becomes necessary if we are to accept travel as perpetual, observe the intersections of physical travel with other mobilities and explore the continuing influence of travel upon an individual's lived experience.

The style of longitudinal research I undertook in my project is commonly referred to as a 'revolving panel design' (Menard 2008). Menard (2008: 6) writes that 'revolving panel designs collect data on a sample of cases either retrospectively or prospectively for some sequence of measurement periods, then drop some subjects and replace them with new subjects'. This 'dropping' of participants is both at the discretion of the researcher, and a part of the reality that not all participants can maintain their involvement in a project over its lifetime, particularly if that lifetime spans a number of years.

Despite the benefits that longitudinal studies offer for investigating the continuing influence of physical travel, a number of limitations of this research design have also been highlighted. While technological approaches offer potential avenues for overcoming some of these limitations, along with advantages, such as being able to reach a global study population (albeit still limited, as internet access is not universal), these methods also hold their own concerns. In the following section I explore a variety of issues that have been raised in regard to longitudinal studies and email research, discussing how they played out within a longitudinal travel/mobilities study. This discussion is informed by a review of methods I conducted with participants in 2005, along with my own personal reflections.

Time and costs

Two of the main reasons cited for the lack of longitudinal studies in tourism research (Ritchie 2005), and more broadly (Bryman 2008, Walter 2010), are the time and cost involved in conducting them. In regard to time, the commitment is not only on the part of the researcher, but also the participant. While the time involved in longitudinal research varies depending on the type of study design being implemented, the use of email interviews offers a number of potential timesavers over face-to-face interviews. Email eliminates the time needed to conduct interviews in person, including aspects such as arranging interviews and travelling back and forth between them (in the case of longitudinal research, over an extended period). Possibly most significantly, they remove the need to transcribe participant accounts (McCoyd and Kerson 2006). Alternately, in the event that transcription is to be outsourced, it represents a significant cost saving. As McCoyd and Kerson (2006) observe, using material that has been developed directly by a participant also removes a degree of researcher manipulation that may take place in the conversion of verbal material to text.

There are, however, other time demands that come from using this method. In reflecting upon a study utilizing both email and face-to-face interviews, McAuliffe (2003) observed a number of aspects that required a significant time investment on the part of the researcher.

> ... reading and re-reading of instalments as they arrived; the formulation of responses and comments; the management of data across computer systems and the attention to confidentiality requirements; the prompting and support of participants to continue writing; the monitoring of data quality and adherence to the research questions; feedback of completed transcripts; and some data cleansing/reduction in preparation for entry into a data analysis package (McAuliffe 2003: 65).

The time demands in my study were similar to those of McAuliffe (2003), although there were also some significant variations. While McAuliffe (2003) conducted extended conversational interviews that took place over a series of emails, providing accounts that spanned from 3,000 to 30,000 words, the major time requirements for my study came in the form of developing a research website and in tailoring interviews to individual participants and their earlier submissions (although, it could be argued that through providing background information on the study the website eliminated the time that would be needed for clarifying various aspects of the study with participants). While it is conceivable that stock questions could have been sent to all participants, I decided I was likely to receive richer responses if interview questions were directed personally to each respondent.

Modifying questions was also necessary to ensure I did not frustrate participants by asking questions they had already answered in previous responses.

In terms of conducting a longitudinal study, email interviews provided considerable time savings in future stages of the research. While there was a considerable investment of time in developing a website and conducting a series of tailored interviews across a variety of themes, this developed a project with few time and cost demands as a longitudinal study. Follow-up interviews simply required a generic email to previous respondents asking whether they were available to participate in another round of interviews. Once demographic information had been collected, and various hypotheses tested in early stages of the study, questions became increasingly open ended. By 2009/2010, the number of questions had been greatly reduced. The focus of enquiry became a reflection upon previous accounts and whether the participant felt they had undergone any transformative experiences in the intervening years. The narrative generated by these open ended questions was sufficient to provide data for the study in a longitudinal format. It also left open the opportunity to ask follow-up questions, and to launch new areas of enquiry if necessary. As each round of interviews was only conducted every two years, it was easy enough to schedule the project around other work commitments, therefore posing little imposition in terms of workload.

An important determinant of the duration of data collection, and additional time demands upon the researcher, is the number of questions presented in each email. Bryman (2008) debates the virtues of sending all interview questions together, as opposed to sending them one at a time. The risk, he writes, of combining all questions is that respondents may leave some unanswered as they are not interested or do not feel they can make an adequate contribution, thus the appeal of sending questions one at a time. The initial interviews in my study were drawn out as I felt it was necessary to limit each email to a maximum of five questions. I employed this strategy as I did not want to place too much demand upon participants in a single interview, and to ensure they had sufficient time to provide detailed and meaningful responses. This decision meant that I had to deliver my questions over a series of three to four email interviews, which given delays in participant responses, drew out the interview process considerably. One benefit to come from these delays, however, was the time it allowed for redeveloping themes and questions, on the basis of earlier responses, before launching each new round of interviews.

While longitudinal methods are often critiqued for being expensive to conduct (see Bryman 2008, Walter 2010), in the model employed in this study, costs were only minor. The main expense was in purchasing and renewing the domain name for the website. There were no content hosting expenses as I was able to utilize free space provided by my personal internet provider. Even these minor costs could be eliminated if researchers can acquire these services through their institution. As such, the main demand of this method upon the researcher becomes one of time.

In regard to time demands placed upon participants, the main drawback of website submissions and email interviews is the time involved in writing an account of one's experiences and answering interview questions rather than simply vocalizing them in an interview. One strategy I employed to reduce the demand upon participants was to not impose deadlines for responses. At the completion of the first stage of the study, a number of respondents remarked that they had enjoyed not feeling rushed. Participants also appreciated the opportunity to complete the interviews over an extended period of time. If they were particularly busy they could complete the interview in parts, and were able to pause to reflect further and reread their responses if necessary. These positive evaluations were also obtained in reviews of email interviews conducted by McAuliffe (2003), McCoyd and Kerson (2006) and Reid, Petocz and Gordon (2008). In terms of a longitudinal study, time demands upon participants reduced over time, as after the initial interviews were conducted, the number of questions were generally limited to one or two emails sent every two years.

There are also benefits for both participants and researchers that can come through the construction of written responses. While one participant found it a difficult method as it took them a considerable amount of time to write about their experiences, most said that they had found it an easy way to participate and that they had benefited from the opportunity to reflect upon their travel experiences and associated influences. In addition, McAuliffe (2003) argues that the extra time email interviews allow for responding can lead to more detailed and focused answers as participants are able to concentrate upon a researcher's questions rather than trailing off on tangents, as is common in face-to-face interviews. In doing so, this helps to cut down on the amount of extraneous data to be analysed.

Other limitations that need to be considered include access to computers and email facilities within a private and secure space and the need for participants to read and write in the language of the researcher so they can adequately interpret questions and form detailed responses. Although, the latter is a limitation of all interviews, as McCoyd and Kerson (2006) found, email interviews can provide a better opportunity for people whose language skills are not as strong as they are able to take their time to consider questions and develop responses.

Recruitment

It was one thing to build a website containing forms for participants to detail their transformative travel experience(s); it was another to source a viable number of respondents within a relatively short period of time. To accomplish this I decided to promote the research as broadly as possible. This included promotion through personal and industry contacts, online travel groups and discussion/message boards and other researchers within the field. To my surprise, this had quick and rewarding results. Marketing the website also took on a life of its own, as details of the project were included in several travel newsletters by editors who had happened across the original call for participants. Some recipients also forwarded the call for participants to family and friends they believed may be interested in the study.

Bryman (2008) writes that online methods generate concerns about confidentiality, particularly given incidents of fraud and hacking surrounding the internet. One of the main recruiting strategies I employed centred on assuring participants of the importance of the research and my trustworthiness as researcher. The website became a critical tool in achieving this as it allowed me to provide a significant amount of background information on the study, ethics, myself and the institution/departments of which I was a member (researchers, such as Curasi 2001 and O'Connor and Madge 2003, argue that directing participants to the reseacher's website can help to increase response rates). It also permitted me to keep my call for participants brief, as I could simply refer those who required further clarification to the website. In addition, the website gave me the opportunity to display photographs of my own travels and, therefore, show my membership of the 'travel community'. There appeared to be a degree of increased acceptance and trust in our communications as a result of being able to do so. All of these strategies helped to eliminate the idea that respondents were sending personal information to a complete stranger and putting their privacy at risk.

An unexpected benefit of targeting online travel groups/forums was having access to a group of participants who not only had a keen interest in travel but were familiar with discussing their experiences both generally and in an electronic format. What is more, they appeared to be adept at quickly developing online relationships and were happy, and confident, in conveying detailed accounts of their experiences and emotions. I also found these participants had a keen interest in the topic of investigation and were eager to see its outcomes. This all played an important role in their involvement, and in terms of a longitudinal study, continuing commitment to the research. In saying this, however, my participant base was sourced from a broad range of outlets and respondents who had not found the study through membership of online travel groups still possessed similar skills in 'online expression'.

Attrition

A challenge presented by both longitudinal research (Ritchie 2005) and email interviews (Mann and Stewart 2000, McAuliffe 2003, McCoyd and Kerson 2006) is keeping participants involved for the duration of the study. In terms of email interviews, emails can be easily overlooked and forgotten, particularly given my decision not to set response deadlines and to provide continual reminders to respondents that they could withdraw at any stage of the research should time demands become too much. In order to ensure the success of the study, I often had to send several reminder emails. I approached this delicately as I did not want to annoy participants. As such, reminders were sent at weekly or fortnightly intervals depending on the project deadlines at that particular stage of the study.

Mann and Stewart (2000) write that it is important to maintain contact with participants to assure them that their contributions are valuable, particularly given that email interviews are still an unfamiliar format. In the first two years of the study I sent newsletters to participants reporting its progress to both maintain contact and assure them of the importance of the research. This was positively received in the methodology review; however, it becomes another aspect of time commitment on the part of the researcher that needs to be considered.

In regard to email interviews conducted as a longitudinal study, it is not possible to keep all participants involved. Two of the most common reasons for participant attrition were changed email addresses and participants being too busy to complete interviews. To cater for this dropout, as discussed earlier, I utilized a revolving panel design, recruiting new participants during each round of interviews. I also remained as flexible as possible with the time provided for responses, and continued to send 'gentle' reminder emails as necessary. Some participants wished to continue but were too busy at a particular time (in some cases they were travelling again and not able to contribute until their return). I always tried to accommodate these participants at a later date, but coordinating this required meticulous records. I kept a detailed spreadsheet to record all communication with participants and to monitor the completion of various interviews. This was married against digital and paper files for each participant. These were essential for launching future rounds of interviews over the course of the project.

As a catalyst for keeping participants involved, at the beginning of each new round of interviews I would send them their responses from two years beforehand, asking them to provide a written reflection. Not only did this yield interesting data, most found it a rewarding aspect of their continuing involvement in the study. I also tried to provide participants with some form of outcome from the previous stage of research before launching a new round of interviews. In 2007 this was in the form of a summary of findings to date, and in 2009/2010 it was a recent publication on the research. Of course, if this form of feedback is provided to participants, its potential influence upon responses needs to be considered. I determined that my project was evolving to such a degree that the findings from previous analysis would have little effect. Providing this output to respondents also gave me an opportunity to gain their feedback on the study's findings.

Depth of interviews and researcher/participant relationship

One aspect of email interviews enjoyed by many respondents was the anonymity this form of data collection allows. Some told me they could not have revealed the same information in a face-to-face interview as they would have been too intimidated by meeting someone for the first time, and concerned about their reactions. For one participant, the study was the first outlet they had found to discuss emotional issues surrounding their travels and transformation. In fact, they had found the interview process 'cathartic' (the therapeutic effects of participating in interviews have been explored by a number of researchers; see for example: Hutchinson, Wilson and Wilson 1994, Birch and Miller 2000, Haynes 2006). These findings were echoed by McAuliffe (2003) who, when comparing email and face-to-face interviews, found email interviews enabled more honest responses and a longer relationship with the participant. In a comparison of email and face-to-face interviews, McCoyd and Kerson (2006) argued that the anonymity of email interviews enables more extensive and in-depth communication. In addition, they found as email interviews usually take place over an extended period of time, a greater amount of information could be gathered (although as acknowledged earlier, this was a point of frustration for one of my participants who felt it took too long for her to type out her experiences).

Reid et al. (2008) write that email interviews are sometimes criticized for their inability to unpack issues in as much depth as face-to-face interviews. They are also critiqued for not allowing participants and researchers alike to immediately clarify questions and responses. Conversely, researchers such as James and Busher (2006) argue that there is an extra layer of depth to responses resulting from the additional time email interviews allow for participants to consider and formulate their responses. I found that while it was not possible to ask immediate clarification questions, I could simply work these into the next email (although, this does require more time than it would in a face-to-face interview). Like James and Busher (2006), I found that email interviews were able to elicit quite detailed, succinct and considered responses.

Another advantage of email interviews is the removal of certain biases and reactions that arise in face-to-face interactions between the researcher and participant. For example, the use of technology hides personal attributes, such as physical characteristics and ways of speaking (Reid et al. 2008). McCoyd and Kerson (2006: 398) feel this results in 'less contaminated interactions' between the researcher and respondent. Although, it should also be acknowledged that there are also biases that may arise through the interpretation of written material, including judgements upon the participants' opinions, beliefs and practices.

In a comparison of face-to-face methods and email interviews, McAuliffe (2003) found that one main point of difference between the two styles of interviewing was the inability to read emotions within text as opposed to during a direct encounter:

> The major contrast in conducting the face-to-face interviews was not in the content of the data or structure of the discussion, but in the confrontation of raw emotion. Reading emotive language, as powerful as this can be, is quite different from coming face-to-face with anger, despair, helplessness, confusion, frustration, fear, and sadness ... [T]his dimension may well have become lost in the analysis had only email dialogues been conducted (McAuliffe 2003: 65).

This is a significant limitation of this form of research, which will obviously vary in degrees of importance depending on the topic being investigated. Alongside this, and with particular relation to conducting a longitudinal study, there are significant limitations to the amount of detail that can be gathered about a participant's experience before, during and after travel – particularly given the complex amalgam of emotions, sensualities and embodied experiences involved in physical travel. There is a certain level of complexity that cannot be delved into in terms of the lived experience within short email responses every two years.

To address this in my project, I complimented the collection of participant stories with my own experiences of physical travel. Having realized the limitations of email accounts in my initial study, and given my conversion to traveller after reading the evocative stories of my participants, I decided to conduct a series of my own journeys as a part of the research design. This added a richness of analysis to the experience of physical travel and 'return' that would have otherwise been unavailable by drawing upon email interviews alone. In saying this, even face-to-face interviews would be insufficient in gaining such richness. Implementing this design also provided me with a pool of travellers, met during my experiences, with whom I formed close relationships and could observe aspects of their ongoing journeys, physical and otherwise. This included contact through social networking websites, online chat/calls and visits to their places of residence.

Conclusion

As becomes overwhelmingly apparent in this book on lifestyle mobilities, the traditional idea that a traveller moves from one static place to another, with eventual return home to resume life as normal, is somewhat problematic. Travellers inhabit, move through and 'return' to spaces that are, to varying degrees, mobile. Investigating these overlaying mobilities, however, requires methods that are themselves mobile and that can investigate a traveller's life journey over an elongated period of time. Following recent calls made by writers such as Urry (2007) and Büscher et al. (2011), researchers need to explore new methods that can investigate mobile lifestyles and how physical travel intersects with other forms of mobility.

Longitudinal studies utilizing email interviews offer one potential avenue for achieving these goals. In my study, such methods were able to reveal the fluidity of transformation through travel; I was not only observing a particular moment in time, but how reality continues to alter over one's life course and intersects with other mobilities. It enabled me to look at the transformations individuals identify through travel and how these perceptions alter with time and with new experiences. These methods helped to illustrate how the transformative experiences connected to physical travel can be compared to ongoing life journeys and transformation – how physical travel experiences, and consequential transformations, inform and influence falling in love, having children, work roles, relationships with family and friends, dealing with illness, transitioning to new life stages, future physical travel experiences and, in one particularly interesting case, a soldier's experiences in Iraq. Conducting interviews via email allowed me to draw upon a global participant base incorporating diverse physical travel experiences and participants from non-English-speaking backgrounds.

As can be ascertained from the discussion above, however, a longitudinal email study is not the be all and end all; like any methodological design, these methods come with their own unique set of benefits and limitations that need to be considered and catered for in any study for which they are deemed suitable. That said, the potential benefits they have for investigating traveller experiences in a landscape of perpetual travel and lifestyle mobilities is one well worth exploring. What is more, internet technology offers other methodological opportunities for conducting longitudinal research: online text chat, internet calls and live video calls using webcams. Again, however, these technologies all hold their own advantages and limitations that would have to be assessed on a case-by-case basis. For example, while email is widely available and simple to use, the necessity of more complex and costly hardware, software and applications may limit the study population under investigation given varying access to technology and infrastructure, along with knowledge of its use. This is of particular concern given growing pushes to capture perspectives from 'less-developed' countries. In addition, video interviews would still have to be transcribed and there would be a host of ethical considerations around their use. That said, no doubt as technology evolves and becomes more accessible, new opportunities will arise and researchers should not be afraid to pilot these in their work. If appropriate for a given project, exploration and honing of these technological advances as research methods are likely to lead to contributions as important as those findings generated from the data they are gathering.

References

Ateljevic, I., Pritchard, A. and Morgan, N. (eds) 2007. *The Critical Turn in Tourism Studies: Innovative Research Methods*. Oxford: Elsevier.

Bauman, Z. 2000. *Liquid Modernity*. Cambridge: Polity Press.

Birch, M. and Miller, T. 2000. Inviting intimacy: the interview as therapeutic opportunity. *International Journal of Social Research Methodology*, 3(3), 189–202.

Bryman, A. 2008. *Social Research Methods*. Oxford: Oxford University Press.

Büscher, M., Urry, J. and Witchger, K. (eds) 2011. *Mobile Methods*. Abingdon: Routledge.

Curasi, C.F. 2001. A critical exploration of face-to-face interviewing vs. computer-mediated interviewing. *International Journal of Market Research*, 43(4), 361–375.

Franklin, A. 2004. Tourism as ordering: towards a new ontology of tourism. *Tourist Studies*, 4(2), 645–657.

Franklin, A. 2007. The Problem with Tourism Theory, in *The Critical Turn in Tourism Studies: Innovative Research Methodologies*, edited by I. Ateljevic, A. Pritchard and N. Morgan. Oxford: Elsevier, 131–148.

Franklin, A. and Crang, M. 2001. The trouble with tourism and travel theory. *Tourist Studies*, 1(1), 5–22.

Hannam, K. 2009. The End of Tourism? Nomadology and the Mobilties Paradigm, in *Philosophical Issues in Tourism*, edited by J. Tribe. Bristol: Channel View, 101–115.

Haynes, K. 2006. A therapeutic journey?: Reflections on the effects of research on researcher and participants. *Qualitative Research in Organizations and Management*, 1(3), 204–221.

Hutchinson, S.A., Wilson, M.E. and Wilson, H.S. 1994. Benefits of participating in research interviews. *Journal of Nursing Scholarship*, 26(2), 161–166.

James, N. and Busher, H. 2006. Credibility, authenticity and voice: dilemmas in online interviewing. *Qualitative Research*, 6(3), 403–420.

Lean, G.L. 2009. Transformative Travel: Inspiring Sustainability, in *Wellness and Tourism: Mind, Body, Spirit, Place*, edited by R. Bushell and P.J. Sheldon. Elmsford, NY: Cognizant Communication, 191–205.

Lean, G. 2012a. The Lingering Moment, in *The Cultural Moment in Tourism*, edited by L. Smith, E. Waterton and S. Watson. Abingdon: Routledge, 274–291.

Lean, G.L. 2012b. Transformative travel: a mobiliities perspective. *Tourist Studies*, 12(2), 151–172.

Leed, E.J. 1991. *The Mind of the Traveller: From Gilgamesh to Global Tourism*. New York: Basic Books.

McAuliffe, D. 2003. Challenging methodological traditions: research by email. *The Qualitative Report*, 8(1), 57–69.

McCoyd, J.L.M. and Kerson, T.S. 2006. Conducting intensive interviews using email: a serendipitous comparative opportunity. *Qualitative Social Work*, 5(3), 389–406.

Mann, C. and Stewart, F. 2000. *Internet Communication and Qualitative Research: A Handbook for Researching Online*. London: Sage.

Mavrič, M. and Urry, J. 2009. Tourism Studies and the New Mobilities Paradigm (NMP), in *The Sage Handbook of Tourism Studies*, edited by T. Jamal and M. Robinson. London: Sage, 645–657.

Menard, S. 2008. Introduction: Longitudinal Research Design and Analysis, in *Handbook of Longitudinal Research: Design, Measurement, and Analysis*, edited by S. Menard. Burlington, MA: Elsevier, 3–12.

Minca, C. and Oakes, T. (eds) 2006. *Travels in Paradox: Remapping Tourism*. Lanham, MD: Rowman and Littlefield Publishers.

O'Connor, H. and Madge, C. 2003. 'Focus groups in cyberspace': using the Internet for qualitative research. *Qualitative Market Research: An International Journal*, 6(2), 133–143.

Reid, A., Petocz, P. and Gordon, S. 2008. Research interviews in cyberspace. *Qualitative Research Journal*, 8(1), 47–61.

Ritchie, J.R.B. 2005. Longitudinal Research Methods, in *Tourism Research Methods*, edited by B.W. Ritchie, P. Burns and C. Palmer. Wallingford: CABI, 131–148.

Robinson, M. and Jamal, T. 2009. Conclusions: Tourism Studies – Past Omissions, Emergent Challenges, in *The Sage Handbook of Tourism Studies*, edited by T. Jamal and M. Robinson. London: Sage, 693–701.

Rojek, C. and Urry, J. (eds) 1997. *Touring Cultures: Transformations of Travel and Theory.* London: Routledge.

Tribe, J. (ed.) 2009. *Philosophical Issues in Tourism.* Bristol: Channel View.

Urry, J. 2007. *Mobilities.* Cambridge: Polity Press.

Walter, M. 2010. Surveys, in *Social Research Methods*, edited by M. Walter. South Melbourne: Oxford University Press, 151–181.

Chapter 8

Travelling in the Caucasus: Mobile Methodologies and Lifestyles in the Field

Eleni Sideri

Introduction

Mobility as an analytical framework was partly introduced in order to conceptualize the economic and political transformations defined by Hannam, Sheller and Urry (2006) as state rescaling. These changes concern state relations at an international level, as well as the transformation of public space within sovereign countries. The opening of markets, the emergence of electronic, dematerialized capital, flexible labour and technological innovations in communication and transportation, besides political shifts, such as the fall of the Berlin Wall, created new social, economic and political geographies. Brenner (2004: 64) argued that the 'mobility turn' today stems from universal change, which 'has entailed neither the absolute territorialization of societies, economies, or cultures onto a global scale, nor their complete deterritorialization into a supraterritorial, distanceless, placeless, or borderless space of flows'.

Instead, it seems that this restructuring of the relations between the global and local challenged the international order, as it was established in the post-Westphalian period when bounded territories of national sovereignty became an expression of natural almost innate identities. The naturalization of space, time and identity became a highly criticized concept in the 1990s because it concealed the complexities and multiplicities of the above categories. At the same time, this view often overlooks the 'geometries of power', in other words the fact that not only space is embedded in power relations but also power is spatialized (Massey 2009: 19). These geometries, as the chapter discusses, contribute to the construction and experience of space, time and identity and produce or cancel mobility.

As Tesfahuney (1998: 501) stated, '[d]ifferential mobility empowerments reflect structures and hierarchies of power and position by race, gender, age and class, ranging from the local to the global'. It also reflects, I would add, historical formation and cultural perceptions of travel and its infrastructure (means and processes of mobility, roads and transportation systems, travel paraphernalia) and how the latter is entangled with different aspects of life and politics. In this context, mobility could help us disentangle lifestyle as a category that was often linked to upper social classes and consumption helping us reveal the social nuances, different histories and present political and economic agendas often filtered and experienced through the notion of lifestyle.

This chapter compares three moments of ethnographic mobility: my journey to mountainous Georgia, travel with the United Nations Observers Mission in Georgia (UNOMIG) to the de facto state of Abkhazia and my commute from central Tbilisi to a neighbourhood of the capital where I resided. In these three instances of mobility, I find intersections of colonial histories, post-Cold war geopolitical and economic agendas of transformation of the post-Soviet space and emerging post-socialist lifestyles which could postulate the temporal and spatial complexities entangled in different mobilities and lifestyles.

I will use these cases as an epistemological strategy in order to postulate how the practice of (im)mobilities could be, on the one hand, the object of analysis regarding various socioeconomic processes and socio-political practices (Jones and Murphy 2010) and, on the other hand, the object of affect between the ethnographer, the people, their lifestyles and the place. My account will demonstrate how mobile ethnography could help us comprehend not only discourses or imageries, but also the 'every day' we try to capture in the field in a more embodied way by unpacking the category of lifestyle which is interwoven with the experience of the everyday.

Mobile ethnographies

Time and space are closely interdependent not as homogenous and linear experiences of 'reality', but as 'distinct simultaneity' (Massey 2005: 89); that is to say, the place of encounter of different experiences of space and time is filtered through specific power relations. Such an approach could not consider (im)mobilities as idiom of the 'global' or the 'local' since both categories are interdependent and interwoven. Similarly, (im)mobilities could be neither organized systems nor personal practices. Instead, they are interlinked expressions of both constituted by material conditions and technologies, immaterial symbols, past histories and new imageries, political economies and personal stories of movement and stillness. It is the synergy of these factors at a particular moment that allows or cancels mobility. The line between the two forms constitutes what Sarah Green (2009: 18) calls 'borderli-ness', a place 'where things have got to so far, in the multiple, unpredictable, power-inflected, imagined and visceral way that everyday life tends to occur'. Investigating the borderli-ness of mobility and immobility seeks both for a historical analysis of structures and an examination of social embodied and engendered practices which are, in turn, experienced as different lifestyles. But how do we approach these considerations in terms of methods?

Fieldwork was the distinctive feature of social anthropology that distinguished it from other social sciences. Fischer and Marcus (1986) pinpointed the need for a revision of ethnographic practices. This was due to the conceptualization of the world in the 1970s as a 'world system', pushing the ethnographer to follow people, ideas or products and not to limit her/himself in a bounded site. The so-called crisis of representation in the early 1980s raised serious questions about ethnographic methods, the ways of writing and representation. The increasing interconnection of economic, political and cultural spheres, known as globalization, laid the foundations for the pursuit of methods that could better respond to these 'new' conditions. Within this context, multi-sited ethnography emerged as the most appropriate approach to record more fully the interwoven relations not only of the global to the local, but their multiple internal heterogeneities and mutual interconnections.

Marcus (1999) pointed out that multi-sited ethnography should not be considered a new methodological tool. Instead, what seems to have been revised is the perception of the research imaginary. In other words, our perception of the field should escape from the idea of the site as bounded, a limitation which was possibly consistent with the epistemological prejudices of traditional ethnography, but hardly could be applied to the more fluid economic, political and cultural world of the 1990s. Gradually, it became noted that these phenomena were not new, but are historically formed and reworked in order to meet present requirements (Kennedy and Roudometoff 2000, Amit 2002).

In this framework, research in two or more sites does not guarantee an automatic solution to methodological and representational problems. As Marcus (1995, 1998) stressed, multi-sited research can result in a traditional study of two or more different sites, which will be delineated rigorously and turned into closed fields of observation and knowledge. Instead, consistency with criticism of all levels and types of mediation that generate these 'sites' as such and develop relations of intimacy and otherness could help overcome boundedness (Madianou 1989). As Mateus Candea noted (2007), multi-sited research cannot escape from the daily problems of fieldwork that forces us to make everyday choices regarding the sites of research or the people to meet or how we move from one site to another; options are often governed by funding, political issues and unexpected encounters.

These problems underline the random and arbitrary nature of multi-sited research that are often not included in ethnographic writings which, as De Certeau (1988) emphasized, we tend to turn into holistic theoretical accounts, although they are often based on the fragmentary nature of experience. In this context, the production of the field-site should be represented as a series of entries and exits within diverse social contexts, networks and selves rather than a unified entity with defined borders. In this sense, mobility becomes almost intrinsic in multi-sited ethnography in terms of both practical movement, but also, imagining the field as more flexible and interconnected.

But could we have a mobile ethnography distinguished from what we call multi-sited ethnography? If so, in what sense? According to Urry (2007: 4), 'the mobility paradigm contributes to the multiple conceptualisation of social sciences as an array of ideologies and methods that involved the mobility of people and ideas'. I would add that a methodological focus on (im)mobilities compels us to reconsider their historical, cultural, social and personal plurality in their diverse expression in field life, embedding this concern in our methods. As Ingold and Lee

(2006: 68) encouraged us, we should 'understand the routes and mobilities of the others' as well as ours. For this reason, (im)mobility does not remain a category we study, an object to reflect upon, but an experience of the field. We do not follow the sites, but space-time lived experiences and how our mobility takes part in or generates them. We do not study different lifestyles but we merge into them. The corporeal experience of mobility could minimize the distance of subject/object through the ethnographer's body and lifestyle, as this chapter will argue.

Tbilisi-Kazbegi: lifestyle as authentic culture

My fieldwork in Georgia was centred in the discourses and practices of diaspora among the Greek-speaking communities. Although I was based in the capital, I travelled frequently and by different means. My fieldwork, though, started with a language course. The Summer Language School I attended in 2003 at Tbilisi State University also organized a cultural programme for the students to familiarize themselves with Georgian culture and hospitality. This included short visits to places of historical interest, including the Georgian town of Kazbegi[1] (1740m above sea level, near the Russian Federation border). Our class consisted of seven people of various nationalities (European and American), academic backgrounds and ages, who came to Georgia for completely different reasons.

Our visit to Kazbegi was enthusiastically anticipated even by the members of staff, who regarded this place as the heart of the 'Georgian spirit'. The school rented a *marshrutka*, a shared taxi that follows a particular route within the cities and the countryside. *Marshrutkas* were introduced in the Soviet Union in the 1930s, but their popularity had increased since the 1990s due to the general failure of the post-Soviet public transport. Our seating arrangement was always hierarchized: the director, an esteemed professor of Georgian medieval literature, was seated next to the driver, and a young female assistant sat behind him next to the students. The Military Highway, as the road to Kaszbegi is known, was beautiful, but also gravelly and full of holes. We stopped at several archaeological sites of interest, such as the castle of Ananuri and the Jvari pass (attraction point at 2379 metres). Every few kilometres, there was a farmer, alone or with his family, selling fruits or vegetables (often the only means of economic survival in the post-Soviet years), as well as tourist souvenirs, such as little wooden crosses or *chokhas* (shepherd's coat). A fellow student, a young American dancer, bought a hat. 'It would be fantastic to wear it on cold days in New York', she told me.

When we arrived in Kazbegi, we were all thrilled with our hostel, which seemed better organized than other accommodation we had stayed in. The manager told us that he invested in Kazbegi because he hoped to attract the alpinists of Mount Kazbek (more than 4000m) and the Gergeti Glacier (2950m). The dinner was light because in the morning we would set out to climb the hill to Tsminda Sameba

---

1   The town was renamed Stepantsminda in 2006.

church (2170m). It took almost an hour and a half to reach, walking along a zigzag path through the forest. The fourteenth-century church at the top is one of the most important historical sites in the area. 'The real Georgians don't take the car up there', the director said to the laziest member of our group. Moreover, he advised us not to talk during our trekking, because our breathing would suffer, and to admire the scenery. He also told us that, despite his age (he was in his 70s, but robust), he used to find his 'soul' there.

The visit to Kazbegi retraces the Georgian history of Modernity, reflecting on its present and future. First, it is important to look back at the pre-colonial and colonial history of the area, the movement of populations and troops through the narrow pass. The Georgian Military Highway (206km), which connects the Georgian capital with Vladikavkaz (North Ossetia territory of the Russian Federation), played a significant role in the Russian–Circassian War (1763–1864) as well as the economic modernization of Transcaucassia (South Caucasus). This makes it almost emblematic in the Georgian and Russian imagination. It was constructed between 1799 and 1817 (some works continuing until 1863) by the Russian military. However, the road, which has been well known since antiquity, was mentioned in the works of Strabo and Pliny as the gateway from Asia to Europe. Its construction was costly and exceeded the otherwise poor road infrastructure in the empire (Bryce 1878, Mitchell 2006).

The landscape is not only breathtaking, but also much enveloped in colonial history. As Lermontov underlines (Nasmyth 1998: 12), 'Beyond[2] stands a massive amphitheatre of mountains ... with Mt Kazbek at one end and the twin peaks of Elbruz at the other. What a delight to live in a place like this!' Similar views, though shaped by personal and political ideology, were expressed in the work of other colonial writers (Nasmyth 1998: 33–46, Ram and Shatirishvili 2001, Manning 2004). For the Georgian people, this road captures something of the national psyche. The Georgian intellectual and important public figure, Ilia Chavchavadze, in *Letters of a Traveller* (1861–1871), argued in support of the Caucasian people's values and authenticity as they struggled against a Russian culture, which, anxious to imitate the European spirit, seemed to have lost its soul. Rather, the mountain inhabitants had preserved their culture and identity. Thus, the geographic and political marginality of the Caucasus has been transformed into a positive entity able to resist Russian acculturation and external influence.

Symbolically, the road, which bridges histories, peoples, trade and ideas, is inextricably linked to the history of violence and annexation of Georgia by the Russians, as well as the ambiguous and troublesome relationship between the two peoples. Their historical and cultural connection to Europe has produced Orientalist discourses of superiority and inferiority. In the Georgian psyche this road and its mobilities are celebrated for its purity and authenticity. Even during the Soviet period, writers, including those on history and folklore, considered the mountains as a feature of the distinct Georgian identity that resisted the regime's

---

2   Lermotov refers to Pyatigorsk, a Russian town at the foothills of the Caucasus.

rapid urbanization and modernization. Hence, the ambiguous idealization of the mountains as under-developed and, yet, a source of purity, has remained.

Post-Soviet Georgia in early 2000 was looking for a new way out of ethnic conflicts and underdevelopment. Tourism was considered one of these ways. Sergei Arutiunov (2007: 306) seems to consider tourism as a platform upon which a viable future for the Caucasus could be built after centuries of colonial wars and conflicts. This constitutes a step away from the traditional and violent means of solving problems in the region. Tourism, nevertheless, has become an emblematic form of mobility within global economy and culture (Rojek and Urry 1997, Clifford 1997) – just like the hat that my fellow student bought as a souvenir to take to New York – which exoticizes and commodifies the Caucasus on a transnational scale.

Tourism as a cultural practice often sustains essentialism and stereotypes about locations and identities which could intensify conflict, depending upon the political conditions, instead of resolving them (Sideri 2012). In this framework, the road to Kazbegi is thus transformed into a pilgrimage to the authentic Georgia, a place which, in the words of the school director, captures the 'Georgian soul'. The tourists are invited to experience the taste of the 'real Georgian life', whether through travelling by *marshrutka* or by climbing the mountains. Both practices are invested with economic and cultural capital which tries to combine Georgian history and development in the post-Cold War era despite the fact that they both represent infrastructural failures in post-Soviet Georgia. In this framework, what it is represented as Georgian lifestyle seems to stem from the intersection of both the post-Soviet national agendas of economic modernization and the global development of mass tourism that feeds itself from the consumption of the 'new', 'exotic' and 'unspoiled'. In this context, lifestyle is produced by different power relations which transform through commoditization of authenticity and essentialization, turning local place and culture into a translocal experience.

Zugdidi-Sukhum(i)[3]: lifestyle at the border

After bureaucratic delays and help from the academic community and NGOs in London and Tbilisi, I found myself in the UN headquarters in Zugdidi (western Georgia). I arrived by taxi because the daily train took very long and the *marshrutka* timetable was inconvenient. However, the driver did not believe that I could travel to Sukhum(i): 'Even our president can't go there!' He waited until I reached the front gate of the UNOMIG station, as if he wanted to persuade himself that such a travel was possible, where I was asked for my passport. The guard checked it and I passed through.

---

3   I use the pronunciations of both the Abkhazian and Georgian people.

The UN convoy, which included two jeeps, patrolled the Zugdidi-Gali-Sukhum(i)[4] route twice a day, crossing three check points; at the Enguri bridge (on the Georgia/Abkhazia border), in Gali and in Sukhum(i). We drove along the dilapidated road from Zugdidi (western Georgia) to Sukhum(i) on a sunny afternoon. My co-passengers, who were two UN soldiers, a German medical doctor, a Pakistani engineer and a young Ukrainian soldier, asked me about my research in Georgia. There was also an ethnic Georgian, who was from the Gali region (an area within the de facto state with a dominant Georgian population) and commuted every day with the UN convoy. He remained silent. As we approached the Enguri bridge, I tried to speak to him in Georgian, but he seemed unwilling to use the language. The guards from both sides checked my papers and confirmed my visa with the de facto state's Foreign Office. The UN officers tried to be polite saying 'Gamardzoba' ('Hi!') to all the guards in Georgian, which was appreciated on the Georgian side. However, the Abkhazians answered annoyed in Russian.

During my stay in Sukhum(i) several people asked me about those living on the other side of the border: the economic or social conditions, what the Georgians or Abkhazians said about each other. Returning from Abkhazia, I was invited to many family gatherings in order to show the videos and the photographs I had taken of the internally displaced people living in Tbilisi. Despite the minimal geographical distance between the two territories, the local population on both sides considered the borders, in the period of my visit, as impenetrable. But a 'stranger' with the 'right' passport and connections could show the 'objectivity' of an outsider and, for this reason, she/he is seen as less of a threat. Being mobile in between these two spaces is a privilege that automatically excludes you from the two dominant national categories (Georgian and Abkhazian) and connects you to the wider international order (diplomats, NGO workers, military, journalists) involved in the resolution of the conflict. This privilege also becomes a source of imagination for the people who are not allowed to cross the bridge from either sides.

Grant and Yalçin-Heckman (2007) argued that outsider interests, like the imperial agendas deployed in the Caucasus, treated the region as an 'absent presence' and overlooked local interests, strategies and alliances. The term 'frozen' also insinuates immobility and stillness; an idea that is not unfamiliar to anthropology. Claude Levi-Strauss (1968) categorized societies into cold and hot depending on their social cohesion and cultural production. Through this distinction transformation became embedded in Western societies, as something enmeshed in the vision of modernity concerning progress, change and speed.

If we consider the term 'frozen conflict' along this line of argument, it seems to go beyond the translation of a political impasse and becomes rooted in a tradition of cultural evaluation and hierarchy embedded in European colonization, which

---

4   As the status of this region is not yet clear after the Georgian/Abkhazian conflict (1991–1993), officially, the borders are closed and there is only one entry point from Russia to the de facto state of Abkhazia used for humanitarian purposes.

overburdened the Caucasus with the stereotypes already discussed. There is further emphasis, in the Foucauldian sense, upon the eclectic but genealogical relation between the political and the epistemological that remains to be revealed in this context. For example, how much of our understanding of 'frozen conflicts' is filtered through the presuppositions and power hierarchies produced in the Cold War and the post-Cold War periods, which allowed certain people mobility, while others, like my taxi driver, would not even imagine it.

My moment of mobility in an immobile, frozen area was historically and politically structured within the context of post-Cold War politics and a system of international governance and security. My visit to Sukhum(i) was mediated via electronic communication within academic and NGO networks in the UK, which provided access to the Abkhazian authorities and the UN offices in Tbilisi, as well as a fellow Greek UN soldier who happened to be in Sukhum(i). This mobility, therefore, within a debated territory was facilitated by a global political network of 'foreigners', albeit 'conflict experts' in different capacities (soldiers, UN local personnel and academics). The fact that locally and historically specified movement is internationally structured and monitored, shows to what degree technologies, techniques and regulations make mobility or immobility possible but also, how much immobility is often connected to other forms of mobility like refugeeness to Greece in the case of the Sukhumian Greeks, which was the purpose of my visit. The crossing of Enguri bridge was indicative to the degree that many experts involved in conflict resolution remain disengaged from the actual relations between the different sides (for example, the issue of language used at the borders). This disengagement is not indifferent to the cosmopolitan lifestyle of these mobile transients who became representatives of the mobile turn, but in reality, they form part of the privileged few. In this context, the ethnographic mobility acts as a form of mediation that could open up new imageries concerning the other side of the border despite the suspicion, trauma and prejudices that exist in both sides.

For example, my mobility further generated imaginative journeys on both sides of the borders. The information, photographs, memorabilia and videos I took served as a window for all people, and in particular Georgian Internally Displaced People (IDPs), to share memories and reconnect however momentarily. In these journeys of the mind, where past and present are weighed against each other, older geographies are challenged. The crossing, real and symbolic, of borderli-ness is the space where everyday life occurs, as Green underlined (2009), since it pushes everything beyond borders and, thus, it gives the opportunity for new possible places and lifestyles to be produced or imagined.

From Rustaveli to Tsereteli Avenue: lifestyle on the move

At the beginning of the twentieth century when European Modernity faced its peak with the emerging urban centres and the politics of homogenization and fear, Simmel (1971) argued that the stranger is a symbol of an external, potentially subversive, but also more objective observer. The stranger moves in real or imaginative maps or become still depending on social, cultural and political traditions of inclusion and exclusion. The stranger is a universal category in the sense that it is well embedded in any process of social identification, but at the same time, it is historically produced by specific cultural understandings and political conditions. 'All societies produce strangers, but each kind of society produces its own kind of strangers, and produces them in its own inimitable way' (Bauman 1995: 1). Bauman further defines 'the stranger' as one who does not fit the 'cognitive, moral or aesthetic map' of a specific society. But none of these maps could be seen as close, well-defined systems, without ambiguities and flaws. Instead, they are constructed daily through personal trajectories and commuting. What happens to this category in relation to mobility? How much does mobility challenge the understanding of our mental maps?

Hetherington (1997) used the term 'places of movement' in order to stress mobility as opposed to being rooted in one location. The *marshrutka* is a good example of this. In the trip to Kazbegi, it was considered as an almost cognitive vehicle which brought tourists in touch with Georgian culture. Here, I will examine it as a vehicle which helps us disrupt the idealization of the latter. As I explained in my first case study, the shared taxi became very popular in the post-Soviet period. In Tbilisi, they were chosen for economic and time-management reasons. It was one of the first forms of transport that my Georgian friends taught me how to use when I arrived. The room I was renting was situated outside the Georgian capital in the Tsereteli Gamziri, in the wider area of Didube. The passengers of each *marshrutka* could ask the driver to stop at any point of the scheduled route by calling 'gaacheret sheidzleba' ('Stop, please!'). The fare was cheaper than that of other taxis, but higher than alternative public transport.[5]

The river Mtkvari cuts Tbilisi into two. Tbilisi was always considered one of the major cultural centres of the wider Caucasus. The colonial architecture provides some of the most impressive examples in the central avenue, Rustaveli's Gamziri. Since the 1990s the city centre has been renovated,[6] especially the old quarter with its stone-paved streets and multicultural character. Many foreign restaurants and bars have opened, giving the neighbourhood a cosmopolitan ambience. However, the journey to my neighbourhood introduced the visitor to a less salubrious reality. Very often, when Rustaveli's avenue had electricity, the passage of Tabidze's khidis (Tabidze bridge) was marked by the noise of generators indicating that there was no electricity in this part of the city and my trip home, via the bridge to Mardzanishvili's street and then from Aghmashenebelis Gamziri, past the Dinamo Stadium – where the bazroba (market) may be found – and on to Tseretelis Gamziri (Tsereteli Avenue) was often accompanied by the noise of these generators.

---

5   In 2001, the rise in prices of *marshrutkas* provoked strong reactions and strikes (Civil.ge 2011).

6   This renovation also provoked controversy (Collin 2008).

On one particular evening in late autumn both the weather and scenery seemed gloomy. It was rainy but still quite warm, something which must have burdened the electricity system as it was off for the most part of the day. The political situation was explosive with the elections in less than 10 days, creating more worries than expectations. A couple of meetings I had were cancelled, the books that I was looking for in the National Library could not be found and doubts regarding the success of my fieldwork were wearing me out. My *marshrutka* was full. Men had given their seats to women and were standing, or rather trying to, because the vehicle was packed. A middle aged woman wearing a fur coat was getting annoyed by those passengers with bags full of vegetables. The traffic was heavy and more people were getting on at every stop.

When we arrived at Mardzanishvili street we realized that the odyssey would continue since a water pipeline had burst and water was pouring into the roads. It took us more than 15 minutes to arrive at the Mardzanishvili metro station (it usually takes less than five minutes) and to witness that, although the road was drier, the line of *marshrutkas* and cars was huge. I sighed deeply, and I was not the only one. The woman seated next to me did the same thing almost simultaneously. We looked at each other understandingly and smiled. In that place of movement, people (engendered and socially hierarchized), objects (bags, fruits and vegetables and coats), the sights of colonial buildings, the bazroba, the smell of food and the noise of generators all pointed to social and historical differences brought together through bodily proximity. Each of the passengers might have a different mental map of the city (Urry 2003b, Büscher 2006, Germann Molz 2006, Kaplan 2006), which was being restructured in post Soviet Georgia and its introduction to neo-liberal economics which tried to turn part of Tbilisi to commercialized, thematic sites of memory and nostalgia, such as, the 'Old Tbilisi', the 'colonial Tiflis'. During this itinerary, we all shared a divided, in all the above aspects, space which in that moment of bodily exhaustion seemed to create mutual compassion.

Conclusion

The last case of mobility underlines how the sensory, corporeal, emotional and kineaesthetic (Vannini 2009) could contribute to the understanding of the complexity of what constitutes 'everyday life'. The sensory, together with the emotional (the sigh), could create a shared place and a moment of empathy with the people we study, transgressing for that moment the subject/object line, and creating a place of intimacy. The journey by *marshrutka* comprised a series of brief encounters with people, objects and sensory experiences, which forced me to contextualize the 'mudane' in an 'assemblage of acts', means and actors (Jain 2009: 92). Each case of (im)mobility constitutes an assemblage of different acts and meanings attaching to different lifestyles. This provided the opportunity to challenge positions and identities developed in the field and to reconsider the relations produced.

In this chapter, the notions of mobility and immobility were closely examined, in particular the ethnographer's position as a tourist, an expert/mediator and a commuter. Each act of mobility, as a tourist in Kazbegi, as member of a UN Mission, as inhabitant of Tbilisi were interdependent with the infrastructure and the means of transport (*marshrutka* or jeep), the people and the objects, and the social, economic and cultural history of Georgia. Each of these cases of mobility, although different, stem from the complexities and ambiguities of post-Cold War period (post-socialist economy and politics) revealing the ways (im)mobilities are interwoven, context specific, historically produced but also socially experienced. Using as focus of study, the ethnographic (im)mobility , the line between subject/ object and real/imaginative could be challenged not only theoretically, but also in a more sensory and emotional way. In this way, lifestyle which has been often attached to social difference and consumption turns into a category where different spatial and temporal relations come together and form the everyday for different categories of people.

The trip to Kazbegi postulated the ways the introduction of market and the development of a tourist industry renegotiates Georgian culture for different people (local academics, tourist entrepreneurs, farmers) commercializing it and re-essentializing it vis-à-vis new political relations (Georgia/Russia) and agendas (rewriting the national history) and economic opportunities (tourist flows). Crossing the Enguri bridge, something impossible for the members of the Abkhazian and Georgian communities underlined how much fieldwork is a politicized act. The paradox of my mobility uncovered the boundaries and limitations of present lifestyles and producing imageries for the possibilities of new one. Finally, commuting in Tbilisi postulated how much corporeality and senses contribute to new ways of understanding the field unravelling the interconnections of different places (tourist, old colonial Tbilisi) and lifestyles (interwoven with the emerging economic and social divisions in post-socialist Georgia) and impeding their homogenization. These three cases of ethnographic mobility methods pointed out to a more experiential and multi-sensory learning which compels us to consider new forms of knowledge beyond the spoken, more situated, immediate and collaborative.

References

Amit, V. 2002. An Anthropology without Community, in *The Trouble with Community. Anthropological Reflections on Movement, Identity and Collectivity*, edited by A. Vered and N. Rapport. London: Pluto Press, 13–66.

Arutiunov, S. 2007. Afterword, in *Caucasus Paradigms: Anthropologies, Histories, and the Making of the World Area*, edited by B. Grant and L. Yalçin-Heckmann. Munster: Lit Verlag, 301–307.

Bauman, Z. 1995. The Making and Unmaking of Stranger. *Thesis Eleven. Critical Theory and Historical Sociology*, 43, 1–16.

Brenner, N. 2004. *New State Spaces: Urban Governance and the Rescaling of Statehood*. Oxford: Oxford University Press.

Bryce, J. 1878. Transcaucasia and Ararat. *Being Notes of a Vacation Tour in the Autumn of 1876*. London: Macmillan.

Büscher, M. 2006. Vision in Motion. *Environment and Planning A*, 38(2), 281–299.

Candea, M. 2007. Arbitrary Locations: In Defence of the Bounded Fieldsite. *Journal of the Royal Anthropological Institute*, 13, 167–184.

Certeau de, M. 1998. *The Practice of Everyday*. Berkeley: The University of California Press.

Civil.Ge 2011. *Marshrutka Drivers on Strike in Tbilisi* [Online: Civil.Ge]. Available at: http://www.civil.ge/eng/article.php?id=23181 [accessed: 26 February 2011].

Clifford, J. 1997. *Routes. Travel and Translation in the Late Twentieth Century*. Cambridge, MA: Harvard University Press.

Collin, M. 2008. The Battle for Tbilisi's Soul [Online: BBC]. Available at: http://news.bbc.co.uk/2/hi/europe/7478392.stm [accessed: 10 June 2011].

Fischer, M.M.J. and Marcus, G. 1986. *Anthropology as Cultural Critique: An Experimental Moment in the Human Sciences*. Chicago: Chicago University Press.

Germann Molz, J. 2006. 'Watch us Wander': Mobile Surveillance and the Surveillance of Mobility. *Environment and Planning A*, 38(2), 377–393.

Grant, B. and Yalçin-Heckmann, L. 2008. Introduction, in *Caucasus Paradigms: Anthropologies, Histories, and the Making of the World Area*, edited by B. Grant and L.Yalçin-Heckman. Munster: Lit Verlag, 1–21.

Green, S. 2009. Lines, Traces and Tidemarks: Reflections on Forms of Borderliness. *EastBordNet Working Papers* [Online: EASTBORDNET], 1(1), 1–19. Available at: http://www.eastbordnet.org/working_papers/open/documents/Green_Lines_Traces_and_Tidemarks_090414.pdf [accessed: 25 August 2010].

Hannam, K., Sheller M. and Urry, J. 2006. Editorial: Mobilities, Immobilities and Moorings. *Mobilities*, 1(1), 1–22.

Hetherington, K. 1997. Place of Geometry: the Materiality of Place, in *Ideas of Difference*, edited by K. Hetherington and R. Munro. Oxford: Blackwell, 183–199.

Ingold, T. and Lee, J. 2006. Fieldwork on Foot: Perceiving, Routing, Socializing, in *Locating the Field: Space, Place and Context in Anthropology*, edited by S. Coleman and P. Collins. Oxford: Berg, 67–85.

Jain, J. 2009. The Making of Mundane Bus Journeys, in *The Cultures of Alternative Mobilities. Routes less Travelled*, edited by P. Vannini. Farnham: Ashgate, 91–111.

Jones, A. and Murphy, J.T. 2010. Practice and Economic Geography. *Geography Compass*, 4 (4), 303–319.

Kaplan, C. 2006. Mobility and war: the 'cosmic view' of air power. *Environment and Planning A*, 38(2), 395–407.

Kennedy, P. and Roudometof, V. 2002. Trasnationalism in a Global Age, in *Communities Across Borders: New Migrants and Transnational Cultures*, edited by P. Kennedy and V. Roudometof. London: Routledge, 1–27.

Levi-Strauss, C. 1968. *The Savage Mind*. Chicago: The University of Chicago Press.

Madianou-Gefou, D. 1998. Reflection, Difference and Anthropology at Home, in *Anthropological Theory and Ethnography. Modern Trends*, edited by D. Madianou-Gefou. Athens: Ellinika Grammata, 365–437 [in Greek].

Manning P. 2004. Describing dialect and defining civilization in an early Georgian nationalist manifesto: Ilia Ch'avch'avadze's 'Letters of a Traveller'. *The Russian Review*, 63(1), 26–47.

Marcus, G.E. 1995. Ethnography in/of the world system: the emergence of multi-sited ethnography. *Annual Review of Anthropology*, 24, 95–117.

Marcus, G.E. 1998. After the Critique of Ethnography, in *Anthropological Theory and Ethnography. Modern Trends*, edited by D. Madianou-Gefou. Athens: Ellinika Grammata, 67–109 [in Greek].

Marcus, G.E. 1999. *Ethnography through Thick and Thin*. Princeton: Princeton University Press.

Massey, D. 2005. *For Space*. London: Sage.

Massey, D. 2009. Concepts of power and space in theory and political practice. *Documents d'Anàlisi Geogràfica*, 55, 15–26.

Mitchell, L. 2006. Exploring the Georgian Military Highway. *Hidden Europe* [Online: Hidden Europe], 9, 2–7. Available at: http://www.hiddeneurope. co.uk/exploring-the-georgian-military-highway [accessed: 12 June 2011].

Nasmyth, P. 1998. *Georgia: In the Mountains of Poetry*. New York: St Martin's Press.

Ram, H. and Shatirishvili, Z. 2001. Romantic topography and the dilemma of empire: the Caucasus in the dialogue of Georgian and Russian poetry. *The Russian Review*, 63(1), 1–25.

Rojek, C. and Urry, J. 1997. *Touring Cultures: Transformations of Travel and Theory*. London: Routledge.

Sideri, E. 2012. The land of the Golden Fleece: conflict and heritage in Abkhazia. *Journal of Balkans and Near Eastern Studies*, 14(2), 263–278.

Simmel, G. 1971. *On Individuality and Social Forms with an Antroduction of D.N. Levine*. Chicago: The University of Chicago Press.

Tesfahuney, M. 1998. Mobility, racism and geopolitics. *Political Geography*, 17(5), 499–515.

Urry, J. 2003. Social networks, travel and talk. *British Journal of Sociology*, 54(2), 155–176.

Urry, John. 2007. *Mobilities*. Cambridge: Polity Press.

Vannini, P. 2009. *The Cultures of Alternative Mobilities. Routes Less Travelled*. Farnham: Ashgate.

SECTION III
Moorings, Mobilities and Belonging

Chapter 9
Traveller Trails:
Locating the Lifestyle Traveller

Kathryn Erskine and Jon Anderson

Introduction

Through an examination of the 'lifestyle traveller' (Cohen 2010, 2011) this chapter seeks to explore how geographical relationships are changing from 'roots' to 'routes' (Massey 2005, Ingold 2006) and the implications these changes have for our understanding of place within a globalizing world. By exploring travel as a preferred lifestyle choice, we seek to unravel what place means to the 'über-mobile' (Gogia 2006: 365); does place remain as a significant component of identity, or is it rendered redundant through a lifestyle based on movement? Essentially, we ask, how important is mobility? Is movement the definitive trait of lifestyle travellers, or can mobility infer a different kind of transit rather than literal movement? Does a commitment to mobility serve to disrupt attachments to place, or can the two mutually co-exist? In short, what roles do notions of place and mobility play in the identity of the travelling lifestyle?

The lifestyle traveller as defined by Scott Cohen (see 2010, 2011) is one who actively pursues travel indefinitely, rather than as a temporal or 'cyclical break' from normality (2010: 64). Such a preferred lifestyle choice exemplifies the alternative and 'networked patterns of social life' (Duffy 2004: 32) that characterize the twenty-first century, with such individuals serving as a corporeal example of increasing global mobility. Such commitment to movement raises questions regarding what place means to the traveller, mirroring debates that have focused on the erosion of 'place distinctiveness' associated with the processes of globalization (Relph 1976). By considering the lifestyle traveller, such heightened flows can be explored tangibly to examine whether the preoccupation with stability as indicative of place attachment still carries weight (see Relph 1976, Buttimer et al. 1980, Hay 1998) or whether mobility can be about finding new and meaningful places. This chapter therefore explores the extent to which place attachment and mobility are mutually exclusive phenomena or whether they may be combined in various ways (Gustafson 2006).

The chapter is based on interviews with 23 lifestyle travellers conducted in 2010. Interviews occurred across South East Asia and Australasia, on the 'beaten track' for independent travel where exotic destinations combine with opportunities for casual employment. Interviews were conducted whilst engaged in travel down the East Coast of Australia and across to the West Coast; and in Malaysia, Indonesia and Thailand. Recruitment occurred through the opportune meeting of lifestyle travellers 'on the road', but was focused through the social networking site 'Couch Surfing'. Here messages could be posted on various location 'walls' asking for respondents. Interviewees were educated and generally from Western democratic countries and were all voluntary travellers rather than forcibly exiled from home locations.

The chapter will first examine the difficulty in defining or categorizing lifestyle travel, recognizing that there cannot be one homogenous overarching criterion applicable to all. The chapter will then consider the key motivations to lifestyle travel, before examining how self-progression is central to sustaining this practice. As we will see, for the lifestyle traveller, mobility *within* places and mobility *between* places is equivalent to freedom. Lifestyle travel provides the freedom to carve individualized paths and trails through the world, to break free of routine and settlement in order to sustain a lifestyle based on change, novelty and progression.

Lifestyle travellers

Beginning to define the lifestyle traveller poses much difficulty as there is little academic agreement on the distinguishing features of general categories such as 'tourist' and 'traveller'. For Erik Cohen (2004: 23), a tourist is defined as a 'voluntary, temporary traveller, travelling in the expectation of pleasure from novelty and change experienced on a relatively long and non-recurrent round trip'. Tourist and traveller in this guise are represented as part of the same continuum of which little distinction is made. As Richards and Wilson (2004: 49) state, 'it is often easier to say clearly what one is not than what one is', rather than, as Clifford (1997: 65) identifies, 'reduce always diverse and hybrid insides to a stable unity'. In this way travellers are more commonly defined in relation to tourists, emphasizing a morally superior agenda whereby the tourist is presented as 'unadventurous and lacking initiative and discrimination', whereas the traveller is associated with discernment, respect and taste. For Rojek (1993: 175), 'while travel is seen as a resource in the endeavour of self-realization, tourism is considered to actually confirm one's view of the world rather than transforming it'. This is echoed by O'Reilly (2005: 167) who argues the fundamental distinction between tourist and traveller is in their approach, with the traveller seeking a 'transformative experience' to promote self-reinvention, which the tourist lacks.

Tourism can also infer a shorter period away from home, often staying in hotels and resorts. By comparison, travel may signify a longer period away from home and a more independent kind of travel – travellers often become synonymous with the 'tell-tale knapsack' and preference for cheaper hostel accommodation (Attenborough 2006). Budget also tends to be a major distinction between the two broad groups with tourists having more money to spend on shorter breaks, whilst travellers may operate within a tighter budget to sustain a longer journey.

Whilst the tourist may return 'home' following a two-week break, and the traveller return after a two-month trip, both groups accept this return 'home' rather than challenging it. In contrast, the lifestyle traveller is different. For the lifestyle traveller, travel is extended into an 'ongoing lifestyle practice' that supersedes conventional episodic bouts of backpacking (Cohen 2011). Whereas tourists and travellers accept a return to 'normality' once their travels are complete, the lifestyle traveller rejects this return, transforming their travel into their 'norm' and way of life.

However, even such 'preferred lifestyles' (Cohen 2011) vary in length, pattern and degree of travel, illustrating how fluid and interchangeable the practices categorized by the term 'lifestyle travel' can be. Within this project there were various types of 'lifestyle traveller' identified in part by the ways in which they punctuate their travel. All respondents paused their travel activities for some period of time, rather than be on the move continuously. For some this involved sojourns within a new place, for others it involved visiting friends in locations they had visited before, whilst some individuals opted for brief returns to their original location. As the following respondent outlines, some briefly returned home for family reasons:

I was supposed to go straight from India to Africa, but was too tired, and my sister had a baby while I was gone, so I went home for a bit. (Kirsty)

Whilst others returned for employment to sustain their mobility:

come home, work to get enough money to travel, go travelling, use that money, come home work to get enough money to travel ... (AJ)

Or to take the opportunity stop and reflect on their experiences, rather than moving directly onto the next place:

... but it's nice to sort of see and experience different countries as opposed to whizzing through them. (Simon)

Despite the different pace, pauses and other punctuations to their movement, the important commonality between these individuals was their overarching commitment to travel rather than to a career or home ties; as the following respondent sums up:

I didn't necessarily expect to have travel as an identity but now it very much is and when I talk to people back home you know, they say, 'well what do you do?' and I don't say, 'oh I'm a chef, I'm a secretary', I say, 'I travel'. And it feels kinda (silly) but I don't know how else to describe my lifestyle choice and I couldn't really picture what I would be if I wasn't travelling. (Miriam)

In essence travel is considered the definitive trait of these individuals' lives – it is an active and conscious choice that they have made to vacate a routine and ordered life in one place for an existence centred on movement. This raises questions in relation to the motivations for such alternative and mobile lifestyles (see Benson and O'Reilly 2009: 614), and the importance of place and mobility to these individuals.

Spontaneous travel

For some interviewees, travel as a lifestyle evolved organically. For these individuals, their identity as a lifestyle traveller was never planned, but had simply come into being as one bout of backpacking became prolonged indefinitely, as Simon outlines:

> it was just intended as a gap year but I think now it has moved into something a bit more permanent ... I don't think we'd ever thought beyond that at all. (Simon)

For these individuals, the idea of lifestyle travel was not something they originally aimed for or considered appropriate for them. Gap years or other fixed-term travel were seen as more socially permissible and a strategy that offered a safety valve of return should they not enjoy their experiences. However, through positive travel encounters a realization grew that lifestyle travel was not only possible, but enjoyable; as Miriam explains,

> I realised just how easy it was to live abroad and how easy it was to travel and that I didn't have to stay in the US I could go anywhere. (Miriam)

This perspective introduces ideas of freedom, spontaneity and compulsion as key factors that influence the development of lifestyle travellers. For Miriam, stepping out of 'normality' perhaps meant she was able to choose whatever kind of lifestyle she wanted as she had escaped societal pressures telling her what was or was not acceptable. For others it was more about falling in love with the lifestyle and a refusal to give it up – that it was a kind of 'addiction' – '*it's kind of intoxicating in a way*' (Jenni). Others enjoyed the feeling of not having set plans and objectives which a travelling lifestyle afforded:

> I was very anti-future ... I was always convinced you needed to relax and let the world take you to where it was gonna take you to because eventually that was going to happen anyway so it's been a very organic sort of travel for the last 8 years. (Aviv)

In this way travel could provide the *'ultimate freedom'* (Heath) in allowing movement and direction to flow naturally, a completely unrestricted and unfettered existence based on forming routes rather than being rooted. The spontaneity of the lifestyle traveller became an appealing 'pull factor' to individuals, with ongoing travel regarded as a positive addition to their lives.

Transformative travel

However, as O'Reilly (2006) has outlined, travel is often not simply associated with the 'pull' of spontaneity but also associated with the 'push' factors of leaving the roots and routines of home. For En Tze, this was the key motivation for travel: *'I wasn't changing at home, I was just like kind of stifling myself, so getting away was good'*. For many lifestyle travellers, the need for personal growth and transformation could be satisfied through movement: lifestyle travel not simply offered a 'way out', but a 'way to grow'. The notion of transformative travel therefore closely resonates with ideas of 'finding oneself' through travel (see Desforges 1998, 2000, O'Reilly 2006), a concept which was widely discussed by the interviewees:

> ... I think finding yourself is part of growing up, whether you stay at home or if your come here, like getting to know yourself, you can do that at home as well. (Chris C)

> The point is not to find yourself, the point is to create yourself ... I don't know if there was anything there pre-existing that I was supposed to find but I definitely created myself along the way. (Marco)

The debate over the possibility of 'finding' one's identity is echoed within social science literature. For Maxey (1999: 199), there can never be a whole or authentic self which can be known or 'found', '... there is no fixed "me" of which I am fully cognizant'. For Bauman (1996: 18), identity is 'bio-degradable plastic' continually under reconstruction and redefinition. These fragmented and malleable approaches to identity resonate with interviewees' reluctance to subscribe to the notion of 'finding oneself', as this implies some kind of end state, perhaps frustrating the very purpose of lifestyle or on-going travel. Whilst interviewees acknowledged the transformatory qualities afforded through their travels, finding a complete or unified self was not their objective, they were more interested in constructing or discovering the different selves they would encounter through their travel experiences.

Escape attempts

However, for some interviewees, lifestyle travel was a form of escape – a means to run away from undesirable situations at home. As the following respondents outline:

> I was in love with this boy ... he didn't love me back ... so I just thought of the furthest possible location and I went there and I haven't really stopped travelling since. ... I would say it's definitely more escapist from than searching for something. (Aviv)

> I was running away from a life that I felt I was being forced into ... just the typical mundane go to college, to university, get a job, get married, have kids, settle down, die. (Chris C)

Escape for these lifestyle travellers was thus about shedding societal expectations and roles, rather than freeing themselves from state oppression or being forcibly exiled. Their self-induced exit was motivated by a wish to experience a more satisfying life. For Chris, escape was synonymous with avoiding conformity to societal stages, to escape the rules of 'normality' so that he could create his own kind of 'freely chosen game' (Bauman 1996: 18). This relates to the desire to be free and create new kinds of identities based on individuality rather than being structured by society (see, for example, Beck and Beck-Gernsheim, 2002). By opting out of normality through physical dislocation from home Chris felt he could shirk off feelings of being tied or constrained to people or place, that there were no longer expectations on him:

> I don't like feeling trapped by people or society. When you're in another culture that doesn't apply to you cos you're just a foreigner so you're free of all that, no-one expects you to do anything. (Chris C)

Motivation change

'Spontaneous Travel', 'Transformative Travel', and 'Escape Attempts' are just three overarching factors used by individuals to explain their lifestyle travel choices. In practice, these key factors interplay with each another to forge a dynamic range of motivations for each lifestyle traveller. As a consequence, all three may be significant or become more relevant to travellers at different points along their journey. This emphasizes that while such motivations can be central to initiating travel, they do not necessarily serve to sustain travel, with other influences 'en route' perhaps becoming more or less significant; as Chris explains, it's getting to the point it was so long ago that I wanted to get away that I've almost forgotten why I wanted to go in the first place. (Chris C)

For Jenni, factors that served to perpetuate her travel included compulsion, learning, self-fulfilment and novelty:

> ... like the more you travel the more things, more places you want to see ... new experiences really [*compulsion*], and get some more knowledge about what's going on in the world [*learning*], getting new ideas of what I want [*self fulfilment/novelty*], just not getting stuck in the same circle as such [*progression, or escape from routine*]. (Jenni, authors' emphases)

Jenni appears to crave novelty of experience in order to continually challenge her understanding of the world. These experiences prevent her from remaining static in terms of her self-identity – she is constantly challenged with new cultures and different ways of being. As a consequence, she avoids getting 'stuck' in a routine. Such yearnings are corroborated by En Tze and Aviv in discussing the experience of being 'rooted' in place, how feelings of claustrophobia and self-doubt occur when mobility is restricted through being settled:

> It keeps me moving 'cos I know that if I stay still like I just end up in a rut [*progression*]. (En Tze)

> So when I'm (home) I start to worry 'what am I doing with my life?', 'who am I really?' and no matter how many great projects I have on, all of that starts to get to me because I am back where I started – whereas if I'm travelling ... [*progression*]. (Aviv, authors' emphases)

For these individuals, travel is considered synonymous with self-progression which a more rooted permanence within place could not actively provide, and, in practice, may actively retard. However, does avoidance of a static and sedentary 'normality' necessarily mean that it is literal movement that is solely desired? Is rejection of stability (in the sense of an unchanging identity) always a prerequisite for mobility (in the sense of geographical movement from place to place)? For the case of the lifestyle travellers interviewed, interesting dynamics in the relations between mobility, place and identity were explored.

Mobility, place and identity

Whilst all interview respondents were committed to lifestyle travel, they also sought to dwell temporarily in one location for an extended period of time:

I think we've learnt more about places when we've lived there ... you kind of get a sense of what it's all about, you tune in to their way of life, whereas you see all these people coming through and they're just sort of seeing the High Street end of it. (Simon)

I like the challenge of trying to establish myself somewhere and of really finding things that are unique to me, including memories there. (Miriam)

I guess I wanted to do some travelling where I got to live somewhere as opposed to just moving around, like actually being in one spot and getting to know someplace more than as a tourist. (En Tze)

For these respondents, lifestyle travel is about experiencing variety and alternative lives for themselves in a place. Such an aim demands a longer stay than conventional tourism would allow but crucially not an indefinite stay. This suggests that lifestyle travellers dip in and out of normality on their own terms in order to keep a 'continuity of change' and avoid staying the same. They desire a flexibility to reinvent their selves and this wish for instability therefore involves stints of movement offset with pausing in place. This offers interesting implications on the relationship between self and place: that place is considered important for self-progression but for only as long as it offers novelty to incite identity-change.

Mobilities within place

In this way, mobility is about the freedom to get to new places, to not be rooted in any one locale but rather to travel to, then establish many 'home like' or meaningful places through developing connections, creating relationships and familiarizing oneself with a place. Lifestyle travel therefore enables regular challenges of relocating a life – from a place which has become familiar, to a new location which is strange, unknown, and therefore, exciting. Such dis- and then re-location promotes feelings of self-achievement and personal growth. This geographical mobility thus gives a freedom to the individual to experience and test many lives, rather than simply living out one life in one place; they can essentially *'drop into someone's life and live it'* (Heath), before moving on to another version of themselves as and when they please. For them, the appeal is about continuing this sense of change, promoting fluidity and an evolution of the self through their ability to relocate as often as they desire. As Miriam explains:

there are so many people and so many, even countries that seem very similar but can be really different and there's languages to learn and food to try and just, there's an exhilaration of moving to a city and knowing that there's no-one in the whole country that you know that you could call if you had an emergency, that you don't have a job, you don't have a flat and you have $2000 in the bank and you have to somehow sort yourself out and you know even if you only have a couple of those it's better than sky diving, the rush! (Miriam)

For Miriam freedom to test herself/ves in new places is synonymous with fulfilling a personal challenge, to see how far she can push herself when isolated from familiarity. By submerging herself in the unknown she can carve her own paths and develop new networks, forcing herself to actively pursue her own way in a place and achieve goals of self-development and satisfaction. In this sense, the challenge of lifestyle travel is more about the process of making paths and integrat*ing*, rather than the end result of integrat*ion*. Once integrated, stasis within a place is likely, so geographical mobility will be sought (as will be discussed further below).

This raises a number of important issues. Firstly, this allows us to conceive that it is the mobilities through, in and across place that are important to the lifestyle traveller, rather than mobilities passively between places. Lifestyle travel involves movement to new places rather than seeking mobility for the sake of it. It involves a contained and periodic mobility where lifestyle travellers accept or opt for a temporal normality in order to further their own personal journey. Immobility (through remaining in place) does not hinder or stunt their movement as they are still pursuing an 'inward voyage' (Cohen 2010: 69), a development of the self through being in an 'Other' place. Movement for them symbolizes the ability to test and create identities through immersion in place, and self relocation is driven by their exposure to the multiple situations, cultures and relationships that they hover within:

... when I do fully learn a language and learn a town and make connections that's when I tend to like dis-anchor and go to the next place. And um, yeah that's been a bit of a pattern for me ... (Aviv)

Secondly, these issues illustrate both the fixity and fluidity of place, from the perspective of the lifestyle traveller. There is not space in this chapter for an extended review of the changing ways in which place has been conceptualized (for this, see Anderson forthcoming; Massey 2005, Cresswell 2002). Suffice it to say, like identity, place is no longer seen as wholly fixed and static, but dynamic and subject to change, influenced by the interactions and relations of its members. In this way lifestyle travellers are changing places through their presence in them, that their engagements with local people and fellow travellers, as well as their activities, mould and make senses of place that can change the direction, pace and feel of place, alongside the movements of its inhabitants. Places thence provide a medium for lifestyle travellers to weave their way in the world, as a medium for identity games to be played out – no matter how fleeting – as a way in which to 'know themselves' through the trails they weave. However, places can also be seen to be limited in their ability to change at a pace fast enough to fulfil these individuals' desire for personal growth. Once they have established themselves in one location they can no longer be themselves in this place as part of these selves require the novelty and challenge that only travel to new places enables.

Thus, for many lifestyle travellers, being on the move within place to promote self-growth and stimulation is what is important, and as Rachel describes, to 'conquer' place:

> when I travel my goal is to conquer a place like I really, I want to be able to leave and be like oh yeah I lived there 3 years ago, you should totally go to this bar or definitely check this out, I want to be able to share that experience with somebody. (Rachel)

In this way, place is conceived as a challenge to be met, with success being achieved when that place is subjectively fully known and thus exhausted of all its possible avenues and experiences. This suggests some kind of end state where place is acquired and 'defeated', that there is a fixed finite point to place in lifestyle travel.

Mobilities between places

Such a phenomenon introduces the notion of place saturation, that remaining in place once networks and constellations have been fully explored serves only to hinder self-progression. By staying indefinitely, or becoming 'trapped' in place, lifestyle travellers are limited in their ability to grow and transform since the challenge and novelty of it is removed, frustrating the very qualities that were originally sought:

> I do notice that when I stay somewhere too long I start to feel nervous, like I'm not accomplishing enough, and then when I start somewhere new and difficult I feel fulfilled. (Aviv)

> things should be moving, right, I'm relaxing at home, I'm now in a stable, relaxed work and its almost a sense of I'm coming to a grinding halt when, right where I'm travelling to, I'm gonna go now! (Cameron)

As a consequence, comfort for the lifestyle traveller appears to be a state of being '*un*comfortable' or outside of their comfort zone – it is about the challenge that being within a place involves. As Heath outlines:

> it's kinda like for some reason I find myself less comfortable in the most kind of stable, and the most comfortable in the most unstable places. (Heath)

Mobilities in place for the lifestyle traveller thus tend to have a 'shelf life' – an (unknown) expiry date which passes when the individual establishes a 'home-like' feel in a location and a sense of regularity or 'normality' sets in:

> I like to just to stay for a few months, but not for a long time! Then I'll still continue travelling. Cos the novelty will wear off after a few months of being there, not from the people that I care about but just the regular, doing the things you have to do, it's not very interesting cos you always know there's gonna be so many different things you could be doing. (Jenni)

> I don't have to be somewhere for 2 or 3 years to get a sense of home, like Melbourne feels like home, Canberra feels like home, Edinburgh feels like home, places where I've spent long enough to get an association or feel a sense of identification with a place, they're home, so yeah I like to keep that moving, keep it fresh. (Cameron)

> everywhere is a bit sentimental for me, but I don't really see myself moving back to any of those places you know it's almost like that times done … I get restless living in a certain place … so it just feels more comfortable to keep moving … (Miriam)

Feelings of familiarity – or over-familiarity – with place thus seem to represent feelings of stagnation, suggesting that there are only a finite number of things to do and selves to explore within a place. In this way, the 'shelf life' associated with place expires when a place no longer offers novelty – that there is no longer new things to see and do, and therefore inspire change – or when a place no longer offers the potential to explore identity. In this way, the person place relationship may have exhausted all possible avenues and serve to feed only one aspect of their identity – such as 'worker' for example – thus limiting their possibility to create new and contrasting identities. This is nicely summarized by En Tze who described how having pre-existing networks comprising of family members served to *stifle* his experience in Singapore, and that this ready-made 'home' from 'home' essentially suppressed his ability to grow.

> I just started travelling again and I really should've looked for work but I find it really hard to make myself stop travelling, I looked for work in Singapore for about a month but after 3 weeks I was going slightly insane I couldn't imagine being there for a year long contract so I just kinda took off … I find it, I dunno quite stifling and when I'm there its all family, everyone I know is family, and I end up staying in like apartments, I'm not in hostels, I'm not meeting people, I've not got a job so wasn't meeting anybody new, and this is just, drives me nuts, just sit all day reading, I mean it was like I was back in the US only without any friends.

For En Tze, the process of establishment within place centred on meeting new people, and it was this process that was important to him, those feelings of 'newness' and the unknown were what he was seeking. Familiarity with Singapore thus hampered his ability to weave new and personalized trails through the place as such constellations based on family were already formed, removing any excitement he may have felt from finding his own way. Perhaps new paths could have been laid had En Tze decided to pursue a new and individualistic sense of Singapore outside these pre-fabricated networks, yet for him, the trails were stale, well trodden and not conducive to self progression.

The lifestyle that these travellers have created thus tends to be centred upon the freedom to be mobile both within and across places. Once immobility occurs, feelings of restriction follow, suggesting that it is the ability to relocate across new selves, induced by keeping things '*fresh*' within place, that is the imperative component of identity formation. Place still strongly configures how the lifestyle traveller views and tests a sense of self, yet is dependent on the capacity to which they are able to remain mobile.

This is emphasized by Jen, whose love of travel and being in new places is based on being able to '*be whoever you want to be and no-one knows you*'. Through this testing and selecting of personas, she is constantly engaged in getting to know herself, allowing different aspects of self to manifest through being in new and foreign situations. For her, it is a battle of the selves, a game to be played out to see '*which part of your personality is gonna win out … so you have to re-define yourself*'. This perhaps explains En Tze's lack of motivation to carve new trails in Singapore as an 'old' place, as less colourful and dynamic relocations manifest by being in a familiar place. The ability to be mobile across selves is restricted by 'knowing' and being 'known' within place.

Conclusion

This chapter has set out to explore what mobility means to the lifestyle traveller, what this mobility involves, and ultimately what consequences these issues have for notions of place in the globalizing world. We have seen how mobility is imperative to the lifestyle traveller, it is how they define and live their lives; yet these mobilities vary in pace, momentum and direction depending on what they are seeking at any point of their journey. For the lifestyle traveller, mobility is equivalent to freedom: freedom to explore, freedom to relocate across selves, and freedom to move between, across and through places. Mobility in this sense is thereby the freedom to carve individualized paths and trails through the world, to break free of routine and settlement to sustain a lifestyle based on change, novelty and progression which permanence and fixity within place cannot provide.

For lifestyle travellers initial mobility may be sought to escape 'home' or shed societal pressures and expectations, whilst sustained lifestyle travel becomes oriented around an agenda of 'creating selves' for which a range of different mobilities are essential. *Mobilities within place* are fundamental to lifestyle travel as through this 'static' change individuals get to know and discover new selves; it is how they learn, grow, and gain satisfaction through creating something from nothing. *Mobilities between places* allow the physical relocation of these networks to new and exciting locales which can offer possibilities for further growth and change. Places in this way are amalgamations of the dynamic and multiple mobilities or paths that lifestyle travellers weave, promoting an inward voyage through the exploration of new paths mixed with current or existing ones. By relocating to new places lifestyle travellers are confronted with novelty and challenge, submerging themselves in the unknown to test their adaptability and learn about new aspects of themselves through developing connections. In this way place and mobility cannot be divorced but are involved in a co-constitutive relationship, with mobilities colouring place, and places providing an outlay for mobilities to manifest and become meaningful within.

Thus, for the lifestyle traveller, place has become something that is both fixed and in flux. Places are fluid in the sense that they allow travellers to gain a sense of belonging within them, yet they are also (relatively) fixed as their customs and routines are able to be subjectively explored and known by the lifestyle traveller. Places' pace of change therefore do not correlate with lifestyle travellers' pace of identity establishment and need for novelty. As a consequence, it becomes more necessary for lifestyle travellers to instigate their own movement and relocate to different places in order to find fresh opportunities and new roles to play.

References

Anderson, J. 2012. Relational places: the surfed wave as assemblage and convergence. *Environment & Planning D: Society and Space*, 30(4), 570–587.

Attenborough, K. 2006. Wildlife Special: The Backpacker, in *Bangkok Recorder Magazine – Bangkok Exposed. RSS Newsletter*, Wednesday Aug 2 2006. Available at: www.bangkokrecorder.com/magazine (accessed: 4 June 2011).

Bauman, Z. 1996. From Pilgrim to Tourist – or a Short History of Identity, in *Questions of Cultural Identity*, edited by S. Hall and P. du Gay. London: Sage Publications, 18–36.

Beck, U. and Beck-Gernsheim, E. 2002. *Individualization*. London: Sage.

Benson, M. and O'Reilly, K. 2009. Migration and the search for a better way of life: a critical exploration of lifestyle migration. *The Sociological Review*, 57(4), 608–625.

Buttimer, A. and Seamon, D. 1980. *The Human Experience of Space and Place*. London: Croom Helm.

Clifford, J. 1997. *Routes. Travel and Translation in the Late Twentieth Century*. Cambridge, MA: Harvard University Press.

Cohen, E. 2004. *Contemporary Tourism: Diversity and Change*. Oxford: Elsevier.

Cohen, S. 2010. Chasing a myth? Searching for 'self' through lifestyle travel. *Tourist Studies*, 10(2), 117–133.

Cohen, S. 2011. Lifestyle travellers: backpacking as a way of life. *Annals of Tourism Research*, 38(4), 1535–1555.

Cresswell, T. 2002. Introduction: Theorizing Place, in *Mobilising Place, Placing Mobility*, edied by G. Verstraete, and T. Cresswell. Amsterdam: Rodopi, 11–33.

Duffy, R. 2004. Ecotourists on the beach, in *Tourism Mobilities: Places to Play, Places in Play*, edited by M. Sheller and J. Urry. London: Routledge, 32–43.

Gogia, N. 2006. Unpacking corporeal mobilities: the global voyages of labour and leisure. *Environment and Planning A*, 38(2), 359–375.

Gustafson, P. 2006. Place Attachment and Mobility in *Multiple Dwelling and Tourism: Negotiating Place, Home and Identity*, edited by N. McIntyre, D. Williams and K. McHugh. Oxford: CABI, 17–31.

Hay, R. 1998. Sense of place in developmental context. *Journal of Environmental Psychology*, 18(1), 5–29.

Ingold, T. 2006. Up, across and along. *Place and Location: Studies in Environmental Aesthetics and Semiotics*, 5, 21–36.

Massey, D. 2005. *For Space*. London: Sage.

Maxey, I. 1999. Beyond boundaries? Activism, academic, reflexivity and research. *Area*, 31(3), 199–208.

O'Reilly, C. 2005. Tourist or Traveller? Narrating Backpacker Identity in *Discourse Communication and Tourism*, edited by A. Jaworski and A. Pritchard. Clevedon: Channel View Publications, 150–170.

O'Reilly C. 2006. From drifter to gap year tourist. Mainstreaming backpacker travel. *Annals of Tourism Research*, 33(4), 998–1017.

Relph, E. 1976. *Place and Placelessness*. London: Pion.

Richards, G. and Wilson, J. 2004. Travel writers and writers who travel: nomadic icons for the backpacker subculture? *Journal of Tourism and Cultural Change*, 2(1), 46–68.

Rojek, C. 1993. *Ways of Escape: Modern Transformations in Leisure and Travel.* London: Macmillan.

Urry, J. 2003. *Global Complexity.* Cambridge: Polity Press.

Chapter 10

Trans-Pacific Bluewater Sailors – Exemplar of a Mobile Lifestyle Community

Barbara A. Koth

Many Westerners in wealthy countries dream of sailing off to tropical isles and anchoring offshore of sparkling sand beaches in turquoise waters teeming with dolphins and coral. It is the prototype idyllic paradise, the retiree's dream, the flight of fancy at an office desk on a dreary winter afternoon. Certainly there is a skill-based threshold for entry to sailing, but even among sailors few denizens enmeshed in the postmodern production economy extricate themselves from onshore lives and sail oceans in small boats. Despite the romance, lure of exotic ports, and postcard sunsets, most sailors recreate on weekends in local waterways or hug coastal shores. As is the parlance in bluewater (i.e. oceanic) sailing circles, it is 'a different breed' of sailor that heads offshore over the horizon to adventures yet unknown. Trans-Pacific sailors comprise a mobile, lifestyle community, perhaps utopian in nature.

The sea is part of human cultural experience inspiring literature and art that materialize historical mobilities. Fiction classics such as *Treasure Island* and Melville's *Moby Dick* build the romantic and dangerous lure of the open ocean; storytelling about factual events at sea (e.g. *Mutiny on the Bounty*, *Two Years Before the Mast*) are no less compelling. Tales of incredible voyages such as Thor Heyerdahl's *Kontiki* wanderings, Shackleton's journeys to Antarctica and early circumnavigations are embedded in the Western psyche, for some from childhood. Literary themes of these expeditions, building on fiction traditions, often centre on exploration of the unknown and male camaraderie and maturation (Bender 1988). Young men and boys were, in fact, sent to sea for 'cure of their ethical ailings', to be tamed from rebellion and defiance (Taylor 1993). Extremes of social class were represented in trading; upper classes served in the merchant marines, and financial rewards for crew could be irresistible to men with few options (Redicker 1987). The historic representations in literature recast grand adventure, in the face of uncertain survival, as the seduction. Hardship conditions as Evans (2007) describes – onboard physical toil and exposure to elements, sleep deprivation on watch schedules, limited food rations and cramped living quarters – still exist to a lesser extent in working boats (Maguire 2011) and ocean passaging, but the mystique of open ocean sailing endures. It is still not risk-free given the vagaries of weather forecasting, unchartered reefs and collision dangers (e.g. whales, containers).

While the name of the landfall may be identical, today's voyage is certainly not an enactment of the passages of history. Innovative mobility forms have become more broadly achievable through transformations enabled by technology and communications (Hannam, Sheller and Urry 2006). While ocean racing is driven by advances in boat design and construction, widespread availability of GPS (Global Positioning System) units for several hundred dollars is central to the increasing popularity of offshore touring by sail. When integrated with a chart plotter, advanced anti-collision radar and an EPIRB (Electronic Positioning Indicating Radio Beacon) to target any emergency recovery efforts, the simple sextant and compass navigation aids of sailors as late as the 1970s look prehistoric. Communication innovations increase margins of safety, such as SailMail allowing email contact and receipt of weather forecasts by SSB radio, alongside the now ubiquitous satellite phone. Illustrative of time-space compression in modern life (Harvey 1989), daily contact with the land-based world is possible; sailors post their position on the internet for friends and family (Pangolin 2011) or blog about the day's events. Bluewater sailing is no longer a voyage of isolation, unless so chosen.

The ultimate mobility?

Bluewater sailing can be positioned within the mobility literature, as it meets both definitional elements of migration and circulation (Cridland 2008). More specifically, lifestyle migration, defined by McIntyre (2009: 230) as 'movement of people, capital, information and objects associated with the process of voluntary relocation to places perceived as providing an enhanced, or at least different lifestyle' shows conceptual promise in profiling oceanic sailing. Various authors (Benson 2011, O'Reilly and Benson 2009, Benson and O'Reilly 2009) suggest participants in lifestyle migration are characterized by relative affluence, escape intentions and a search for a better way of life, and creation of a new identity. In practice, bluewater sailors' renegotiation of work-life balance, enhanced quality of life and freedom from prior constraints distinguishes them as practicing lifestyle mobilities.

Not surprisingly, there is little academic examination of the specialized leisure world of offshore yachties, a uniquely independent subculture physically distant from the structures of modern society by travel to remote locations (Axup and Viller 2005). Cornell (2008) estimates there are 800–1,000 non-commercial boats crossing tropical Pacific waters by sail at any one time, with many more in the Atlantic Ocean, a shorter 14- to 25-day crossing. A standard westbound 10,000 nautical miles 'Milk Run' traverses the Pacific, with landfall from North America or the Panama Canal at the Marquesas Islands of French Polynesia, continuing through Tahiti and the Society Islands, to the Cook Islands, Tonga, Fiji, and perhaps Vanuatu. The crossing may be done in one rushed seven-month season, or more intensive multi-year explorations, typically returning to popular summering grounds in New Zealand (or the Marshall Islands) during cyclone season. At the western edge of the Pacific, sailors face at least four choices, to: 1) continue westward global circumnavigation through the Straits of Malacca into the Indian Ocean; 2) return to North America fighting the trade winds back to Hawaii via the Line Islands; 3) sell the boat and travel or return to home base; or 4) place the sailboat on a yacht-carrying commercial freighter for transport to a home port or the next region of sailing interest such as Thailand or Turkey.

The small numbers of boats, fragmentation of itineraries and the independent nature of individuals who choose this highly transient lifestyle make this a difficult group to study (Koth 2010). There remains a paucity of inquiry on this individualistic yet highly communal 'leisure' subculture. Conceptual foci to date have centred on the formation of community within a utopian paradigm, yachting lifestyle and motivations, and traditional economic development implications (e.g. Northland Marine Development Group 2008, Koth 2011). Macbeth (1992) first applied subculture theory to hypothesize entry of cruisers into a lifestyle realm following an introduction phase shaped by popular media and literature, and an acceptance phase characterized by skill building. He posits the importance of having no job 'in the background' as an important distinction in building an alternative 'whole of life', one of ambiguity and periodic hardship offset by powerful opportunities for self-actualization. Macbeth later (2000) makes analogy to utopian community in exploring creation of an alternative life that is partially escapist from modernity, while simultaneously creating an ideal characterized by self-reliance, physical activity and connection to nature.

Lusby and Anderson (2008) studied Caribbean cruisers to profile the offshore sailing community, focusing on belongingness derived from shared experience. One element of self-identification with community is hypothesized to come from 'generalized reciprocity' whereby cruisers help each other with the future expectation they too will assist and be assisted. Refinements in their work (2010) hypothesize a set of motivational drivers for bluewater sailing: a freedom theme incorporating autonomy, challenge and escape, and love of the sea. Uniquely, women mentioned spirituality and healing in poignant stories of connection with the universe, but all respondents described deeply satisfying 'peak' immersion experiences. More narrowly, Jennings (2007) calls for gender-based differentiation in defining the benefits of extended offshore cruising, while Werth (1987) profiles the historic-laden mystique of solo ocean-traversing sailors, mostly male.

Parallels can be drawn with other networked mobile leisure communities, especially the grey nomads of Australia or caravanning by North American retirees. Motorhome owners are distinctive in also bringing their residence and possessions with them 'on the road' when they camp, and have strong codification of group norms (Onyx and Leonard 2007, Higgs and Quirk 2007, Hardy and Gretzel 2008). Cohen (2011) profiles lifestyle backpackers that travel lightly, with perhaps a tent or sleeping bag, to unspoiled destinations, following routes opened by transit services. In comparison to their land-based peers, oceanic sailors travel farthest from the core, traversing some of the loneliest places on the planet. In leaving land, they depart from the margins carrying inventories and advantages of modernity with them (e.g. fibreglass boats, mechanical spares, global communications, cryovaced food and foulweather gear made of high-tech fibres), but they remain subject to the laws of nature and chance. Time-old adages about putting your affairs in order before setting to sea still hold, as there is no guarantee of return for ocean crossing sailors. As such, bluewater sailors represent an extreme of lifestyle migrants in terms of physical dissociation with the postmodern world and amplified risk and as such exemplify lifestyle mobility.

Methodology and movement

This research targeted middle-class sailors in small- and mid-sized sailboats who can be physically located in popular ports, or maintain an internet presence, in contrast to more difficult-to-reach social isolates that mimic voyages of the past, interacting primarily with traditional cultures. Survey methodology was employed to reach two subsets of international sailors – English-speaking cruisers berthed in the Whangarei, New Zealand harbour during the cyclone season, and sailors in the southern Pacific during the peak season (July/August) with access to internet list serve groups. Whangarei, popular for its plethora of marine services and ease of community integration, is a northern international port of entry for boats coming from Pacific islands. Study periods were chosen when boat crew would be most likely to be onboard having just completed the crossing from Tonga or Fiji (November), or preparing for the next season's departure (April/May). One data collection period used face-to-face interviews, and the other utilized personal delivery of self-completed surveys after marina referrals to the researcher, with 43 cruisers' completions of the questionnaire.

Bluewater sailors subscribing to the Yahoo! list 'pacificpuddlejump' were also targeted for survey completion. Pacificpuddlejump (1,070 members) is directed at westbound cruisers headed to the South Pacific, with lively e-communication and a compilation of resources to assist that passage. Each year a 'class' of puddlejumpers depart the Americas, although users may subscribe for years as they prepare their boat and improve their skills. For many, trans-Pacific community formation, both physical and virtual, starts before setting sail into Pacific waters. Mobility is thus both real and imagined (Hannam et al. 2006). Given the bandwidth constraints of at-sea email delivery systems, sailors on pacificpuddlejump were asked to contact the researcher with intent to participate, and 20 did so. Difficulty in obtaining even a relatively small number of responses from face-to-face and internet contact can be expected, and statistical analysis of the two subgroups showed no significant differences, with the exception that the pacificpuddlejump list subsample is skewed toward those having been at sea for a lengthier time.

The author provides an observational context for survey results from personal experience as a transpacific sailor. In the two years prior to the study, she sailed as co-owner and first mate on a 44-foot, 16-ton sailboat *Gypsy Soul*. Ten years of saving and planning prior to purchase of a used boat in California was followed by three months of preparation in Ensenada (Mexico) and a shakedown cruise along the Baja Peninsula. This accelerated schedule after purchase represents time compression in comparison with the lengthy multi-year preparation periods common among sailing peers. The first season's passaging included Puerto Vallarta (Mexico) to New Zealand, with a second season in Fiji and Vanuatu. Prior immersion in the sailing lifestyle, and cooperation with marina owners, allowed the author to achieve a 100 per cent response rate for interviews with yacht owners berthed in Whangarei.

Profiling bluewater sailors

Minimal research to date means sailor profiles of nationality; onboard social affiliations, boat characteristics, experience levels and income have been largely anecdotal. Respondents were asked what country they considered home and U.S. citizens dominated the sample (46 per cent), with Canadians accounting for another 10 per cent. Nineteen countries were reported; Europeans comprised 28 per cent of respondents with the largest generating countries being the United Kingdom, Germany and Sweden. At remote anchorages and island ports, there was evidence that language clusters assume more importance than nationality, in that stable subgroups form around non-English speakers (e.g. the French boats, the Scandinavian boats). Seventy-five per cent of questionnaires came from captains (versus crew), of whom five were female, with an additional four instances of co-captaining. Couples comprise the most common sailing social unit (79 per cent), including two boats with two couples aboard. Data comparisons with real-world observation corroborates the study's weaker representation of solo single-handers (16 per cent), families with children (8 per cent), and unrelated friends (3 per cent; comprised of 20- and 30-year-old cohorts). Consistent with historical portrayals (Werth 1987), all study singlehanders were male, despite the author's informal contact with several female singlehanders (always with pets). Children's ages in familial groups ranged from infancy to teenagers, with their independence in international settings and instantaneous formation of playgroups – including local children, demonstrating the reverse of a reduced mobility trend regarding daily interaction patterns of youth in wealthier countries (Barker et al. 2009).

Most cruisers (84 per cent) are sailing on monohulls versus multihulled catamarans, and the average boat length is 13 metres (43 feet), ranging from nine to 25 metres. The offshore subsample averages 19,400 nautical miles (nm) travelled on the present voyage. For perspective, a circumnavigation is considered to be at least 21,600nm, and the direct line in a Pacific crossing from Mexico to Australia is approximately 6,500nm. But notation is made that sailboats traverse far greater distances to achieve point-to-point landfall. Sailors in the study have 'been out' an average of almost five years (59.3 months), with a modal response of 4.2 years. Range is extremely variable from three months to 20 years, with

10 per cent voyaging over 10 years to date. The author posits a sample bias toward sailors with high experience levels, with most having crossed the Pacific Ocean.

The survey did not ask for income as it is not a polite question within the egalitarian sailing community. Despite stereotypes of wealthy retired businessmen, anecdotally we know many are middle-class couples, from diverse occupations, who traverse oceans in 15–30-year-old boats they have purchased after a lifetime of dreaming. Participant observation (meeting families of four on 27-foot boats, failure to hire out for labour-intensive boat tasks despite low local wage rates) and open-ended results provide some evidence of the attention to fiscal issues faced by middle-class sailors. Financial tensions were mentioned frequently in questions about desired port attributes (e.g. cheaper marine services, better currency exchange rates), trips home ('the cruising kitty can't afford it') and visitors ('most of our family don't even have passports'). The supposition is that many bluewater sailors are well educated professionals or self-employed, but that the significant expense of running an ocean-going yacht requires a financial plan and some frugality in living and travel costs.

Motivations

Culture in many traditional societies remains enmeshed with the sea, but what compels modern man or woman to venture into the open ocean for non-commercial purposes? Certainly passion and a sense of exploration, discovery and curiosity enter into the equation, while others find solace and leisure fulfilment by setting sail. Respondents were asked to consider a statement summarizing previous motivational research (Lusby and Anderson 2010): 'ocean cruisers sail because of (1) freedom and an independent life, and (2) love of the sea'. In open-ended replies, there was widespread acceptance of the former theme ubiquitous in the mobility literature, although 10 per cent of the sample articulated a love-hate relationship with the sea due to bad weather, the onus of decision-making and constant repairs. Freedom was often defined as 'positive freedom' (Sagera 2006), the choice *to* exert autonomous control and self-determination, in contrast to freedom *from* constraining structures. These dimensions served only as a starting point, with the 63 respondents detailing 40 core aspects of bluewater sailing that provided a motivational set for individual journeys. Adventure and exploration, exposure to new cultures and seeing the world, the most frequently cited themes (n=12 each) emergent in content analysis, could be conceptualized as meeting the desire for novelty and 'newness'. An interviewee explains how they feel on intermittent return visits to Europe:

> There is such a grey predictability to it all. Every day is like the day before it, the sameness. The 7:01 train arrives at 7:01. In sailing, even at anchor, the day never plays out as planned.

The mobility of the bluewater sailing lifestyle directly contrasts with schedule-driven life ashore, and the daily knowingness of survival and maintenance tasks demanded by twenty-first century integration. Long-distance sailing absorbs a sense of adventure and newness given the immediacy of action dictated by weather, functionality of equipment in the moment, crew capabilities and stamina, and what sailing peers are doing. In some cases, true exploration occurs, exemplified when sailors encountered new volcanic land being formed mid-ocean near Tonga in 2008.

Another theme is the simple love of boats and sailing (n=7), however, the sailing lifestyle cannot solely be explained in terms of preferred recreation specializations. The sea may simply allow a means of achievement of lifestyle goals, or its materiality and natural rhythms may be a motive source in itself. A similar number of cruisers report affinity for the act of movement, describing sailing as the 'best way of extended travel because you see the world and take your home with you'. Long-term dream fulfilment, the challenge of self-sufficiency, sociability and normative functioning of the sailing community, and interaction with local people round out the list of commonly reported motivations. The final two items, a drive for authentic contact, is indicative of a repeated pattern of hyper-mobility interspersed with a quest for grounding and mooring. In addition, each of the following received multiple mentions: lifelong learning, the opportunity to be outdoors in the environment, building a life beyond employment demands, the remoteness of the Pacific, a mode of budget travel, the simple drive for change (from boredom, through divorce) and the daily way of life. Adjectives used in describing the onboard way of life were 'slow', 'simple', 'variety', 'fun' and 'sustainable', echoing Pye's (1960) famous excerpt:

> Washing your face in an inch of water, feeling the salt in your flying hair, the warmth of the sun through an ancient shirt, turning out in the night to silence a tin that rolls with the rolling ship, seeing the same faces from four feet across the cabin sole day after day, week after week; if these things don't seem worthwhile, give up your dream of the southern seas and ... catch the nine-fifteen.

The sailors' terms evoke a style of living that predates modernity; the words assert a reversal of critiques of the modern age (Creswell 2006), a satisfaction in everydayness.

The survey also incorporated a 5-point Likert scale (1 = very unimportant; 5 = very important) to indicate levels of support for motivational statements extracted from the literature. Five elements were measured: connection with nature, satisfying way of life, independence, community and spirituality. Importance was high for four of the five motivational elements with similar patterns exhibited for both genders, with the exception of statistically significant means difference in women's desired connection with nature. Women derived greater satisfaction with the connection to nature that the sailing lifestyle offered, a finding partially predicted by research about the more intimate relationship that

Western women have with wildlife. If Cresswell (2010) holds up classic images of technological mobility in motorized modes, sailing is perhaps one of the few types of transportation, with cycling and walking, where immersion in the feel, sound and life of nature are omnipresent. Further, more women (42 per cent) placed the highest importance level on belongingness in the sailing community, compared with 30 per cent of men. The reverse is shown whereby more males (44 per cent) label the independence/challenge element of bluewater sailing as 'very important'; 34 per cent of females did so. Several men pencilled in related comments that the challenge and dream aspect of sailing can push back societally-defined limitations and the stereotypes of aging, a theme echoed under the escape dimension. The 'spirituality aspects that sailing offers' were scored lowest, but still, at least one-in-five termed spirituality of importance.

The dimension of escape

Mobility incorporates the concept of emotional distancing in addition to corporal departure from a home base. The data on the escape dimension shows a bi-modal U-shaped distribution, with approximately equal numbers (45 per cent) agreeing and disagreeing with the statement 'I escape through sailing'. The pattern holds for both genders and most respondents report strong feelings at the extreme ends of the Likert scale (i.e. scored one or five). Predictably, Pacific sailors are most often escaping from work obligations, materialism and stresses of the busy, hectic 'rat race'. But the less frequently reported aspects provide insight into the anomie of modernism for many: escape from ordinariness and a 'quotidian' life, a regulatory culture, a society lacking insight and reflection ('mind pollution') and an urban existence isolated from nature. One articulate quote mentioned 'escape from being old and scared of dying'. Conversely, a similar proportion vehemently rejects the escape label: 'We have nothing to escape from. We have a great house, great families, had fantastic jobs and good incomes. There is nothing to run away from, just something to create'. A similarly illustrative quote: 'We have always liked our lives. We are not running away; we are pursuing the uncommon'. The Zen-like perceptions of one poetic sailor is captured in description of escape 'from everything and from nothing'.

Creation of community

The motivational profile suggests extreme importance of the oceangoing sailing community, especially for women, with strong social bonding occurring. Findings support Larsen et al.'s (2006) contention that strong social ties can persist over distant spaces removed from the home environment, with strong formation of social capital. North American East Coast boats and European yachts are likely to have met during the Panama Canal transit experience or cruising in the Caribbean.

Many North American bluewater cruisers prepare their boats and gain experience (for months or years) in well-serviced Mexican west coast ports prior to the crossing. Some will have joined the Baja Ha-Ha cruise-in-company event to test their skills in passaging from San Diego to central Mexican ports, and built their social network by participating in associated educational programs. The pacificpuddlejump Yahoo! list in fact differentiates each year's crossing with the designation 'Class of 2012' (with t-shirts), a nomenclature used by the sailors themselves to position identities. The seasonality (April to November) and directionality (east-to-west taking advantage of tradewinds) creates a meet-disband-reform model, repeated at periodic intervals. Most insurance policies mandate that tropical sailors spend six months in non-cyclone zones, so the community forms at popular island anchorages, disbands for long-distance passaging (although radio contact may be maintained), reforms episodically, and then regathers for the nontransit season. At remote anchorages, socializing occurs in the cockpit with cruisers bringing creative cuisine from oft-depleted provisions (bonding in scarcity), and 'boat cards' (business cards) are exchanged. In the author's experience, conversation centres on storytelling about sailing experiences, and problem solving (bonding in technological challenges); the land-based world recedes into irrelevance. Again, moorings, both short- and longer-term, are material as well as a metaphor for intermittent stability and engagement. Travel decision-making is often made based on knowledge and tips shared during these communal phases, in particular about management of mobility controls such as best ports for international entry and customs protocol.

When in port in a developed country, this complex community exhibit behaviours of both seasonal resident and tourist. Visual identifiers for the sailors can be deep tans, worn clothes stained by paints and chemicals, colourful island garb and sarongs, the ubiquitous Crocs and deck shoes, and boat shirts with embroidered names for formal occasions. The lack of a vehicle in port means reduced mobility on land and more face-to-face contact with fellow members of the lifestyle community. Cruisers walk long distances or use public transit, have bicycles outfitted for carrying supplies and function geographically within a limited dockside area. Continuing the habit of scheduled radio contact while at sea, major ports may have radio 'scheds,' self-organized VHF radio programs where information is disbursed, and assistance requested (how can I ship ...?, does anyone know how to fix ...?). Communities across the Pacific arrange events for sailors, and typically a pub or two is claimed by long-distance sailors. Some continue journeying in the off-season with independent land travels, or in the company of cruising friends. Temporary entry into the community is allowed when captains request crew assistance on long ocean passages. About one-fifth (22 per cent) of sailors make crew additions while crossing the Pacific, primarily to perpetuate mobility – to enhance safety margins, share watch responsibilities or meet insurance requirements.

Fluidity of decision-making and movement

Unstructured travel itineraries and flexibility in cruiser movement are the norm; most captains are uncertain regarding intentions for circumnavigation, the future length of time to be spent in the sailing lifestyle, or even identification of the next port at the end of cyclone season. The most frequent response category is 'uncertain' for these three variables, with one-third unsure whether they will sail around the world in a voyage that typically takes three to five years. The commitment to the lifestyle is evident in the fact that 40 per cent of the sample are circumnavigating, despite exponentially increasing piracy dangers and recent sailing deaths in the Horn of Africa region. Similarly, 40 per cent reply 'no idea' in estimating the expected duration of the present voyage. When outliers are removed ('20 years', 'forever'), respondents plan to sail, on average, for an additional two and a half years. Twelve per cent plan to sail more than five years longer. Even identification of the next port of call is uncertain for many (24 per cent), sometimes phrased as 'today Vanuatu, tomorrow who knows?' The flexibility in movement can partially be attributed to lifestyle elements, as well as the strength of and trust in the sailing network. The author recalls that the strongest influence on itinerary planning (which Tuamotan atolls to visit, routing option from the Society Islands to Tonga, which cyclone-free port, where to do international check-ins) was recommendations and advice from fellow cruisers. With the exception of a decision to be out of cyclone latitudes during specific timeframes, always at the mercy of weather conditions, ocean sailors generally have no deadlines for completion. It is a sense of pride for many sailors to slow down and live 'in the moment', taking advantage of serendipitous conditions (meeting a boat with friends from a previous anchorage, good winds, traditional festival or seasonal wildlife display). In totality, this means that Pacific yachts are generally headed westward for a season, with multiple options within a flexible itinerary, subject to input from sailing peers. During the cyclone and major repair season, new plans are made, to then be altered under very broad sailing goals.

Interface with the home world

Findings provide insight to shifting identifications in relation to place attachment and the nature of interface with the 'home world'. The concept of 'home' is tenuous for some sailors with fluid identities not based on a single passport or primary land residence. Transnationalism, a variant of world citizenry, is evidenced in several data patterns. Firstly, a segment who consider their home country to be 'nowhere' or 'where I am at the moment' (n=2) is extremely uncommon in this author's research experience. The number who report dividing their non-boat time between two home countries (n=2), in addition to boats captained by a person who reports holding dual citizenship (n=4) means 10 per cent of the sample live in at least three potentially intersecting lifestyle and land-based worlds. The globalization of transpacific sailing is also perpetuated by international crew compositions, in particular when owners supplement onboard personnel for lengthy (e.g. Mexico to French Polynesia) or more dangerous (e.g. to New Zealand) passages. In fact, the most commonly reported mechanism for finding additional crew (in New Zealand) was meeting local sailors. Further evidence of this transglobal lifestyle is provided by data on the yacht's port of registry, with three boat owners specifying the sailboat had never visited its home waters. Given the worldwide marketplace for pleasure yachts, some bluewater sailors had travelled from a residential base to a locale with a competitive boat trade, and started their global voyage from this location.

Although 76 per cent of respondents report they live aboard and sail year-round, sampling bias is evident; in New Zealand surveys and interviews would have been completed only by those onboard the boat at the time. A more accurate interpretation is that *at least* 24 per cent live on the yacht and sail for only part of the year – those that report part-time status (16 per cent), other variations such as working or travelling by land in New Zealand (8 per cent), in addition to the unoccupied boats that were unavailable to the sampling frame at the time. Several respondents articulated how the 'two lives – sailing and nonsailing – enrich each other'. Those that participate in the sailing lifestyle on a part-time or seasonal basis may have a regular connection with a land base, for example 'flying back' for part of a year. The interface with traditional tourism and bluewater sailing becomes evident when noting the majority of respondents (57 per cent) had left the boat to travel internationally in the last year, and 45 per cent were visited in tropical or New Zealand ports by friends and family. This latter finding suggests the home milieu can be transplanted to the yacht as centrepiece for maintaining far-flung social relationships.

Interface with the world of work

As predicted anecdotally, most captains (63 per cent) report retirement status, but four respondents discussed retirement in vague terms, often labelled as 'temporarily' or 'both yes and no', and thus defy precise classification. Standard conceptualizations generate a work/not work dichotomy; retirees do not work, and workers do engage in paid activity. However, 14 per cent of the sample exhibits indistinct boundaries between paid employment and retirement. There are cases of both self-classified working retirees, as well as the self-categorized 'employed', who are not working or are unemployed at present while sailing. In the latter instance, the labelling suggests the flexibility to re-enter the workforce enroute or seasonally as time appropriate opportunities arise. The minority (36 per cent) who still re-engage with the land-based world to work occasionally emphasized that they choose when to do so, in flexible or consultant professions such as IT, teaching, nursing, marketing, retail, engineering, architecture or company ownership. Onboard work for pay while enroute may include writing, the creative arts and sail repair/rigging. The broad measure of age in the study does not allow correlation with employment status, but interview encounters suggest while youthful traditional retirees who saved for sailing over a extensive career are most common, there are a significant number of younger couples (under 55 years) who have extracted themselves from employment for a sailing lifestyle that can continue only with semi-regular engagement in the working world.

Discussion and conclusion

Throughout the ages humans have travelled the oceans in search of the unknown. Some limited number of society's 'escapees' have always set their sights seaward and set sail, thus marine mobility is not new historically. A global elite, relative to income levels in most of the world, but not necessarily of wealth and privilege, continue these explorations. Niche market is too simplistic a label for modern sailors, driven by mobility, lifestyle, leisure, retirement or amenity aims. External observers can measure the consumption of long-distance cruisers as they interact with the tourism economy while in port, but they purchase a far greater range of goods and services than typical tourists (e.g. seamstresses, pipefitters, marine repair and supply, education for their children), while also being self-sufficient in other realms (e.g. non-perishable food stocks, no accommodation costs). Likewise, the 'drifter' title that implies nomadism, '... having relinquished all idea, desire or nostalgia for fixity' (D'Andrea 2006: 102), does not apply. When measured as deliberate disengagement, sailing does not demonstrate characteristics of social deviancy, as individuals are linked to modern society, and socially supported within the network. Sailing allows the option of being as connected and networked as one wants to be, or as isolated as is desirable. Lifestyle mobility perhaps best targets the sailor's impulse, and as such Cresswell's (2010) six structural facets of mobility can be applied in summary: why, how fast, in what rhythm, by what route, how does it feel, and what frictions are generated in completion?

The motivations for oceanic sailing are a plethora of contradictions. Sailing's globalized way of life contrasts with the independence and physical isolation in visiting some of the most remote places on earth. Self-sufficiency becomes possible because of technology, and skills traded within the sailing subculture. Technology has altered the lifestyle in opening it to more participants, and in connecting the sailors to home bases and to each other. The author posits that oceangoing community and social bonds are often greater than land community because of the intensity of the experience and living in the flow of the moment.

The label 'escape' both draws and alienates sailors. A division exists between the many sailors who expressed deep dissatisfactions with modern society and its obligations, and those who emphasized a quest for creation of a desired personal world. For some, participation in bluewater sailing is an overt critique of acceptance of and immersion in the globalized twenty-first century. The cruising lifestyle, slow paced with minimal regulation, represents the antithesis of societal emphasis on rigidity and formal structure that constrains adventure. Whereas holidays represent breaking away to seek novelty temporarily, the sailing life is novel on a daily basis. The mobile lifestyle assumes value in its contrast to larger society, especially the ability to create enduring community. Many sailors reject consumerism on paper, but purchase sophisticated technologies that allow them to communicate and travel. In contrast are those for whom co-creation of a desirable way of life is foremost. There is something authentic internally, in personality and psyche, that propels these individuals to build a life offshore. Rather than differentiating an alternative, they are immersed in dream fulfilment: 'we are not escaping anything; we led a satisfying life on land and are continuing to do so at sea'.

Many cruisers do not have strict plans; the velocity and rhythm of movement is slow and fluid. In contrast to other forms of mobility, the pace has not quickened over centuries. One still sails at 5–10 miles per hour. Yet there are boundaries that operate to keep boat and crew moving: cyclone season, potential exposure to severe weather, recommendations from and promises to sailing friends, and pressing need for repairs. Routing is predictable, in part a function of service availability. Sailors are not only hyper-mobile in terms of crossing oceans, but they are mobile in terms of air travel to reconnect with home environments or for leisure purposes, as well as land-based exploration in foreign countries. They also attract travellers to them to maintain social connectivity or assist in the task of passaging.

The individually-shaped relationship with work, if any, and potentially tradition-shattering gender roles are key experiential distinctions in bluewater sailing. The current dichotomous language of retirement (is/is not) does not fit for many sailors. One notes that there are dropouts on the Milk Run; they sell boats enroute and rejoin the workforce or their leisured peers, having tested the dream. But when the lifestyle is rewarding, individuals do what it takes to maintain their desired immersion in sailing. Opportunities may arise for employment that can be integrated into a break from sailing, or earlier plans may be extended. There is fluidity inherent in the lifestyle, hence a blurry boundary between work and not-work.

It is also possible that in realizing the lifestyle dream through sailing, gender roles also become more fluid. Captaining an ocean-going boat has always been the right and privilege of men. The numerous reports of shared leadership responsibilities on a yacht suggest women are able to shape an important role. To sail safely, one needs to build a skill level commensurate with the legal and psychological responsibilities of (co-)captaining a sailboat. The data suggest partnerships are forged that challenge historic conventions, and multi-year voyaging statistics also indicate a satisfaction among sailing couples. The author recalls numerous conversations about onboard role delineation, often with men responsible for complex maintenance and repair, and women becoming expert at navigation and communication. When the lifestyle demands performance of all tasks, all operational contributions are valued irrespective of gender.

Certainly, for many of the small number of participants, ocean sailing for pleasure is the ultimate mobile lifestyle, simultaneously occurring within a super-networked community, well linked to the shoreside world. Technological advances aside, the skill requirements, and danger, restrict this immersion to a limited number that accept the risks. Perhaps the act of sailing itself perpetuates the desire. Lonely night watches pondering the stars spur reflection, and consciousness of mortality conceivably creates a drive for experience on the move – independence and connectedness, communion with nature, newness and satisfaction in the moment. Bluewater sailors control their interactions with the land-based world, but in the ultimate irony, they also give final control to the forces of nature, as of old.

References

Axup, J. and Viller, S. 2005. *Formative research methods for the extremely mobile. Appropriate methods for design in complex and sensitive settings*. Paper to the OzCHI (Computer Human Interaction) Workshop: OzCHI 2005, Canberra, Australia, Nov. 21–25.

Barker, J., Kraftl, P., Horton, J. and Tucker, F. 2009. The road less travelled – new directions in children's and young people's mobility. *Mobilities*, 4(1), 1–10.

Benson, M. 2011. The movement beyond (lifestyle) migration: mobile practices and the constitution of a better way of life. *Mobilities*, 6(2), 221–223.

Benson, M. and O'Reilly, K. 2009. Migration and the search for a better way of life: a critical exploration of lifestyle migration. *Sociological Review*, 57(4), 608–625.

Cornell, J. 2008. *World Cruising Routes*. Camden, Maine: International Marine/ McGraw-Hill.

Cridland, S. 2008. *An analysis of the winter movement of grey nomads to northern Australia: planning for increased senior visitation*. Unpublished PhD thesis. Townsville: James Cook University.

Cresswell, T. 2006. *On the Move: Mobility in the Modern Western World*. New York: Routledge.

Cresswell, T. 2010. Toward a politics of mobility. *Environment and Planning D: Society and Space*, 28(1), 17–31.

D'Andrea, A. 2006. Neo-nomadism: a theory of post-identitarian mobility in the global age. *Mobilities*, 1(1), 95–115.

Evans, A. 2007. Defining Jamaican sloops: a preliminary model for identifying an abstract concept. *Journal of Maritime Archaeology*, 2(2), 83–92.

Hannam, K., Sheller, M. and Urry, J. 2006. Editorial: mobilities, immobilities and moorings. *Mobilities*, 1(1), 1–22.

Hardy, A. and Gretzel, U. 2008. *It's all about me: understanding recreational vehicle usage on the Alaska Highway.* Paper presented at the 18th Annual Council for Australian University Tourism and Hospitality Education Conference, Surfers Paradise, Queensland, Australia, February 11–14.

Higgs, P. and Quirk, F. 2007. Grey nomads in Australia: are they a good model for successful aging and health? *Annals of the New York Academy of Sciences*, 1114(1), 251–257.

Jennings, G. 2007. Sailing/cruising, in *Water-based Tourism, Sport, Leisure and Recreation Experiences*, edited by G. Jennings. Burlington, VT: Elsevier, 23–45.

Koth, B. 2010. *Trans-Pacific bluewater cruising: New Zealand on the horizon.* Paper to the New Zealand Tourism & Hospitality Research Conference, Auckland, November 24–26.

Koth, B. 2011. *Destination planning to host bluewater sailors.* Paper to the Islands and Small States Tourism Conference, Suva, Fiji, September 12–14.

Larsen, J., Axhausen, K. and Urry, J. 2006. Geographies of social networks: meetings, travel and communications. *Mobilities*, 1(2), 261–283.

Lusby, C.M. and Anderson, S. 2008. Community and quality of life – the case of ocean cruising. *World Leisure*, 50(4), 232–242.

Lusby, C.M. and Anderson, S. 2010. Ocean cruising: a lifestyle process. *Leisure/Loisir*, 34(1), 85–105.

MacBeth, J. 1992. Ocean cruising: a sailing subculture. *Sociological Review*, 40(2), 319–343.

MacBeth, J. 2000. Utopian tourists – cruising is not just about sailing. *Current Issues in Tourism*, 3(1), 20–33.

McIntyre, N. 2009. Rethinking amenity migration: integrating mobility, lifestyle and social-ecological systems. *Die Erde*, 140, 229–250.

Maguire, H. 2011. *The queasy, the shaky & the loud: 'knowing your boat' through affective mobilities.* Paper to the Association of American Geographers, Seattle, April 8–12.

Northland Marine Development Group. 2008. International visiting yachties survey – Whangarei and Opua. Whangarei, New Zealand, May.

Onyx, J. and Leonard, R. 2007. The grey nomad phenomenon: changing the script of aging. *International Journal of Aging and Human Development*, 64(4), 381–398.

O'Reilly, K. and Benson, M. 2009. Lifestyle migration: escaping to the good life?, in *Lifestyle Migrations: Expectations, Aspirations and Experiences*, edited by M. Benson and K. O'Reilly. Farnham: Ashgate, 1–13.

Pye, P. 1960. *The Sea is For Sailing.* London: Rupert Hart-Davis.

Redicker, M. 1987. *Between the Devil and the Deep Blue Sea.* Cambridge: Cambridge University Press.

Sagera, T. 2006. Freedom as mobility: implications of the distinction between actual and potential travelling. *Mobilities*, 1(3), 465–488.

Taylor, A. 1993. James Fenimore Cooper Goes to Sea: Two Unpublished Letters by a Family Friend. *Studies in the American Renaissance*, 43–54.

Werth, L.F. 1987. The paradox of single-handed sailing – case studies in existentialism. *Journal of American Culture*, 10(1), 65–78.

Chapter 11

Mobile Habitations of Canoescapes

Jessica Dunkin and Bryan S.R. Grimwood

Introduction

This chapter explores modes of inhabiting and moving in and through 'canoescapes', landscapes enacted in relation to the canoe. We take as points of departure intersections and tensions between two case studies: one historical, the other contemporary. The first case travels back in time to the annual meetings and encampments of the American Canoe Association (ACA), peripatetic events that took place at out-of-the-way sites in Ontario, New York and New England between 1880 and 1902. The annual meetings were two-week affairs that brought middle-class urbanites from throughout east-central North America to recreate, socialize and race canoes. The second case follows affluent Canadian canoeists who travelled north in July 2010 to experience the Thelon River in the central Canadian 'barrenlands'. These tourists took part in an 11-day canoe journey with an experienced guide and outfitter.

These case studies reflect the research pursuits of a social historian of gender and leisure and a tourism geographer, brought together not by a shared interest in a particular time or space, but by a mutual curiosity in the nature-cultures of canoeing. In addition to the different eras, landscapes and scales characterizing these examples, the chapter is animated by two distinct voices. In part, these are the product of our personalities, but they also represent disciplinary differences and divergent methodologies. Whereas the first case study draws on archival material – periodical accounts, memoirs and photographs – to reconstruct the practices of camp life, the second makes use of mobile ethnography. In this latter case, Bryan's position as a participant observer enabled him to explore in detail the complex social and material practices related to producing the canoescape. By contrast, the passage of time and the idiosyncrasies of archiving mean that much of what the ACA campers experienced and felt remains hidden from view. Thus, the example of the Association encampments narrates events that are necessarily more global in scope.

In spite of these important differences – and, more than likely, because of them – we believe that the conversations engendered in writing this chapter were invaluable to mobilizing new ideas (certainly for us!). As we compared our research, we noticed points of intersection and tension that raised interesting questions about broader theoretical issues in tourism scholarship, working across disciplines and our understanding of mobilities. In what follows, we draw on our canoescape cases to make three distinct, but related arguments. First, lifestyle mobilities, understood as the condition of 'being corporeally mobile as a lifestyle', are intimately connected to the ideas, practices and material cultures of 'home', an observation that challenges the binaries of home/away and culture/nature that continue to animate much of the travel and tourism literature (Franklin and Crang 2001). Second, while movement and habitation echo through time and across space, indicative of the nature of our *dwelling* (Ingold 2000, Pons 2003), the particular expressions of these practices and their attendant meanings are deeply contextual, reinforcing the notion that the multiple and dynamic modes of *being-in-the-world* are always ripe for description (Merleau-Ponty 1962). Finally, mobilities, and by extension habitations, are practiced and made meaningful in relation to and with others. They are, in other words, profoundly social, a point that is marginal in contemporary theories of mobility centred on the isolated (and often masculine) individual of the *flâneur* (Benjamin 1973), *Wandersmänner* (de Certeau 1984), or *tourist* (MacCannell 1976, Urry 1990).

We begin with narrative accounts of each of the case studies, which reflect their divergent scales and our research realities. Jessica's example, which covers 23 years of an annual, mobile event, takes a more holistic view of the experience, mapping the canoeists' physical and psychological movements in the periods leading up to and following the annual meetings, as well as during the encampment itself. Bryan's case, by contrast, is largely focused on the journey from 'put-in' to 'take-out' in which perception and motion are coupled (Ingold 2007), although he hints at the longer *durée* of the experience. We then discuss the intersections and divergences of these two case studies, and what these trajectories might contribute to the emerging literature on lifestyle mobilities. This analysis is structured by three practices identified as central to the act of inhabiting these disparate canoescapes: imagining/representing, making lines and constructing camp. Within this discussion, we pay particular attention to the interpolations of home and away, of nature and culture.

The encampments of the American Canoe Association, 1880–1902

From its organization in 1880, the highlight of the American Canoe Association's calendar was the annual meeting. Prior to 1903, when the ACA established a permanent encampment on Sugar Island in the St. Lawrence River, the annual meetings moved between locations in Ontario, New York and New England (Figure 11.1). Although there was no official criterion for choosing a location, most sites balanced accessibility and amenities with privacy. The aesthetics of the locations varied widely; the two saltwater encampments on Long Island (1890) and Cape Cod (1902) were a far cry from the 1883 and 1900 meets on the Canadian Shield. Most organizers, however, aspired to locations that resonated with romantic ideals of the day (Jasen 1995).

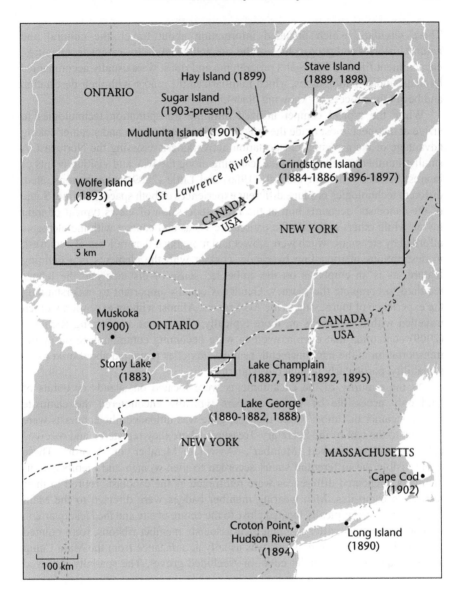

Figure 11.1 American Canoe Association encampments, 1880–1903

Source: Eric Leinberger (University of British Columbia).

The experience of attending a meet began long before arriving at the campsite. The location was announced via one of the organization's official organs (for example *American Canoeist, Forest and Stream*) in the winter months, with more details arriving in the form of circulars to canoeists' mailboxes in the springtime.

These circulars, which included information about travel, the cultural and natural histories and geographies of the site and its environs, campsite amenities, encampment life and the regatta programme and rules, were usually accompanied by maps and/or photographs, which familiarized the reader with their destination and began the process of 'knowing place'.

While the typical camper utilized multiple transportation technologies to arrive at the meet, most made the bulk of the journey by train and steamer, taking advantage of the growing transportation networks crisscrossing the Northeast. A smaller number travelled by canoe, camping along the way and visiting points of interest besides.[1] As Schivelbusch (1986) and Little (2009) have demonstrated, different technologies produce different experiences of both space and time. Some of the canoeists' accounts hint at the rapid succession of views typical of train travel, while others highlight the panoramic vistas and contact with the elements afforded by steamers, which were slower and more open than railcars. By contrast, in descriptions of travelling by canoe, contact with the elements is a defining feature, as is an emphasis on the embodied sense of distance and the labour required to complete the journey. Gender is equally important to understanding the experience of journeying to the ACA meets. Almost without exception women travelled with companions or, more typically, chaperones, reinforcing Richter's (2009) contention that even as women were becoming commonplace on public transportation in the late nineteenth century, anxieties remained about mixed-sex sociability, particularly in such close quarters.

As the majority of the encampments were located on islands or points of land only accessible by water, campers typically encountered the campsite from a steamer or canoe.[2] Once their baggage was unloaded, the canoeists were directed to the tent of the Secretary-Treasurer where they registered and received coloured badges, marked 'Member', 'Associate Member' or 'Visitor'. These made visible the differential status accorded to men/women and members/non-members. Gendered differences were reinforced as the canoeists retired to their respective campsites. Men wearing member badges were directed to the Main Camp, which was typically located close to the centre of site and the Headquarters. By contrast, women, after donning their associate member ribbons, were pointed towards the Ladies' Camp, which was usually at a distance from the Main Camp and Headqaurters in a 'quiet cove' or 'secluded grove'. The spatially removed

---

1   For those taking trains or steamers, the trip generally took one or two days depending on their point of origin and the location of the meet. Travelling by canoe significantly extended the time it took to arrive at the encampment, in some cases to a week or more.

2   Although accounts present the encampments as wild places, much work had been done to prepare the campsites for habitation. Brush was removed, paths were constructed and graded, temporary buildings were raised. The majority of this manual labour was performed not by the canoeists themselves, but by a workforce of local men, typically rural whites. Also present on site, however, were local women, African-Americans, French-Canadians and Aboriginal people who worked as cooks, domestic servants and vendors.

Ladies' Camp reflected women's second-class status in the ACA and anxieties about heterosexual sociability (*New York Times* 16 August 1887, 22 August 1887; *Daily Mail and Empire* 27 July 1900).[3] During the meet, strict rules and the camp police governed travel between the two camps.

Arrival at the encampment could be credibly compared to crossing a threshold as the attendees moved from the imagined community of canoeists into a tangible one (Turner 1995). This was at once a conceptual and embodied movement, as the campers stepped onto the wharf, unloaded their baggage, donned camp clothes and began the process of physically inhabiting the campsite. Tents were the most iconic expressions of habitation. Most years, local carpenters were hired by canoeists to construct platforms as a base for the heavy canvas tents otherwise supported by wooden poles, pegs and guy lines. Canoeists spent hours outfitting their tents. Shelves were built, rugs spread on the floor, strings of Chinese lanterns hung and flags raised. The time passed decorating reveals the importance attributed to these spaces. Equally telling is that fact that the tent flaps were almost universally open during the day revealing the contents to any and all who passed by.

Although tents likely reflected Victorian understandings of domestic space as 'material markers of civilization' and as windows onto 'the individual's soul and the family's moral state' (Raibmon 2003: 71), they might also be interpreted as manifestations of the complex relationship between movement and dwelling at the heart of modern tourist practices (Haldrup 2004, Pons 2003). Even as the canoeists ostensibly sought to escape from domestic and urban environments linked to home, they reproduced aspects of the same while at the encampments. This is also evident in the organization of the men's camp, which recalled a small village with individual canoe clubs serving as neighbourhoods. Some years, the inhabitants erected signposts naming the 'streets' that passed between the neighbourhoods. There were also elements of the domestic and home-making evident in the cooking arrangements. While some campers prepared their meals over an open fire or cookstove and consumed them upon a makeshift table, most ate in the camp mess where a cook provided board for one dollar per day. Although the quality of the food varied, locally-recruited wait staff served meals on china to campers seated at cloth-covered tables adorned with centrepieces.

The encampments as social and recreational spaces had a temporal rhythm. Each day began with a flag raising, meals were taken at regular intervals (typically 7.00 am, 12.00 pm and 6.00 pm), campsites were to be put in order by 10.00 am in time for the garbage cart and the day was closed with taps ringing through the campsite (10.00–11.30 pm), at which point the expectation was for camp-wide silence. Most campers used the 'free' time during the first week to explore the campsite and its environs by foot, canoe or steamer; others took the opportunity to prepare for the upcoming regatta, familiarizing themselves with the racecourses and/or taking part in exhibition races. Most evenings were passed by the campfire.

3　'Ladies' Camp' is a misnomer, as the site also housed families (including men and children of both sexes). Still, it was consistently represented as a feminine space.

These gatherings ranged from casual affairs with a handful of participants to camp-wide events featuring recitations, theatrical performances and singing. On Sundays, it was common practice to attend a Divine Service amongst the trees.

By contrast, a good part of the second week 'was given up to the serious business of racing' (*New York Times*, 26 August 1900). The boat races were a highlight of the annual meeting for members and visitors alike, at times drawing upwards of a thousand spectators from the surrounding area. Programmes featured between 15 and 30 events organized by skill and boat type. The races afforded different, mobile opportunities for the competitors to 'know' the campsite. These experiences were shaped by gender – women were first admitted to competition in 1890, although only a handful of contests classified as 'novelty' races were ever open to them – and race characteristics: the races varied in style (for example paddling, sailing, novelty), duration, course layout (for example triangle, straight line), physical length and canoe type (for example decked, open, war canoe). Spectators watched the contests with enthusiasm from shore and in boats. The end of the regatta was celebrated with a prize ceremony and banquet.

At this point, the annual encampment, for all intents and purposes, was finished. Although a few individuals stayed on site for another week or two, most left sooner in much the same way they had arrived. Many would return the following year, albeit to a different site, and those that did not would be replaced by new faces, inspired perhaps by the accounts of the encampment printed in *Forest and Stream* or the photograph album of a friend.

Day nine: Thelon River, Canada

It is mid-afternoon as our fleet of five tandem canoes glides cautiously towards our final campsite on the river left shoreline. Many times our guide has reminded us that the rocks lingering in the shallows will scuff his canoes if we approach the beach too quickly. Like thousands of strokes prior, these final gentle gestures with the paddle link river to hands, sun bronzed and bug bit, and to arms, shoulders and backs toughened by 270 km of self-propelled Arctic travel.

Our group of 10 – nine clients and one guide – have just canoed through the heart of the Thelon Wildlife Sanctuary, whose namesake, the Thelon River, is a main artery in the Hudson Bay watershed (Figure 11.2). As the Thelon stretches 900 km on its eastward path across the central Canadian sub-Arctic, it traverses boreal forest and tundra biomes, the homelands of the Akaitcho Dene and Caribou Inuit and the jurisdictions of the Northwest Territories (NWT) and Nunavut. The Sanctuary was originally established in 1927 by the Federal Canadian Government to conserve muskoxen and caribou stocks *from* over harvesting and *for* potential agricultural uses (Sandlos 2007). In the decades since, it has endured the devolution of responsibility to the NWT (1948), amended geographic boundaries (1956), changing mineral policies (1986) and the Territorial division (1999) that came with the implementation of the Nunavut Land Claims

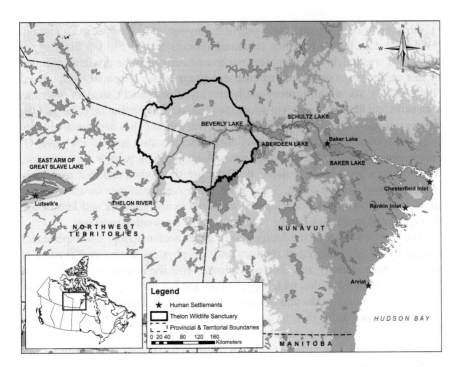

Figure 11.2   The Thelon River and Wildlife Sanctuary

Source: This map was created by Will Van Hemessen using shapefiles provided by GeoGratis, Natural Resources Canada (coastlines and protected areas at 1:7.5 million scale, digital elevation model at 1:250,000 scale) and the DMTI Data Consortium (major water bodies, rivers, populated places and provincial boundaries at 1:50,000 scale), June 2012.

Agreement (MacKinnon 1983, Pelly 1996). Today, the 56,000 km² protected area continues to be represented as one of North America's largest tracts of 'untouched wilderness', a sublime ecosystem in one of Canada's oldest nature preserves (see for example McCreadie 1995: 73–83).

Over the last nine days, our group has canoed the middle section of the Thelon, following the river trails sketched by early European visitors to the area: adventurers, government surveyors, trappers and Royal Canadian Mountain Police officers that advanced the colonization of these lands beginning in the early twentieth century. The first recreational canoeists arrived in 1962 (Pelly 1996), precursors to the commercial outfitting presence that emerged in the mid-1970s when our guide, Alex, established his business *Canoe Arctic* (Hall 2003). Contemporary travel along the Thelon includes roughly 100 independent or commercially guided canoeists annually, a number that reflects the remoteness of the watershed and the short summer season.

Arriving by car and plane, our group first convened at Alex's base in Fort Smith, NWT, two days before boarding chartered aircrafts for the 590 km flight to the 'put-in'. It was quickly apparent that our troupe embodied the privilege afforded by late capitalism, a privilege that enables certain modes of spatial consumption (Baker 2002). We are all professionally employed or retired Canadian urbanites with sufficient financial wealth to afford the necessary transportation costs, and the services of Alex who, in 35 years of Arctic river guiding, has accumulated more lived-experience within the Thelon Wildlife Sanctuary than anyone else alive. Of course, our group is far from homogeneous. Some joined as pairs or with a spouse, while others signed on as individuals. There are six women and four men; only two are below the age of 60. Some have extensive experience on other Arctic rivers, while others have developed specialized skills, attitudes and knowledge through canoe instruction courses, club outings or association meetings.

The first few days of the journey were spent acclimatizing, our experiences shaped by Alex's time-tested routines and the physical strains and rhythm of paddling. Now, activity and efficiency characterize the mornings. People crawl from their nylon tents, don paddling clothing and hooded bug jackets and begin to organize personal packs and dismantle tents. Gear is lugged from tent sites to the kitchen along paths that, in the short span of our use, become trampled and familiar. Such movements and the associated interactions with fellow canoeists make meaningful this space (Opp and Walsh 2010), and give shape to our temporary home.

The canoes are also integral to our mobile inhabitation. Loading equipment and food into canoes is meticulously regimented; gear packs are coded using coloured strips of duct tape and positioned to evenly distribute weight, while the emergency supplies are stationed close to Alex. Canoeists also perform their own individual system of emplacement within the vessels. We develop different ways to sit or recline comfortably, and find spots to store personal effects, such as pocketknives, journals, or bug repellent, for use throughout the day. Unworn life jackets and spare paddles rest behind each bow seat, while cameras are secured ready at the hip and wet socks are hung to dry on the canoe's frame. The habitual arrangements of bodies and materials (re)create the canoe as a place of residency within in this vast landscape.

Also habitual are the athletic movements of our paddling, which propel us between 20 and 40 km per day. As muscle memory sharpens, an acute sense of 'living in the moment' is inspired. We break only to inspect white water, panoramic views and heritage sites, or to stop for lunch at wind-exposed beaches (minimizing buggy encounters) at noon. When we cease paddling each day at 4.00 pm, I remain curious about the paths we have travelled. With Alex alert to our destinations, and the particularities of his expectations and routines, it is hard to consider ourselves *wayfarers*, advancing a new line as we press forward (Ingold 2007). Yet attached to the rhythm of canoeing is the feeling of *being here*; immersed in the moment, on the river, on the move. This observation suggests that our lines are not simply a matter of efficiency, but are also deepened with the desire to absorb, craft and participate in the stories that enliven this place (Ingold 2007).

When we beach at a campsite, Alex sets out to find ideal places for the kitchen and tents. Shoreline gravel bars are kitchen-ready with easy water access, few fire hazards and minimal sand, which is best avoided in food and gear. Only after the canoes are securely anchored on raised ground do we grab our tents and follow Alex's direction up the embankment to beds of tundra moss and grass. Here the wind is more pronounced and discourages the presence of black flies and mosquitoes, at least in theory. Individually or in pairs we look for flat ground to pitch our abodes, calling out occasionally to others when we locate, but pass up, a potentially suitable spot. The placement of tents is never haphazard. Rather, as one female canoeist observed, couples opt for more serene and private perches, such as those with an elevated view of the river, while novice campers tend to set their tents closer to Alex.

While the Thelon's current has determined the macro-trajectory of our journey, a medley of smaller excursions has amassed through purposeful and aimless wanderings on foot. Retracing his discoveries from seasons past, Alex has led various walks to unoccupied wolf dens, waterfalls, Dene chipping sites, Inuit tent rings and old caribou caches and fox traps. But time and space have also allowed for unguided exploration. For instance, as Alex prepares dinner, served each night at 7.00 pm sharp, we have a couple of hours to navigate eskers, hike to views of the river valley or amble along the river's edge. Such roaming occurs individually or in small groups and, upon return, invites the curiosity of others.

When the winds are particularly light, and our bodies assaulted by swarms of black flies and mosquitoes, we tend to abandon these walks for an unsteady bug tent large enough for 10 people to position themselves in relative insect-free comfort (Figure 11.3). More than a shelter or dining hall, the bug tent has been a place for our group to gather and converse, read, debate, laugh, share stories and reflect on daily events. The ways in which ecological features, objects and people interact to give rise to the space within the bug tent echo the 'spinning relations' that Haldrup (2004) suggests people enact when transforming an environment into a home.

Notwithstanding these positive interactions, by day nine, the general mood of our group has become tainted with disappointment. Only two wolves have been caught with the camera, while a lone moose and solitary caribou have been spotted through binoculars. One of the things pulling canoeists northward is the promise of encountering the 'big five' – wolf, caribou, grizzly bear, muskoxen and moose – in the wild. While Alex tried to temper such expectations in his pre-trip information package, his recurrent stories of past encounters encourage our desires.

We have arrived at our final campsite, which like the locations of all our encampments, is marked on Alex's maps and in his memory. Just as we finish unloading the canoes for the last time, a herd of 22 muskoxen is spotted on the opposite shoreline. Exclamations of surprise are quickly muffled so as not to risk spooking our bovid neighbours. The shift in mood is palpable. Faces radiate awe and delight. Bodies move to locate cameras and binoculars and to assume positions along the shoreline for unobstructed, or rather *unpeopled*, lines of sight (Figure 11.4). Shutters snap to secure the moment with the kinds of photographs anticipated but thus far elusive. Once the muskoxen crest the ridge, we load

Figure 11.3   More than a bug tent?

Source: Bryan Grimwood.

Figure 11.4 Photographing muskoxen

Source: Bryan Grimwood.

our enthusiasm into the canoes and silently cross the river. On shore, emulating Alex's slow gait and hunched body, we pursue ever-closer observation and higher-resolution documentation until the muskoxen lose patience and scamper away into the open terrain.

When we return to our campsite, we realize that this encounter, which lasted a couple of hours, has interrupted the flow of our evening routines. Dinner will be served late and tents set up amid thickening clouds of insects. But clearly this is secondary to the magic of the event that just transpired. Over the next two days, I suspect that our meeting with the muskoxen will be recounted and relived as we prepare to depart. Presumably, the memories and images of this encounter will also travel with us as we return south.

Intersections and divergences

During our first reading of these two case studies, we noticed a handful of seemingly important intersections. While both examples described touristic experiences in 'natural' landscapes, we were struck by the prevalence of home and/or the domestic. Recognizing 'home' as a concept embedded in a matrix of multiple meanings and performances (Blunt and Dowling 2006), we observed its imprint in the daily routines of the canoeists, the camps they constructed, the material objects that travelled with them and their efforts to document their experiences for later consumption. Through these relations, canoescapes become inhabited as cultured and social spaces. Conventional discourses perpetuate the apparent truism that tourism entails an escape from the rituals and materialities of everyday life. However, even as travel 'promises to leave culture behind, it never does' (Braun 2002: 131). Moreover, these experiences did not remain tethered to those touristic landscapes, but made the return journey 'home' with the canoeists. In some cases, they were marked on the body: a sunburn, augmented muscles or bug bites; in others, they were represented in a totem of the event: a winning ribbon or a rock from the campsite; still, in others, they were captured in photographs, journals or letters/emails. These observations reverberate with suggestions that tourism is not an *extra*-ordinary experience, but rather a complex of embodied, practiced and everyday relations (Franklin and Crang 2001, Larsen 2008).

Imagining/representing

Habitation *in place* began long before the canoeists arrived at their destination through acts of imagining. In both examples, the organizers or guide produced and dispatched information about the upcoming experience to their charges. Although Alex had access to electronic mail, he often issued such correspondence by post, much as the ACA organizers had done more than a century earlier. Even as these 'circulars' were a window into/onto the experience, they also mapped out acceptable practices within the canoescape through the inclusion of rules and descriptions of camp life. Such disciplining was mediated by the fact that the canoeists accessed/received information about their destinations in other ways as well: by corresponding with friends and relatives, reading books and periodical accounts of similar experiences and, in the case of the Thelon trip, surfing the Internet.

In both cases, the landscapes being visited loomed large in the imagination of canoeing cultures; the Thelon in the present day and the ACA destinations in the late nineteenth century – the Adirondacks, Muskoka, the Hudson River – are/were iconic destinations, amply documented in text and image and thus easily accessible in a representational sense to potential visitors. These representations were/are not benign (Chatelard 2005); canoeists pursued them by travelling to these varied locales, they reproduced them in photographic and narrative accounts and, later, they shared them with others in letters/emails, personal albums, periodicals and conversations. The documentary practices of the canoeists form part of a 'circle of representation', the 'circular process by which particular tourist images are produced, projected, perceived, propagated and perpetuated' (Jenkins 2003: 324). Like Jenkin's (2003) example of backpacking culture, the canoeists were/ are not just consumers of such representations, but were/are active participants in the entwined processes of production and reproduction. In both instances, these practices of cultural production and reproduction were/are intimately tied to the (re)production of colonial power relations, including the erasure of indigenous presence on and title to the land.

Making lines

In addition to being constructed imaginatively, these canoescapes were constituted through myriad forms of movement that were afforded and framed by different technologies of mobility. The ACA encampments and the Thelon River trip were made possible by 'epochal' (Macnaghten and Urry 1998) or 'hegemonic' (Vannini 2009) technologies, such as the train, airplane and automobile, and are thus enmeshed in the (hi)stories of capitalism and colonialism. Yet our concern in this section is to emphasize the overlapping micro-journeys that took place in and produced these canoescapes, but which were not necessarily limited to movement in a canoe. These micro-journeys included: movement within and between the spaces of the campsite, curtailed travel outwards from these sites (for example an after-dinner walk along the shoreline) and local excursions. We might imagine these various scales of movement layered on top of one another, such that the canoescape is not a 'continuous surface' to be traversed, but rather a 'mesh of interweaving lines' each representing the paths forged and followed (Ingold 2007: 75). That such journeys often engaged the spaces of the tent, mess hall, kitchen, and others, reinforced the domestication of the canoescapes.

Much of this movement was undertaken informally, inspired by necessity and/or desire. We think here of solitary after-dinner rambles through the tundra or paddling around the point to attend an evening campfire. However, both case studies also include more formal excursions arranged and/or led by the organizing committee or guide. Canoeists on the Thelon trip, for example, followed Alex on tramps to animal dens and archaeological sites, while ACA members visited local natural and cultural landmarks, such as Fort Ticonderoga on Lake Champlain and Bala Falls in Muskoka, by canoe or steamer. Although both forms of movement were central to the knowing and making of place, informal micro-journeys permitted, or better yet required an 'active engagement with the country' that emplaced the canoeist in a different way (Ingold 2007: 76).

Constructing camp

As much as the canoescapes described in these case studies were spaces of movement, they were also spaces that afforded material expressions of dwelling: the campers erected tents for sleeping and others for eating; they identified or built a kitchen area; they demarcated locations for washrooms. They did so, however, on different scales. Whereas an ACA encampment might accommodate a few hundred campers and, thus, was aptly described as a 'tent village', the campsites on the Thelon trip featured seven tents housing ten individuals. Moreover, the relative permanency of the ACA encampments – in place for at least two weeks – stands in marked contrast to the daily practices of deconstructing and reconstructing the Thelon River campsites[4]. Nevertheless, both approaches engendered the familiarity necessary to facilitate inhabiting. Not only were the material elements of the Thelon sites the same, but there also was a ritual quality to choosing and constructing the camps. That a participant could identify patterns in the geography of the tent locations underscores this point. A similar observation could be made of the ACA encampments although on a larger scale, for even as the location of the annual meeting changed on a yearly basis, the campsites boasted familiar faces and locales, such as the Headquarters and Ladies' Camp.

   As we alluded above, the quotidian processes of constructing camp were spatial and temporal. Both examples were characterized by strict schedules, yet another way in which the meanings and practices of everyday life migrated into the 'site experience'. As the canoeists in both examples performed their daily routines, which involved moving from tent to shoreline to mess tent to headquarters or from canoe to shoreline to tent to kitchen, they produced/inhabited the spaces of the campsites. In other words, constructing camp was not limited to the raising of tents, but was an ongoing process that involved ways of thinking, relating and being in *time* and *space*.

   To be sure, camp life in both examples was ordered by particular configurations of power. On the one hand, it was underpinned and enabled by the labour of others, albeit in markedly different ways. On the Thelon, it was the guide's work

---

   4   To an extent, changing technologies enable such impermanency. The nylon tents carried by the Thelon canoeists provided an ease of movement not possible with the large canvas wall tents used by the ACA campers.

of preparing meals that provided the free time employed to know place, while the lifestyle of the ACA campers was made possible by the efforts of complex groups of marginalized people that included rural whites (many of whom were women), African Americans and French Canadians. At the same time, the practices of camp life were also shaped by the power/knowledge practices of those in positions of authority, namely the ACA organizing committee and the guide, but also more distant forms of authority, such as legislation governing the use of park reserves and border crossing.

Conclusion

Larsen (2008) reminds us that the experience of tourism is not confined to the exotic site experience, but rather is deeply embedded in the practices of everyday life. The canoescapes described herein extended into the participants' daily lives in multiple ways, through circulars, conversations, books, photographs and souvenirs. Similarly, home was not a discrete entity that remained in the south or the city, but was an experience that canoeists mobilized in the form of objects (including canoes), altered bodies, routines, practices and ideas. Such interpolations of home and away are not transhistorical. Rather, as we have tried to demonstrate by situating the annual encampments of the ACA alongside the Thelon River trip, they are contextual, reflecting both time and place. This observation is likely to resonate with other lifestyle mobilities, which are also products of particular moments and locations. Furthermore, as our discussion of intersections and divergences makes clear, the mobile habitations of canoescapes are profoundly social, inflected with the power dynamics and routines that mark everyday life. This is suggestive of the value of studying leisure and tourism from the perspective of lifestyle mobilities. In particular, it opens up analytically rich and dynamic terrain for improving our understanding of movement and practice as social phenomena, and specifically the ways in which such experiences are constituted by and are constitutive of power. Finally, as much as this chapter is about a particular kind of lifestyle mobility, it is also about the challenges and rewards of interdisciplinary scholarship. In reaching across time, space and disciplines, this chapter offers an approach to scholarship that the mobilities literature has called for, scholarship that invites knowledge synthesis and mobilization to better understand human pasts, presents and futures.

References

Baker, J. 2002. Production and consumption of wilderness in Algonquin Park. *Space and Culture*, 5(3), 198–210.
Benjamin, W. 1973. *Charles Baudelaire: A Lyric Poet in the Era of High Capitalism*. London: Verso.

Blunt, A. and Dowling, R. 2006. *Home*. New York: Routledge.

Braun, B. 2002. *The Intemperate Rainforest: Nature, Culture and Power on Canada's West Coast*. Minneapolis: University of Minnesota Press.

de Certeau, M. 1984. *The Practice of Everyday Life*. Berkeley: University of California Press.

Chatelard, G. 2005. Tourism and representations: of social change and power relations in Wadi Ramm, South Jordan, in *Représentation et Construction de la Réalité Sociale et Politique. Palestine, Jordanie, 1948–2000*, edited by S. Latte-Abdallah. Beyrouth: IFPO, 194–251.

Franklin, A. and Crang, M. 2001. The trouble with tourism and travel theory. *Tourist Studies*, 1(1), 5–22.

Haldrup, M. 2004. Laid-back mobilities: second home holidays in time and space. *Tourism Geographies*, 6(4), 434–454.

Hall, A.M. 2003. *Discovering Eden: A Lifetime of Paddling Arctic Rivers*. Toronto: Key Porter Books.

Ingold, T. 2000. *The Perception of the Environment: Essays in Livelihood, Dwelling and Skill*. London: Routledge.

Ingold, T. 2007. *Lines: A Short History*. London: Routledge.

Jasen, P. 1995. *Wild Things: Nature, Culture and Tourism in Ontario, 1790–1914*. Toronto: University of Toronto Press.

Jenkins, O. 2003. Photography and travel brochures: the circle of representation. *Tourism Geographies*, 5(3), 305–328.

Larsen, J. 2008. De-exoticizing tourist travel: everyday life and sociality on the move. *Leisure Studies*, 27(1), 21–34.

Lefebvre, H. 1991. *The Production of Space*. Oxford: Blackwell.

Little, J.I. 2009. Scenic tourism on the northeastern borderland: Lake Memphremagog's steamboat excursions and resort hotels, 1850–1900. *Journal of Historical Geography*, 35(4), 716–742.

MacCannell, D. 1976. *The Tourist: A New Theory of the Leisure Class*. Berkeley: University of California Press.

McCreadie, M. 1995. *Canoeing Canada's Northwest Territories: A Paddler's Guide*. Hyde Park: Canadian Recreational Canoeing Association.

MacKinnon, C.S. 1983. A history of the Thelon Game Sanctuary. *Musk-Ox*, 32, 44–61.

Macnaghten, P. and Urry, J. 1998. *Contested Natures*. London: Routledge.

Merleau-Ponty, M. 1962. *Phenomenology of Perception*. London: Routledge.

Opp, J. and Walsh, J.C. 2010. Local acts of placing and remembering, in *Placing Memory and Remembering Place in Canada*, edited by J. Opp and J.C. Walsh. Vancouver: University of British Columbia Press, 2–21.

Pelly, D. 1996. *Thelon: A River Sanctuary*. Hyde Park: Canadian Recreational Canoeing Association.

Pons, P.O. 2003. Being-on-holiday: tourist dwelling, bodies and place. *Tourist Studies*, 3(1), 47–66.

Raibmon, P. 2003. Living on display: colonial visions of Aboriginal domestic space. *BC Studies*, 140, 69–89.

Richter, A. 2005. *Home on the Rails: Women, the Railroad, and the Rise of Public Domesticity.* Chapel Hill: University of North Carolina Press.

Sandlos, J. 2007. *Hunters at the Margin: Native People and Wildlife Conservation in the Northwest Territories.* Vancouver: University of British Columbia Press.

Schivelbusch, W. 1986. *The Railway Journey: The Industrialization of Time and Space in the Nineteenth Century.* Berkeley: University of California Press.

Turner, V. 1995. *The Ritual Process.* Piscataway: Aldine Transaction.

Urry, J. 1990. *The Tourist Gaze: Leisure and Travel in Contemporary Societies.* London: Sage.

Vannini, P. 2009. *The Cultures of Alternative Mobilities: Routes Less Travelled.* Burlington: Ashgate.

Chapter 12

From Citizens to Wanderers of the World: The Noguchi Case as a Timely Study on Cosmopolitanism

Elia Ntaousani

Introduction

In 2010, according to the World Migration Report, around 214 million migrants were spread worldwide, far more than ever previously recorded (Swing 2010: xix). Although the overall number had increased by nearly 65 million since the year 2000, the refugee population significantly decreased between 2006 and 2008 (15.2 million at the end of 2008, according to International Organization for Migration (IOM 2010: 119, 120, 266), whereas those in an irregular or illegal situation were estimated to constitute some 10–15 per cent of the world's migratory people. Even after counting in the over 36 million persons that were displaced or evacuated due to sudden-onset natural disasters in 2008, it is still clear that more than half of today's migrants have not become foreigners by force of events and circumstances. However, the most striking finding to retain here does not concern the rapidly growing number of people who migrate by choice or inadvertently every year; for, despite the indisputably crescent mobility of international students, chance seekers, professional nomads and medical-health expatriates, a certain tribute has to be paid to the reality that the overwhelming majority of the world's population (upward of 98 per cent) remains immobile (Kelo and Wächter 2004: 20).

What seems to have changed worldwide with the advent of the twenty-first century is instead the state of foreignness as lifestyle. For the first time in history and across much of the world, as an article in *The Economist* points out, to be foreign is a perfectly normal condition:

> The dilemma of foreignness comes down to one of liberty versus fraternity – the pleasures of freedom versus the pleasures of belonging. The homebody chooses the pleasures of belonging. The foreigner chooses the pleasures of freedom, and the pains that go with them (The Economist 2009).

As a matter of fact, a closer look to the IOM's report shall clearly demonstrate that the terms 'migrant', 'international' and 'foreign' are often used as synonyms. Such a convergence of meanings, once very distinctive and even contradictory from each other, testifies to the immense impact that the following parameters have on the features and the understanding of so-called 'cultural identity': a) globalization of goods and services, b) formation of transnational, economical or political entities, and c) the blooming of augmented reality.

With these factors in consideration, the chapter aims to explore the variables of contemporary cosmopolitanism in the current state of globalized, increasingly interpenetrating and highly technological societies, while rooting them not only in displacement but also – and mainly – in journeying. By putting an emphasis on the 'Living and Leaving' lifestyle, rather than on the discourse of 'Longing and Belonging'– a binary of incorporation and rejection, under which Home (*Heim* in German) gets fully naturalized as synonym of fixation or homogeneity and strangeness is *a priori* equated to confinement – I hope to further illuminate the figures of the Traveller, the World Citizen and the Tourist, as well as their cross fertilization, for the purposes of revisiting the categories of both the Self and the Other as '*future* memory' of the Uncanny (das *Unheimliche*).[1]

Isamu Noguchi: on place, home, identity and the self

'I find myself a wanderer in a world rapidly growing smaller' – this striking phrase was written with black letters on the dazzlingly white wall that the visitor had to face when climbing up the stairs of the Museum of Contemporary Art on Andros island, Greece, at the major exhibition dedicated to the work of *Isamu Noguchi: Between East and West* in 2010 (27/06–26/09/2010). Although already dead by the time the Oxford graduate Tim Berners-Lee invented the World Wide Web (1989) as well as by the year the first mobile text message (SMS) was sent over the Vodafone GSM network in the United Kingdom (1992), the influential Japanese-American artist and landscape architect has been aptly termed as 'world citizen'. Yet, neither his extensive travelling across Europe, Asia and South America nor his international reputation alone would have ever been enough to confirm his cosmopolitan characteristics, had he not been shaping throughout his life a largely multicultural identity by unceasingly crossing the borders between East and West, both corporeally and artistically.

---

1   I call here upon the Freudian concept of the Uncanny due to its ambivalence and interchangeability. While being clearly the opposite of *heimlich, heimisch, vertraut* (homely, domestic, familiar), precisely because it is unknown and unfamiliar, 'the unhomely' (das *Unheimliche*) is in some way, according to the father of psychoanalysis, 'a species of the familiar (das *Heimliche*, the homely)' as well. By sharing the same etymological root with *Geheim* (secret, hidden, concealed), das *Heimliche* (the homely) acquires the extra connotation of 'mysterious' and appears therefore as the Uncanny (das *Unheimliche*) that lingers in the core of the familiar (das *Heimliche*) – and vice versa: 'the term "uncanny" (unheimlich) applies to everything that was intended to remain secret, hidden away, and has come into open' (Freud, S. 2003: 129, 132, 134).

Isamu Noguchi (1904–1988) was born in Los Angeles as the illegitimate son of a Japanese poet father. After having spent a troubled childhood in Japan with his American mother, an adventurous youth in New York and Paris, one difficult year of reconnection with his Japanese roots (and of rejected reconciliation with his father) in his late twenties and a life of continuous oscillation among those three poles ever since, Isamu began his autobiographical memoir *A Sculptor's World* in 1968 with the following words:

> Things which are so far back are not like a part of myself, more like the life of somebody else, and should be written by another. To me it all seemed like chance; choice, if any, came much later. How I came to make decisions, I do not know. Perhaps choice, too, is chance, like the rolling of dice. With my double personality and double upbringing, where was my home? Where are my affections? Where my identity? Japan or America, either, both – or the world? (Noguchi 1968: 11).

One might think that Noguchi was blessed with wandering the globe carelessly and free as a bird – especially after having received the John Simon Guggenheim Fellowship at an early stage of his career, thanks to which he was able to spend several months in Paris as Brancusi's apprentice and then another year in the Far East, or later, after having been awarded the Bollingen Fellowship to travel around the world and study public space at the age of 44. Although, according to his chronological records (Kammen 2009: 419), he was given the indeed remarkable opportunity to explore the cultures of China, India, Nepal, Hawaii, Mexico, Jerusalem and Europe (Greece and Rome in particular), one can still read between the introductory lines of his memoir (cited above) the struggle of a bicultural man with a mixed racial background, if not to overcome his fatally ambiguous ancestry and transcend the boundaries of ethnicity at a personal level, at least to sense what it means to belong to a certain country or a nation at all.

His agony of self-awareness focuses equally on the absence of a seamless identity as well as on the tight bond between chance and personal agency, between the characteristics of a place and the formation of a personality. The older Noguchi affirms distantness from or even rupture with his younger modes of existence, thus insinuating that the Self is not to be perceived as an accumulation of personas in prosthetic vascular grafts nor does it constitute their performative interaction in Butlerian terms:[2] more likely, identity refers to a contingent structure, an alternation of layers almost arbitrarily superimposed one on the top of the other,

---

2 According to Judith Butler, there is no pre-existent 'I' and therefore identity is to be seen neither as an attribute that someone *has* nor as a noun that acts on one's behalf but rather as a *doing* itself. The theory of performativity envisions identity as a 'cultural intelligibility of agency within the frame of a constituted social temporality (Butler 1999: 179); one that renders the self culturally "coherent" through a regulated process of stylized repetition of acts and practices inscribed on the surface of the body' (Ntaousani 2010: 11).

through which the latest 'version of' Noguchi is but to be better apprehended. In brief, although both genealogy and the socio-cultural surroundings may illuminate the present self, neither do they predetermine it under the scheme 'cause-effect' nor presume any evolutionary process of construction – whether that refers to a linear order of succession or to some performative shaping through repetition. After all, as Hugh Aldersey-Williams (2009: 15) points out,

> the search for roots implies a narrowing of focus to a single origin, but the roots of a tree themselves branch of course ... . Soon, it is clear that no one story is your true past, nor are you in any meaningful sense the sum of the stories of your ancestors.

More than to identify the polymorphic jigsaw of his ancestral influences, what matters for Noguchi is to build his own jenga tower of personalities, a story that suits him, out of fragmentary opportunities and contingent circumstances. The setting and deconstruction of selves is therefore an act and a never-ending story: Noguchi settles into one 'character' but he does not have to keep it firm until the end – as soon as the geographical, social or cultural scenery changes, he instantly jumps into another. For, according to his vision, identity is not shaped by the individual in isolation, but only composed in response to its spatiotemporal frame. 'He believed that environment affects peoples lives', as Shoji Shadao testifies (Barlow Rogers 2005: 6); and conversely, it is likely that his own 'memories of childhood, of things observed not taught, of closeness to the earth, of wet stones and grass' (Ashton 1992: 169) on one hand, as well as his ongoing experience of not fitting in any single social context, of constantly straddling two cultures, on the other, strongly urged the artist's desire to influence in his turn people's surroundings. That may in fact well be the reason why Noguchi chose to design children's playgrounds, 'the Akari lamps [a still-popular line of lanternlike lighting] and furniture, even though other people thought this was a trivial pursuit and misuse of an important artist's talent' (Barlow Rogers 2005: 6).

Art historians also agree that Noguchi was misunderstood or undervalued, as Dore Ashton and Caroline Tiger affirm in their respective books on the prominent Japanese-American artist (Ashton 1992: 279, Tiger 2007), mainly because he did not represent a single art movement nor did he embody the same personal style throughout his career. A critic once wrote, 'it is as if there are too many Noguchis to hold in the mind' (quoted in Tiger 2007: 98) – probably too many for an era of two World Wars, of national pride and border rigidity, where not to belong to a clear cultural framework or at least to some identifiable group would signify at once lack of security, troubled sociability and a pathologically unstable character.

And yet, this very claim of multiplicity did not contradict the integrity of an otherwise coherent identity. On the contrary, it even reflected both a highly comprehensive artist and 'a cosmopolitan figure whose stage was the world' (Duus 2004: 7), all by underlining the (easiness of) formation of plural selves depending on the whatsoever environments, experiences or influences – and hence, (the easiness of) their alternation. The most fascinating aspect of Noguchi's story is, for us, precisely this vision of identity as a multifarious series of personas that go live for awhile, either shine alone or overlap, and then burn out like candles in the darkness, as if of somebody else's memories; his vision of affections as identity, the imaginary of home as such – yet not the envisioning of ancestral origins as home.

On fluid identities: hybridism, multiplicity, and 'emptiness'

There is no such thing as continuity of a single *dramatis persona* for Noguchi but only fragments of a hybrid *spacetime-occupant* that are exhibited in alternation on one human body; where the body is also not to be seen as a pre-defined locus of agency, but as a permeable surface always already in interrelation with time and space – let the latter be physical, cultural, social or other. I rely here on Latour's and Dant's notion of the 'hybrid' as a collaboration or offspring of two species usually unable to further reproduce (Dant 2004: 62, see also Latour 1996) – a term used by both biology and actor-network theory to refer to entities that result either from cross-breeding or from permanently combining two 'components', respectively.

On one side, just like Dant's car-driver, the *spacetime-occupant* might be more of an assemblage and less of a hybrid in the sense that the whole comes apart when the person leaves its surroundings, while it can get endlessly reformed or re-assembled given the availability of people and environments. On the other, John Urry underlines the interdependency between these components by insisting on a 'hybrid' concept, according to which the 'driver-car' is 'neither the car nor the driver but the specific hybrid or intermittently moving combination of the two' (Urry 2007: 35). In any case, Noguchi perceives and incarnates identity as an embodied relationship between the intrinsic essence of a human being and its corporeal surroundings at a specific moment – or else 'our identity resides in the person most like "us" a moment ago or a step away' (Aldersey-Williams 2009: 14).

Interestingly enough, the world famous artist seems to have been exemplifying for more than half a century the so-called 'closest continuer theory', long before the latter has had the chance to explicitly develop. It is indeed only in 1981, seven years before Noguchi's death, that Robert Nozick publishes his ethical and epistemological treatise *Philosophical Explanations*. In this book, when dealing with the metaphysics of the self and with the question 'how, given changes, *can* there be identity of something from one time to another, and in what does this identity consist', Nozick (1981: 29, italics in the original) realizes that the closest-continuer schema does not focus exclusively on *personal* identity but rather on a generic framework of identity over time, from which the former can hardly get isolated.

Despite reflexive awareness being recognized as a main feature of the self,[3] there is no precedent 'I'; rather the 'I' is synthesized around an early act of reflexive self-referring, a delineation of an entity that happens without the doer coming first to existence – 'an entity coagulates' (Nozick 1981: 88). To my understanding therefore, personal identity occurs as an untiring process of self-grip synchronization, or else of magnetic conjunction, during which the 'I' is at every single moment identical with the self, even if the latter identifies with different *personas* each time – or, anyway, relatively often.

'Things which are so far back are not like a part of myself, more like the life of somebody else, and should be written by another' – I revisit Noguchi's earlier words in order to circle and further stimulate this analysis. 'With my double personality and double upbringing, where was my home? Where are my affections? Where my identity?' The metaphysical and spatial correlation insinuated here is central in *Philosophical Explanations* as well, for Nozick does not embed personal identity in the generic frame of a solely temporal co-incidence: by envisioning the 'I' as a place-holder, the 'closest continuer' model equally provides us with a discourse apt to discuss identity and proximity – that is, to envision the self's conceptualization of oneself as one's own selection, weighting and specification of dimensions within space.[4]

When Noguchi confesses an unbreakable bond between home and identity, however, I am not sure whether he implies that every new self (or better, new version of the self) fills in the same or multiple metaphysical containers, each time that a *dramatis persona* leaves 'home' – previously held by another 'tenant'. On the one hand, if we take the *personas* not as mere representations but as actual incarnations of the self (as separate selves indeed), then we rather presume that they are hooked up to their own space-time, have their own agency and form their own notion of home. Except that in such a model of over-identification, where the selves are identical with themselves in the sense that the *spacetime-occupants* coincide seamlessly – and not approximately – with their *place-holders* (and thereafter with the multiple 'I'), there is no room for 'closest continuity': more likely, identity gets treated as a complete and self-contained existence, losing thus its capacity to interact.

On the other hand, to uphold that the 'I' as a single, ever-changing but conceptually 'empty' container tends to coincide with a different each time hybrid *spacetime-occupant* is to somehow risk regressing to the concept of identity as an act – even if ongoing and responsive – that derives from a pre-existent doer.

---

3   As Nozick (1981: 78) says, 'To be an I, a self, is to have the capacity for reflexive self-reference. Something X which could refer, even to X, but not reflexively, is not an I, not a self'.

4   '... I synthesize myself by specifying, for me, dimensions and metric within a closest-continuer schema, and also view myself as filling in a place-holder and reflexively specifying my own identity over time by specifying the metric in the dimensional space ...' (Nozick 1981: 108).

Emptiness as a descriptor of human identity is, nevertheless, not to be taken here as an absence; 'it is the opposite of the [colonist's] concept of identity as a fullness of presence *ab initio* (from the start)' (Pimomo 2011: 4–5).

By contrasting the contingency of being in Buddhism to the Christian manifestation of God's fullness through self-assertive examples in the Old and New Testament (*εγώ ειμί ο ων*, 'I am that I am' or 'I am he (sic) who exists', The Bible, Exodus 3:14), Paulus Pimomo aims in fact to promote 'emptiness' as the quintessence of interdependence. In something of a similar vein, Petra Munro-Hendry refers to the Dalai Lama in order to contest the world as 'an enduring intrinsic "reality" (the story of history)' and to underpin instead identity as a dynamic process of relationships (Munro-Hendry 2011: 209); for, according to the 'emptiness' approach, 'things and events [are "empty" in that they] do not possess any immutable essence ... or absolute being that affords independence' (Dalai Lama 2005: 47).

Returning now to Isamu Noguchi, one may wonder which the appropriate conceptual tools are for clarifying whether his case follows the 'multiple' or the 'empty' paradigm. In other words, and since the *personas* alternate, how are we going to find out if his fluid identity is experienced as a dynamic process of self-awareness under the form of a conceptually 'empty' place-holder or rather abided with a space-time that changes in conjunction with the multiple selves? And in what does the role of home consist within this scheme anyway?

On home: border concept, corporeal aesthesis and matter of essence

Although the link between the formation of a personality and its surroundings at a specific time plays a central role in Noguchi's life narrative, the spatiotemporal co-incidence described in the 'closest continuer theory' is not sufficient as a pattern *per se* to correlate the 'I' with the alternating selves. 'With my double personality and double upbringing, where was my home? Where are my affections? Where my identity?': the words of the Japanese-American artist echo once more in my mind. By introducing affections as a third and vital factor of unpredictability in the game, Noguchi deeply unsettles the neat framework that was meant to explain the contingency of being as a rationalized process of interaction.

Not only is personal identity bound up with the notion of home and with the generic structure of identity over time, but a double relationship of affections with both home and identity is also at stake. And yet, it is doubtful that Noguchi shared the view of the Norwegian composer Håkon Aanesen (2002: 38), according to whom 'home is one's experiences' – a 'timeroom' of remembrance, where one can always travel as a homecomer. For in a quite similar way to how identity does not sum up to a series of personas, home does not consist in a mere accumulation of affections throughout Noguchi's life either; it is more likely 'a sort of state of mind where you feel most yourself', as Adnan Yıldız (2008: 172) insightfully points out. Except that, unlike identity which deals with the 'I' as with an 'empty' metaphysical container not affording independence, home denies to stand for an intellectual term that awaits to get filled with a geographical meaning. Home as a corporeal aesthesis is rather 'carrying yourself, your existence and your story with all of your inevitable (de)attachments and reflections to create another possibility of your life – [precisely] a form of independence' (Yıldız 2008: 172).

So while identity is taking us to the world, teaching us how to be interconnected and helping us to negotiate with each other, home wraps us up in our personal bundle,[5] cherishes our free will and brings us in dialogue with ourselves. If identity is a tool to open up, then home seems to encapsulate an inward movement towards an *embodied-embedded cognition*.[6] It is important to note at this point that such a slippage of the 'home' concept from an outer category to an inner topology, so to speak, does not obscure the degree of one's responsiveness to its surroundings at a specific time. On the contrary, while embodiment emphasizes the role of the body's internal milieu, embeddedness does not just refer to the interaction between the body and the world as a mutual or balanced exchange but rather indicates how firmly enclosed the human being is within its very environment – if not how fatal the influence of the latter can become in terms of the cognitive process of being 'at home'. We envision, in brief, the embodied-embedded cognition as interplay among home (that is where we feel mostly ourselves), body and the world.

At the same time, however, and because of identity focusing on the Other[7] or of home being conceptually Self-centred, identification seems to designate a dynamic process of contextualization – and therefore, of a socio-cultural, ethical and political confinement – whereas homecoming, homeleaving and homemaking are all but variations of the same repetitive ritual encouraging seclusion (through cocooning) as a form of deliberation from any social contract. This is precisely why Noguchi thinks that, for someone with a background like his own, only in art would it have ever been possible to find any identity at all. In an interview conducted by Paul Cummings during the '70s, the artist explains:

> Well, after all, it is only in art that a person who does not belong with any social contact, you see, could find a viewpoint on life which is free of social contacts. One can be an artist and alone, for example. An artist's life is really a lonely life. It is only when he is lonely that he can really produce. If he is not lonely, he may

---

5   Reference to a quotation that is commonly attributed to Harry Emerson Fosdick (1943), although both John Ruskin and Benjamin Franklin seem to have had formulated similar aphorisms: 'a man wrapped up in himself, he makes a very small package'.

6   Term borrowed from cognitive neuroscience to express a philosophical position related to brain-behaviour relationship, neurophenomenology, situated cognition and dynamical systems theory. See van Dijk et al. 2008: 297–316.

7   The Other here is not used in contradistinction to the Self within a binary – of similarity and difference, inclusion and exclusion. Rather the term is meant to encompass everyone around us, to indicate the Neighbourly Other as the person next (and not opposite) to us – a tribute to the closest continuity scheme.

be a social, nice, person, but you know, he might not be driven to it. After all, in a sense you're driven to art out of desperation. People are naturally lazy; they don't do things unless they are driven to it (*Oral history interview with Noguchi* 1973).

The double lifestyle of desperation, at once monastic and mobile, is thus selected by the artist to reflect, replace and transform not only his melancholy of seclusion, experienced firstly in Japan (biracial background as source of discrimination) and later in America (xenophobia when US joins World War II after the Japanese attack on Pearl Harbour), but also his 'sense of modern humanity's fundamental loneliness, its loss of shared systems of religious belief and communal ritual' (Barlow Rogers 2005: 5). In a way, this pain of being alone within a world full of all sorts of people serves as the (same) *place-holder* that Noguchi views himself to fill in, no matter how many *personas* he may have had to change according to his surroundings and no matter how many forms this very pain has taken throughout his life.

When reflexively specifying his own identity over time, Noguchi realizes that his 'homely feeling' sums up the discomfort of not being able to share the same ancestral heritage and life history with anybody else. In this sense, despite the incontestably spatial dimension implicated in the concepts of home and identity, there is no need for choosing among Japan, the States, both or the world. Home is a matter of essence, his affections, a certain awareness of himself as his own specification of dimensions within space. 'Home is where *you* are', with Lise Gundersen putting an emphasis on the *you* when she speaks about leaving and travelling as a form of belonging and staying: 'Home is the moment you are in' (2008: 27).

The Noguchi Case: from Cosmo-Polites to Kul-Tourist

The fact that, since his death, people have shown a growing understanding of Noguchi in hindsight has probably less to do with the artist's multifariousness itself – namely with his working in a broad range of media (sculpture, landscape architecture, furniture, utility objects) or with his experimenting on different methods, materials and styles (even though it does matter that this diversity did not occur in a chronologically linear way of evolution in the course of his lifetime) – and more with a new reality arising; one in which the once exceptional *Noguchi Case* would now come if not to exemplify, at least to serve as the exemplary citizen of the twenty-first-century world of lifestyle mobilities. For, while in the late nineteenth century walkers were increasingly pitied and travellers were even thought 'to be suffering from a new mental illness, identified as "fugue" or the compulsion to walk and to travel', as John Urry (2007: 82) observes in his *Mobilities*, 'by the twentieth century it is those without the desire to travel who came to be pathologized and treated as lacking sufficient mobile desires'.

Noguchi was actually born somewhere in between, and more particularly within the same decade that the airplane was invented. According to the architect and philosopher who wrote the introduction to the artist's autobiography, Noguchi 'took off' at the age of two or rather was 'taken off by his Japanese-bound mother in what has since proved to be a half century of world peregrinations' (Fuller 1968: 7). Fuller was intuitive enough to pass him on to the next generations as a figure with no peer in his time: 'As the unselfconscious prototype of the new cosmos, Isamu has always been inherently at home – everywhere' (Fuller 1968: 7) – hence what justifies the use of Noguchi's life narrative as a case study to investigate the conceptual turn with regard to contemporary Cosmopolitanism.

Whereas the World-Citizenship ideal had in the past theorized 'cosmopolitan' as an attribute (of an identity) progressively becoming a noun (an identity *an sich*), the Mobilities Paradigm seems nowadays to assign cosmopolitan qualities to one's embedded-embodied cognition (interplay of home, body and the world). On the one side, craving for a global identity that would no longer be defined by nation, local community or religion, as it was envisioned during the Classical Greek era,[8] ended up in the later decades of the twentieth century to link 'the idea of world citizen with a "McDonaldization" of our culture and thus with an increasing lack of identity and an uprooted existence' (Schuilenburg 2011: 23). On the other side, moving across cultures does not necessarily imply also leaving one's cultural home. During the Age of Discovery, for instance, the Europeans sailed across the Atlantic and explored other places 'not to find cultures they might learn from and adapt to, but to establish themselves and extend their culture there' (Pimomo 2011: 1). Except that, according to another Cosmopolitan, the Lebanese-American poet and painter Etel Adnan, daughter of a Christian Greek mother and a Muslim Syrian father,

> the problem is that we now know the world; especially, we now know it is known, inventoried, and possessed. No land remains unowned, or at least unmeasured by the engineers (Adnan 1993: 87).

Geographical and celestial spaces having been almost fully mapped, there is no *terra incognita* left, no outer space where we can project the Exotic and the culturally Other. Identity seems absent or useless in terms of negotiating our interpersonal boundaries, unless we are ready to give up the conceptualization of the 'I' as a part of the binary Self/Other for a scheme that deals with the human being next to us as with someone unique – similar and different at the same time, an *alter* ego. In this sense, the culturally different is no more to be found elsewhere, but within our large family, global from scratch.

---

8   'But Socrates expressed it better, when he said, he was not an Athenian or a Greek, but a citizen of the world (just as a man calls himself a citizen of Rhodes or Corinth), because he did not enclose himself within the limits of Sunium, Taenarum, or the Ceraunian mountains' (Plutarch 1878: 5).

According to the philosopher Byung-Chul Han, who introduced the term Hyperculturality in 2005, globalizing means not only that *Here* is linked with *There*; more likely, a global *Here* is produced, while *There* is being constantly moved and removed – as if looking from a window. Unlike the root of a tree that indicates both a gathering spot and an origin or source, this global *Here* – simultaneously accessible from everywhere – is conceived as a netlike *plexus* without beginning and with no end, an intersection of nerves formed by hyphen (Han 2005: 35). Designating such an un-centred (and not merely decentered)[9] multitude, the rhizomatic nature of the twenty-first century human world is thus better represented by the state of *window-being*. For if 'windowing hypertext' constitutes the contemporary experience of the world, then, Han (2005: 50) goes on, 'windowing takes the house resident from inside to a *hypercultural* tourist'. That is, the contemporary human turns into something more than a nomad: a touristic figure that experiences Kultur (the German word for 'culture') as Kul-Tour, by travelling not only the terrestrial and celestial spaces in a mode of sightseeing but also the cybernetic one, with their home virtually or pragmatically on tour (Ntaousani 2012: 157–158).

Seen within this perspective, and when taking into account that the *utopia* of a single, universal and all-encompassing nation-state has proved to have at once over-simplified and over-estimated globalization's and migration's potential, the contemporary Cosmopolitan appears to consist less of a Citizen and more of a Wanderer of this World in flux and flow: one feels now as a multifarious 'I' who floats around the globe carrying one's own cultural – even if dynamically influenced and ever-changing – home (one's own *place-holder*), with an easiness of forming different selves (*space-time occupants*) along the way. Except that such a shift from an identity-bound to a home-anchored concept entails a rather surprising and seemingly self-contradictory slippage of Cosmopolitanism – from the complexity of dynamic, physical or virtual, interpersonal relationships to a more individualistic experience of the human *terroir*.[10] Are we, as a matter of fact, taking the opposite route of what we were expecting to follow, of someone who moves beyond ethnocentric localities to engage with the global picture? Or else, how is it possible to bridge in a consistent way the cosmopolitan openness to the world with its wrapping up in our intimate (notion of) home?

When speaking about the wide interest in and receptiveness (or tolerance) to customs, beliefs and ideas in other places, the philosopher Kwame Anthony

---

9   The Greek dominion was treated as the centre of the universe in Homeric times, thus functioning in a similar way to the centrality of Europe some centuries later, namely during the Age of Exploration.

10   The reason why I prefer *terroir* to *milieu* is because the former acclaims the vague nuances of the latter, while at the same time suggesting a strong liaison with a specific territory. For more about this term that argues for connectivity with the local in times of immigration and globalization, see Schuilenburg's article on the Right to *Terroir* (2011: 20–28).

Appiah (2007: xi, xiv) insists on the rapidly growing personal responsibility for lives elsewhere. Since we live in an era of everyday mobility, where, in just a few minutes of travelling by airplane, we are passing 'more people than most of our remote ancestors would ever have seen in their entire lives' (Appiah 2009: 88), we seem to face the challenge to learn how to be responsible for not just friends, family and compatriots but equally for fellow citizens, both of our country and of the world. This appears as one credible way to justify why we do not need to 'go native' anymore in order to meet contemporary cosmopolitanism. Another one may well be offered by the anthropologists Begrich and Mühlebach (2002), who write about their inquiry into the Goa trance scene in Switzerland what is here hoped to serve as our concluding food for thought:

> On the one hand, there is Goa, a far away place that freaks in Switzerland recreate in an effort to 'feel at home'. On the other hand, Goa freaks feel just as much at home in moving between places. It is not only the reference point Goa that they celebrate, but their cosmopolitan selves, not only roots, but 'routes' [Clifford 1997]. Home then is travel and travel is home (Begrich and Mühlebach 2002: 119).

References

Adnan, E. 2003. *Of cities and women (letters to Fawwaz)*. Sausalito, California: Post-Apollo Press.

Aldersey-Williams, H. 2009. Who Now: Selfhood and Society, in *Identity and Identification*, edited by H. Aldersey-Williams et al. London: Black Dog Publishing, Wellcome Collection and the Authors, 10–19.

Ånesen, A.H. 2003. In *Homecoming*, edited by H. Aagaard. Athens: Cube Editions, 38.

Appiah, K.A. 2007. *Cosmopolitanism: Ethics in a World of Strangers*. London, UK; New York, USA: Penguin Books.

Appiah, K.A. 2009. Cosmopolitanism, in *Examined Life: Excursions with Contemporary Thinkers*, edited by Astra Taylor. New York: The New Press, 87–113.

Ashton, D. 1992. *Noguchi East and West*. Berkeley and Los Angeles, California: University of California Press.

Barlow Rogers, E. 2005. Three Modernist Designers. *SiteLINES, A Journal of Place*, 1(1), 2–8.

Begrich, R. and Mühlebach, A. 2002. Travel as Home: An Anthropological Inquiry into the Goa Trance Scene, in *Here, There, Elsewhere: Dialogues on Location and Mobility*, edited by D. Blamey. London: Open Editions, 117–128.

Blickle, P. 2002. *Heimat: A Critical Theory of the German Idea of Homeland*. Woodbridge, Suffolk: Camden House.

Butler, J. 1999. *Gender Trouble: Feminism and the Subversion of Identity*. 10th anniversary edition. London: Routledge.

Clifford, James. 1997. *Routes: Travel and Translation*. London: Harvard Press.

Dant, T. 2004. The Driver-car. *Theory, Culture and Society*, 21(4–5), 61–79.

Duus, M. 2004. *Isamu Noguchi: Journey without Borders*. Princeton and Oxford: Princeton University Press.

Fosdick, H.E. 1943. *On Being a Real Person*. London: Harper and Brothers Publishers.

Freud, S. 2003. *The Uncanny*. London: Penguin Books.

Fuller, B. 1968. Foreword to *Isamu Noguchi. A Sculptor's World*. New York: Harper and Row.

Goodbody, A. 2011. *Heimat in the 21st century: has place-belonging a place in our globalised world?* Norms, Identities and Representations Research Cluster Interdisciplinary Workshop: Place and Identity, Department of European Studies and Modern Languages, University of Bath, UK, 12 May 2011. Available at: http://www.bath.ac.uk/esml/news/pdf/place-identity-workshop-05-2011-goodbody.pdf [accessed: 5 July 2011].

Gundersen, L. 2008. The Palace you Left, the Latitude of Home, Music as a Home and the Coordinates of Here, in *Home is the Place you Left*, edited by Elmgreen and Dragset. Köln, Germany: Walther König, 21–28.

Han, B.-C. 2005. *Hyperkulturalität: Kultur und Globalisierung*. Berlin: Merve.

International Organisation for Migration (IOM) 2010. *World Migration Report 2010: The future of migration: building capacities for change* [Online: International Organisation for Migration]. Available at: http://publications.iom.int/bookstore/free/WMR_2010_ ENGLISH.pdf [accessed: 2 October 2011].

Kammen, M. 2009. Artistic Inspiration and Transnational Memories in the Twentieth Century, in *Transnational American Memories*, edited by U.J. Hebel. Berlin: Walter de Gruyter, 405–424.

Kelo, M. and Wächter, B. 2004. *Brain Drain and Brain Gain: Migration in the European Union after Enlargement*. Study commissioned by the Academic Cooperation Association for the European Conference Braingain, The Hague, 29–30 September 2004. Available at: http://www.aca-secretariat.be/fileadmin/aca_docs/documents/reports/Migration.pdf [accessed: 2 October 2011].

Lama, D. 2005. *The Universe in a Single Atom: The Convergence of Science and Spirituality*. New York: Morgan Road Books.

Latour, B. 1996. *Aramis or the Love of Technology*. Cambridge, MA: Harvard University Press.

Munro Hendry, P. 2011. *Engendering Curriculum History*. New York: Routledge.

Noguchi, I. 1968. *A Sculptor's World*. New York: Harper and Row.

Nozick. R. 1981. *Philosophical Explanations*. Cambridge, MA: Belknap Press of Harvard University Press.

Ntaousani, E. 2010. *Critical Theory of Gender (zur Kritik des Genderbegriffs)*, 8th European Social Science History Conference, Ghent, Belgium, 13–16 April

2010. Available at: http://www2.iisg.nl/esshc/programme.asp?selyear=10&pap= 7341 [accessed 4 July 2011].

Ntaousani, E. 2012. Kul-Touring and the Exoticisation of the Familiar: On Otherness, Alternative and Alternation, in *Landscapes of (Un)Belonging: Reflections of Strangeness and Self*, edited by O. MacGarry and A. Stasiewicz-Bieńkowska. Oxford: Inter-Disciplinary Press, 153–164.

Oral history interview with Isamu Noguchi, conducted by Cummings P. 1973. Archives of American Art, Smithsonian Institution, 7 November–26 December. Available at: http://www.aaa.si.edu/collections/interviews/oral-history-intervi ew-isamu-noguchi-11906 [accessed 6 October 2011].

Pimomo, P. 2011. *A Way Out of the Contradictory Foundations of Colonial and Postcolonial Difference*, 3rd Global Conference: Strangers, Aliens and Foreigners, Diversity and Recognition Project, Inter-Disciplinary.Net, Mansfield College, Oxford, 27–29 September 2011. Available at: http:// www.inter-disciplinary.net/wp-content/uploads/2011/08/pimomospaper.pdf [accessed 8 October 2011].

Plutarch. 1878. Of Banishment, of Flying One's Country, in *Plutarch's Morals, vol. 3*, translated from the Greek by Several Hands, corrected and revised by William W. Goodwin. Boston: Little, Brown, and Co. Available at: http://oll. libertyfund.org/title/1213 [accessed 12 October 2011].

Schuilenburg, M. 2011. The Right to *Terroir*: Place and Identity in Times of Immigration and Globalization. *Open Cahier of Art and the Public Domain: (Im)Mobility: Exploring the Limits of Hypermobility*, 10(21), 20–28.

Swing, W.L. 2010. Foreword to the *World Migration Report 2010: The future of migration: building capacities for change*. Geneva, Switzerland: International Organization for Migration. Available at: http://publications.iom.int/bookstore/ free/WMR_2010_ENGLISH.pdf [accessed: 2 October 2011].

The Bible. Exodus 3. The Septuagint / LXX / Greek Old Testament. Available at: http://sepd.biblos.com/exodus/3.htm. Holy Bible, King James Version, Cambridge Edition. Available at: http://kingjbible.com/exodus/3.htm [accessed 8 October 2011].

The Economist 2009. Being foreign: the others [online from the print edition, undisclosed author, 17 December]. Available at: http://www.economist.com/ world/international/displaystory.cfm?story_id=15108690 [accessed: 2 October 2011].

Tiger, C. 2007. *Isamu Noguchi*. New York: Chelsea House, Infobase Publishing.

Urry, J. 2007. *Mobilities*. Cambridge: Polity Press.

van Dick, J., Kerkhofs, R., van Rooij, I. and Haselager, P. 2008. Special Section: Can there be such a thing as embodied embedded cognitive neuroscience? *Theory Psychology*, 18(3), 297–316.

Yıldız, A. 2008. Homely Spaces for Homeless Kids, in *Home is the Place you Left*, edited by Elmgreen and Dragset. Köln, Germany: Walther König, 171–172.

SECTION IV
Complexities of Wider Identities

Chapter 13
Mobilities, Lifestyles and Imagined Worlds: Exploring the Terrain of Lifestyle Migration

Norman McIntyre

Introduction

Lifestyle migration has been used to indicate the re-location of people either within a country or across international borders motivated primarily, if not exclusively, by quality of life considerations (Benson and O'Reilly 2009, McIntyre 2009). Research in this area has encompassed a progressively expanding range of migrants including retirees (King, Warnes and Williams 2000), second-home owners (McIntyre et al. 2006), lifestyle entrepreneurs (Shaw and Williams 2004, Stone and Stubbs 2007) and 'urban refugees' (Loeffler and Steinecke 2007). This phenomenon is constructed typically as a manifestation of the counterurbanization movement (Berry 1976, Mitchell, 2004), which has in varying degrees and at different times characterized the late twentieth and early twenty-first centuries worldwide. This emphasis on *migration* and *counterurbanization* creates two problems for conceptual clarity. The first is that the term *migration* focuses debate on the *mobility of people*, which neglects the broad array of other *mobilities* (Urry 2000, Sheller and Urry 2006) or *flows* (Castells 2000, Appadurai 1996) that are associated with this voluntary relocation including the movements of capital, information, knowledge and skills. Secondly, the emphasis on rediscovery and colonization of rural areas is problematic to the extent that it neglects the counter flow to large urban areas of professional and managerial elites attracted as much by lifestyle considerations as by employment opportunities (Castells 2000, Perlik and Messerli 2004). I argue that this neglect has limited a theoretically integrated analysis of this phenomenon and its wider implications.

A key focus in exploring the phenomenon of amenity and/or lifestyle migration has been the motivations underlying the desire to relocate (for example Moss 2006). This emphasis on defining macro-drivers of amenity migration (for example environment and culture) has sidelined what are likely the broader goals of relocation for individual migrants, namely, enhancing or changing lifestyle and potentially re-defining self . In this context, the work of Appadurai (1996) on the role of *imagination* and *imagined worlds* in motivating migration will be explored.

Following on earlier work (McIntyre 2009, Williams and McIntyre 2012), this chapter discusses the concepts of *lifestyle mobilities* and *imagination*. It explores how these conceptualizations can broaden the theoretical scope of lifestyle migration and enhance our understanding of the reasons underpinning its growing popularity and provide insights on the issues and conflicts, which accompany its expansion.

Lifestyle mobilities

Recent research (for example Moss 2006, Benson and O'Reilly 2009), while recognizing the importance of the linkages between mobility and lifestyle, has restricted its assessments to migration or the movement of people. While migration is an essential component of mobility, it is nonetheless only one of a number of *mobilities* (Urry 2000) or *flows* (Appadurai 1996, Castells 2000) that characterize reflexive modernity (Bonss and Kesselring 2004). Urry (2000: 1) argued that to understand the complex and surprising nature of the world today, there was a need to explore 'the diverse mobilities of peoples, objects, images, information and wastes; and the complex interdependencies between, and social consequences' of their interactions. This is not to suggest that everything is 'on the move' as these diverse mobilities depend centrally on immobile infrastructures which constrain, channel and regulate (for example international borders) or enable (for example transmission towers, roads, airports, garages, fibre-optic cabling) the movement of people and things (Sheller and Urry 2006). Although networks of mobile flows and immobile infrastructures have existed at all periods in the past, the speed, scale and volume of these flows today are unparalleled in human history (Appadurai 2000).

Following on the work of Urry (2000) and Moss (2006), McIntyre (2009: 4) introduced the term *lifestyle mobilities*, which he defined as 'the movements of *people, capital, information and objects* associated with the process of voluntary relocation to places that are perceived as providing an enhanced or, at least, different lifestyle'. Using the 'mobilities paradigm' (Urry 2004) and the dimensions of global culture (Appadurai 2000), I am proposing a preliminary conceptual frame for lifestyle mobilities (Figure 13.1).

In this conceptualization, I have borrowed the suffix 'scapes' from Appadurai (2000) which encapsulates both the scalar and fluid nature of the five dimensions of global culture he proposed: *ethnoscapes* (for example lifestyle migrants); *technoscapes* (for example social media and transportation technology); *financescapes* (mobile capital), *mediascapes* (mobile media) and *ideascapes* (imagined worlds). I am proposing another dimension particularly applicable to lifestyle migration: *experiencescapes*, which comprise the varying experiential, personal and financial characteristics that potentially accompany the mobility of lifestyle migrants. These characteristics (for example capital, skills, knowledge, power and influence) are represented in the intersection of the *ethno* and *experience scapes* in Figure 13.1. Similarly, the intersection of the *techno* and *idea scapes* represents the role of mobile media (for example destination and property marketing) in developing the imagined worlds of lifestyle migrants, the intersection of the *experience* and *ideascapes* represents the *imagination* which Appadurai argues is a key influence in motivating migration and, finally, the intersection of the *ethno* and *techno scapes* represents transportation technology (for example budget airlines, highways) which has democratized mobility and mobile phones and social networking sites (for example internet phones, MSN chat, Facebook) that have enhanced social interaction and overcome distance for friends and relatives across the world.

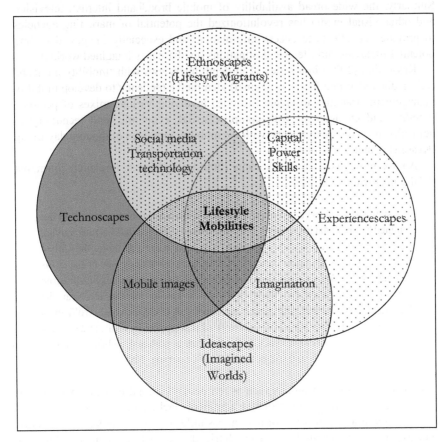

Figure 13.1   A conceptual model of lifestyle mobilities

Consider, for example, the not uncommon effects of capital flows on housing values associated with lifestyle migration. For example, George (2004; quoted in George et al. 2009: 54) noted that in the former fishing port of Lunenburg, Nova Scotia after its designation as a UNESCO World Heritage Site:

> The beautiful old historic homes, one of the major attractions in the town, [were] now becoming a negative in driving property values to a point that very few … who are not affluent or retire[d]

can afford to buy properties in the Old Town.

Other examples both positive and negative for communities can be found in the transfer of technological and business expertise as in Rasker's (2006) 'footloose entrepreneurs' and in the shifting patterns of political power in rural communities (Smith and Krannich 2000, Müller et al. 2004, McIntyre and Pavlovich 2006). Similarly, the widespread availability of mobile broadband internet, television and other visual media has revolutionized the potential of marketing agencies to provide and clients to access information, and especially images, depicting potential lifestyles and lifestyle destinations (mediascapes/imagined worlds).

Kesserling (2006) in a series of in-depth interviews with 'mobility pioneers' (IT, media and armed forces personnel) identified a tendency to develop mobility management strategies to create lifestyles involving various mixes of personal mobility and engagement with complex social, economic, and technological networks to enable them to cope with the mobility pressures of modern day living (Kesselring and Vogl 2004).

An example used by Kesselring (2006) involved a freelance journalist (Wolfgang) who:

> ... established residence on one of the Balearic Islands [his home in the sun] but retained his small flat in Germany as a 'base camp' ... [he] spends his time moving between the Balearic Islands, Germany, Italy, and, more and more, the United States and Russia. From his base in a middle-sized German city, he manages his seminars and makes journalistic investigations; an Italian enclave is his favourite location for recreation and Buddhist exercises. During the last few years he has become acquainted with places and people all over the world. Wolfgang's experience represents a multiplex network of places, people, ideas, and cultures ... [his use of] technologies such as the Internet, e-mail, and mobile telephones permit him to be away and still be accessible (Kesselring, 2006: 272–273).

The lifestyles of many migrants such as retirees and second-home owners are not that dissimilar to Wolfgang's, although admittedly lacking the focus on 'work' and the *constant* motion and transformation. A similar use of technology to socialize with expatriates, to remain in contact with friends and relatives, to manage finances and to remain active in American politics is demonstrated by US migrants to San Miguel, Mexico (Croucher 2009).

Given this, a fruitful area of research might well be to focus on how different kinds of lifestyle migrants manage movement, harness technology, and develop social networks to realize their desired projects and plans (for example keeping in contact with friends and relatives, developing a business) while being 'on the move'.

The terrain of lifestyle migration

In a similar conceptualization of the world today as expressed by Appadurai (1996) and Urry (2000), Castells (2000: 442) argued that:

... our society is structured around flows: flows of capital, flows of information, flows of technology, flows of organizational interaction, flows of images, sounds and symbols. Flows are not just one element of the social organization: they are the expression of processes *dominating* our economic, political and symbolic life.

On this basis, he theorized the existence of two spatial logics: a dominant *space of flows* and a *space of places*. The former he conceptualized as being made up of a network of micro-electronic based devices and transportation linkages connecting a hierarchically organized set of hubs and nodes. This is the domain of today's mobile elites, who adopt '... an increasingly homogeneous lifestyle ... that transcends the cultural borders of all societies' (Castells 2000: 447). In contrast, life for the overwhelming majority of people is conducted in places '... whose, form functions and meanings are self-contained within the boundaries of physical contiguity' (Castells 2000: 453).

The *space of flows* with its electronic connectivities, transportation links, and nodes and hubs facilitates the mobility and lifestyle of individuals in professional and managerial occupations (for example software engineers, academics, brokers) who move within and across national borders (Wickham 2008), not simply following employment, but attracted by the:

residential and leisure-oriented spaces ... [and] easy access to cosmopolitan complexes of arts, culture, and entertainment (Castells 2000: 446–447)

found in charismatic large cities (for example London, Tokyo, New York) and high-technology regional centres (for example Seattle, Silicon Valley).

Similarly, the intersection of the *space of flows* with its mobile people, money and information and the *space of places* with, for example, its re-valuing of rural life have re-created the rural spaces of many societies attracting a new breed of migrant; one who is equipped with markedly different knowledge, skills and attitudes and who places lifestyle and natural amenity above or on equal terms with economic concerns (Persson et al. 1997). Although local economic, social and environmental conditions vary widely between centres depending on their position in the hierarchy, research has shown that rural centres with good communications and accessible air travel to metropolitan areas set in attractive natural environments (Rasker 2006, Rasker et al. 2009) are well-placed to attract new techno-industries and benefit socially and economically from the in-migration of knowledge-based workers, professionals, entrepreneurs and affluent retirees.

The instability in and decline of primary production industries and the resulting economic and social stresses have severely impacted many single-industry rural towns (Halseth 1999). For those rural communities which have developed as nodes or hubs on the space of flows, the re-surgence of in-migration flowing from the re-location of service and knowledge-based industries and the influx of second-home owners, retirees and other lifestyle migrants have been a welcome development.

However, these changes in the size and character of the population have also progressively introduced a variety of social and environmental problems for both residents and migrants (Jobes 2000, Glorioso and Moss 2007). Documented issues include a lack of affordable housing, rapid increases in the cost-of-living, undesirable (for some) changes in the character and ambience of places, fluctuating, part-time and seasonally variable populations, and the loss of environmental amenity and access resulting from sprawling sub-divisions, ranchettes and resort development (Gober et al. 1993, Hansen et al. 2002, Stefanick 2008).

These examples suggest that the complex interplay of the influences of the dominant *space of flows* and the indigenization tendencies of individual locales (Appadurai 1996) in the *space of places* variously constructs and re-constructs the terrain of lifestyle migration. In this way, the intersection of these two spatial logics creates a wide diversity of potential lifestyle choices for migrants and both opportunities and challenges for individual places.

Thinking about difference

Motility is 'the capacity of entities [e.g., goods, information, or persons] to be mobile in social and geographic space' (Kaufmann 2004: 76). This capacity or potential depends on *access* (for example communications and transportation), *competence* (for example physical ability, knowledge, organizational skills) and *appropriation* or how individuals interpret and act upon perceived or real access and skills (Kaufmann 2004). These various components are unequally distributed and vary with nationality, gender, age, ethnicity, and so on (Gustafson 2006). For example, Gogia (2006) compared the different mobilities of contracted Mexican seasonal workers coming to Canada to work on farms and Canadian backpackers travelling to Mexico. She points to the conditions that characterize the working and living conditions of the agricultural labourors likening it to 'slavery', emphasizing 'the precarious nature of their mobility' (Gogia 2006: 370), which is circumscribed by many gatekeepers (for example employers, Canadian and Mexican government agencies). In contrast, Canadian backpackers, lured by the promise of exotic adventures and low-cost airfares and living expenses, face few structural or regulatory restrictions on their mobility to and within Mexico and other countries of the South (for example Indonesia, Thailand). She also notes that the ease of access for Western backpackers is quite assymetric, as backpackers from receiving countries such as Mexico or Thailand face considerable restrictions on their access to most Western nations.

Thus, mobility is achieved when movement and motility come together to allow people to realize specific projects or plans. Although the lifestyle migrant, the seasonal worker and the backpacker are all mobile subjects, their movement and motility is embedded in the specific geographies, networks, and economic and social conditions that influence how people move and are received differently around the globe (Gogia 2006).

The imagined worlds of lifestyle migration

A key way in which mobility is manifest is in the creation and consumption of imagined worlds (for example place meanings and attachments) which are mobilized through processes of imagination (Figure 13.1). The role of imagination is well recognized in art, myth and legend and has acted throughout time to 'both transcend and reframe ordinary social life' (Appadurai 1996: 5). What is different today is that imagination has entered ordinary life. In our media saturated, mobile world, anything is possible:

> More people than ever before seem to imagine routinely the possibility that they
> ... will live and work in [or travel to] places other than where they were born:
> this is the wellspring of the increased rates of migration at every level of social,
> national and global life (Appadurai 1996: 6).

Further, he argues that:

> ... the imagination ... has a projective sense about it, the sense of being a prelude
> to some sort of expression ... the imagination, especially when collective, can
> become ... a staging ground for action (Appadurai 1996: 7).

As has been argued elsewhere (Williams and McIntyre 2012), the desire for an improved lifestyle or enhanced quality of life is a key driver of migration. In this regard, the notion of 'imagined worlds ... the multiple worlds that are constituted by the historically situated imaginations of persons and groups spread around the globe' (Appadurai 1996: 33) is important in understanding the processes that are instrumental in motivating people to visit places, create a second residence, or settle permanently.

The potent mix of personal mobility fuelled by modern electronic media provides a wealth of 'imagined worlds', which are the foundations of lifestyle migration. Destination marketing is designed to communicate a world that appeals to individuals in specific target audiences. Presenting a mix of visual and print narratives depicting a sanitized, often romanticized, perhaps even ideological sense of place designed specifically to entice lifestyle migrants. Quality of life markers such as aesthetic, romantic and often natural surroundings, up-market accommodation, outdoor activities, and healthy lifestyles are central components of such media.

Not unusually, these idealized images often conflict with the lived reality of everyday life in amenity destinations. In such towns in rural or peri-urban areas, competition over housing and services, overcrowding, traffic, cost of living, and loss of amenity and access have led to perceptions of diminished quality of life in some sections of resident populations (Jobes 2000, Glorioso and Moss 2007, Gurran, 2008). Migrants often react negatively and even obstruct resource or other developments which they view as in conflict with their imagined worlds of bucolic or pristine nature.

Mobilities and imagined worlds

The growth in lifestyle migration and the resulting competition between destinations to attract high technology footloose industries, affluent retirees and second-home purchasers to enhance economic development draws small communities, cities, and countries inexorably into a cycle of self-promotion. Central to this endeavour is capturing the imagination of potential markets through the construction and dissemination of desirable experiences and lifestyles. However, as indicated above, the dilemma associated with the success of this self-promotion is a threat to the very qualities upon which the lifestyles and experiences enjoyed by locals and migrants alike depend.

While there is much common ground among residents and in-migrants in appreciation of and concern for the amenity landscape (for example Blahna 1990, Fortmann and Kussel 1990, Jones et al. 2003, Thompson 2004, McIntyre and Pavlovich 2006, Williams and Van Patten 2006), resource and/or tourism related developments are a consistent focus of conflict in many communities. Most commonly, protagonists are divided into in-migrants and locals (for example Gallent and Tewder-Jones 2000, Hall and Müller 2004, Stedman 2006). However, research is pointing increasingly to the need for a more nuanced view of such complex and contentious situations (George et al. 2009, Milne 2001). The imagined worlds within and among locals and lifestyle migrants often differ thus creating a complex and often conflicting mix of visions of how a place is and should be. Such 'communities of sentiment' (Appadurai 1996: 8) are often mobilized in collective action as a result of perceived threats to the integrity of their various imagined worlds. In such situations, the imagined worlds of mobile newcomers and those of the emplaced traditional inhabitants, can variously conflict and align as controversial situations develop.

Prior to any proposal, be it for tourism or for resource development, the various imagined worlds may be largely subliminal, co-existing in an uneasy but generally amicable climate, occasionally manifesting themselves in minor conflicts over untidy, run-down homes, unruly dogs, illegal burning, and disrespect for cultural artefacts and local customs (Tate-Libby 2010). However, development proposals and the ensuing political controversy raise the various versions of a place into consciousness necessitating their articulation and differentiation by exaggerating distinctions, denigrating opponents and emphasizing negative aspects of opposing ideascapes (Ramp and Koc 2001, Satterfield 2002).

In many such disputes, there are those whose imagined place is based on preservation or conservation of former lifestyles and traditions, and natural and cultural heritage (George et al. 2009, Tate-Libby 2010) pitted against those whose imagined worlds are centred on the opportunities for employment, real estate investment, and the business opportunities that tourism or resource development potentially offers.

An example from Lunenburg, Nova Scotia, Canada (George et al. 2009), documents a local community's successful efforts to resist wholesale gentrification of the historic fishing waterfront by affluent in-migrants and associated developers through retaining a significant portion of the Old Town port area as a working waterfront to support a renewed marine industry:

> ... what the community doesn't want to do is freeze itself in time and become a
> tourist community or museum (Tradewinds, 2005; quoted in George et al. 2009:
> 61).

In this, the local action group expresses a vision of a diversified economy which embraces both the opportunities provided by tourism and lifestyle migration *and* the renewal of an industry which was a central component of the history and traditions of the community.

As a tourist destination develops, the community makeup becomes more complex, not uncommonly including some mix of indigenous peoples, long-term residents, lifestyle migrants, business owners, alternative lifestyle followers and tourists of various descriptions. Consequently, the varieties of imagined worlds multiply and the potential for conflict over the scale and style of any proposed developments increase. At the same time, the enhanced profile of the destination inevitably attracts the interests of national and even multinational tourism developers further exacerbating this potential. Byron Bay, formerly an economically depressed coastal settlement on the easternmost point of the Australian mainland has over the last 30 years been subjected to a series of 'invasions'; initially by alternative lifestyle followers, then by 'cashed up' lifestyle migrants and most recently, it has achieved 'mythical' status as 'the must visit' backpacker destination of Australia (Westerhausen and Macbeth 2003). In the early 1990s, the 'Battle for Byron Bay', initiated by a proposal to develop a 'Club Med', split the local community into pro and anti development lobbies pitting the imagined worlds of an authentic, socially tolerant, counter cultural meeting place against that of conventional mass tourism destination (Westerhausen and Macbeth 2003). Although, the proposal was defeated, interestingly by a coalition of local business people intent on maintaining local control of the tourism industry, the 'battle' continues to this day to create a sustainable tourism industry which is sufficiently inclusive to encompass multiple imagined worlds and resilient enough to resist the omnipresent threat of resort cycle decline.

Fundamentally, Milne (2009: 200–201) argues that underlying all these conflicts:

> ... there is a central tension which is seldom made explicit: between support for
> urban types of development, and resistance to development that is grounded in
> a valuing of the rural and what this place ... has been in the not too-distant past.

By 'urban types of development', Milne (2009) does not mean the spread of cities but rather the infusion of 'urban lifestyles' into rural areas as a function of enhanced mobilities. This effect is seen in the displacement of current residents and traditional industries, and the up-scaling of former resource complexes (for example waterfronts, warehouses) and historic areas by in-migration of affluent buyers, usually from urban locales (George et al. 2009). These changes bring the cappuccino bars, up-market restaurants and bookshops, state-of-the-art outdoor gear stores, and the shopping malls and chain stores to former mining, fishing or agricultural communities. The resulting creation of a more interesting and diverse place to live and the provision of new employment and business opportunities that attract in-migrants and enable young people to remain in the community are welcomed by some, because they view these changes as enhancing their quality of life. Others are less enthusiastic and mourn the loss of the local culture and ambience of life that once characterized the community (Whitson 2001).

The above discussion suggests quality of life markers (for example climate, nature, facilities, employment, security, family ties, and tradition) are the key building blocks of the imagination that motivate lifestyle migrants to relocate, and which cause locals to contest developments. These powerful, political images or ideascapes constructed by individuals and nurtured and amplified by electronic communication and mass media enter into the collective imagination in real places initiating and maintaining political action in defiance of those local and global forces that seek to question their authenticity and imperil their continued existence.

Conclusion

In advocating the term lifestyle mobilities, I argue for a more broadly based theoretical perspective than is evident in current conceptualizations of lifestyle migration (for example Benson and O'Reilly 2009). This broader perspective necessitates not only an understanding of lifestyle migrants' mobility performance (that is, movement) but also the mobility management strategies that they develop and use to enhance their 'motility' or mobility potential (Bonss and Kesselring 2004). Further, our studies need to take into account the networks, scapes, and flows that influence temporary/cyclical and permanent migrations including the mobilities of money, culture, technology, skills, knowledge and information which accompany and support these movements. In essence, we need to engage the broader perspectives of reflexive modernity with its complexity and non-linearity, its ambiguity and risks, and its uncertainties and unpredictability.

A key aspect of the modern world is the flows of information and images in the mass media, which provide vast and complex repertoires of images and narratives to tourists and lifestyle migrants throughout the world. These images and narratives form the basis of imagined worlds; 'fantasies that become prolegomena to the desire for ... movement' (Appadurai 1996: 36). Central to understanding lifestyle mobilities is recognizing the importance of these mediascapes and exploring their role in motivating migration itself and their influence in seeding and maintaining conflicts over how places are understood and managed.

Urry (2004) has suggested that a new 'mobilities paradigm' is being formed within the social sciences. In this chapter, I have argued that viewing lifestyle migration through this lens enables us to look both to the relevance of this new paradigm in understanding the phenomenon itself and also, how insights from lifestyle motivated re-location can inform the developing paradigm more generally.

References

Adler, P.A. and Adler, P. 1999. Transience and the post-modern self: the geographic mobility of resort workers. *Sociological Quarterly*, 40(1), 31–58.

Appadurai, A. 1996. *Modernity at Large: Cultural Dimensions of Globalization.* Minneapolis, MN: University of Minnesota Press.

Ateljevic, I. and Doorne, S. 2000. Staying within the fence: lifestyle entrepreneurship in tourism. *Journal of Sustainable Tourism*, 8(5), 378–392.

Benson, M. and O'Reilly, K. 2009. Migration and the search for a better way of life: a critical exploration of lifestyle migration. *The Sociological Review*, 57(3), 608–625.

Berry, B.J. 1976. *Urbanization and Counterurbanization.* Beverly Hills, CA: Sage Publications.

Blahna, D. 1990. Social bases for resource conflicts in areas of reverse migration, in *Community and Forestry: Continuities in the Sociology of Natural Resources*, edited by R.G. Lee, D.R. Field and W.R. Burch, Jr. Boulder, CO: Westview Press, 159–178.

Bonss, W. and Kesselring, S. 2004. Mobility and the Cosmopolitan Perspective, in *Mobility and the Cosmopolitan Perspective: Documentation of a Workshop at the Reflexive Modernization Research Centre*, edited by W. Bonss, S. Kesselring and G. Vogl, 9–23. Available at http://www.cosmobilities.net [accessed: 26 February 2011].

Bunting, T.E. and Mitchell, C.J. 2001. Artists in rural locales: market access, landscape appeal and economic exigency. *The Canadian Geographer*, 45(2), 268–284.

Butler, R.W. (ed.) 2006. *The Tourism Area Lifecycle; Conceptual and Theoretical Issues* (vol. 2). Clevedon, UK: Channel View Press.

Castells, M. 2000. *The Information Age: Economy, Society, and Culture, Volume 1. The Rise of the Network Society.* 2nd edition. Oxford: Blackwell Publishing.

Croucher, S. 2009. *The Other Side of the Fence: American Migrants in Mexico.* Austin TX: University of Texas Press.

Dewhurst, P. and Horobin, H. 1998. Small Business Owners, in *The Management of Small Tourism and Hospitality Firms*, edited by R. Thomas. London: Cassell, 19–38.

Fortmann, I. and Kussel, J. 1990. New voices, old beliefs: forest environmentalism among new and longstanding rural residents. *Rural Sociology*, 55(2), 214–232.

Gallent, N. and Tewder-Jones, M. 2000. *Rural Second Homes in Europe: Examining Housing Supply and Planning Control*. Farnham: Ashgate.

George, E.W. 2004. Commodifying local culture for rural tourism development. The case of one rural community in Atlantic Canada. Unpublished Dissertation, University of Guelph, ON., Canada

George, W., Mair, H. and Reid, D.G. 2009. *Rural Tourism Development: Localism and Cultural Change*. Bristol: Channel View Publications.

Glorioso, R.S. and Moss, A.G. 2007. Amenity Migration to Mountain Regions: Current Knowledge and Strategic Construct for Sustainable Management. *Social Change*, 37(1), 137–161.

Gober, P., McHugh, K.E. and Leclerc, D. 1993. Job-rich but housing poor: the dilemma of a western amenity town. *Professional Geographer*, 45(1), 12–20.

Gogia, N. 2006. Unpacking corporeal mobilities: the global voyages of labour and leisure. *Environment and Planning A*, 38(2), 359–375.

Gurran, N. 2008. The turning tide: amenity migration in coastal Australia. *International Planning Studies*, 13(4), 391–414.

Gustafson, P. 2006. Place Attachment and Mobility, in *Multiple Dwelling and Tourism: Negotiating Place, Home and Identity*, edited by N. McIntyre, D.R. Williams and K. McHugh. Wallingford, UK: CABI, 17–31.

Hall, C.M. and Müller, D.E. (eds) 2004. *Tourism, Mobility and Second Homes: Between Elite Landscape and Common Ground*. Clevedon, UK: Channel View Publications.

Hall, C.M. and Williams, A.M. (eds) 2002. *Tourism and Migration: New Relationships between Production and Consumption*. Dordrecht, Netherlands: Kluwer Academic Publishers.

Halseth, G. 1999. 'We came for the work': situating employment migration in BC's small, resource-based, communities. *The Canadian Geographer*, 43(4), 363–381.

Hansen, A.J., Rasker, R., Maxwell, B., Rotella, J.J., Johnson, J.D., Parmenter, A.W., et al. 2002. Ecological causes and consequences of demographic change in the New West. *Bioscience*, 52, 151–162.

Jobes, P.C. 2000. *Moving Nearer to Heaven: The Illusions and Disillusions of Migrants to Scenic Rural Places*. Westport, CT: Praeger.

Jobes, P.C., Stinner, W.F. and Wardwell, J.M. (eds) 1992. *Community, Society, and Migration*. Lanham, MD: University Press of America.

Jones, R.E., Fly, M.J., Talley, J. and Cordell, H.K. 2003. Green migration into rural America: the new frontier of environmentalism? *Society and Natural Resources*, 16(3), 221–238.

Kaufmann, V. 2004. Motility: A Key Notion to Analyse the Social Structure of Second Modernity?, in *Mobility and the Cosmopolitan Perspective: Documentation of a Workshop at the Reflexive Modernization Research*

Centre, edited by W. Bonss, S. Kesselring and G. Vogl, 75–82. Available at http://www.cosmobilities.net [accessed: 26 February 2011].

Kesserling, S. 2006. Pioneering mobilities: new patterns of movement and motility in a mobile world. *Environment and Planning A*, 38(2), 269–279.

Kesselring, S. and Vogl, G. 2004. Mobility Pioneers: Networks, Scapes and Flows between First and Second Modernity, in *Mobility and the Cosmopolitan Perspective: Documentation of a Workshop at the Reflexive Modernization Research Centre*, edited by W. Bonss, S. Kesselring and G. Vogl, 47–67. Available at http://www.cosmobilities.net [accessed: 26 February 2011].

King, R., Warnes, A.M. and Williams, A.M. 2000. *Sunset Lives: British Retirement to the Mediterranean*. London: Berg.

Loeffler, R. and Steinecke, E. 2007. Amenity migration in the US Sierra Nevada. *The Geographical Review*, 97(1), 67–88.

McIntyre, N. 2009. Re-thinking amenity migration: integrating mobility, lifestyle and social-ecological systems. *Die Erde*, 140(3), 229–250.

McIntyre, N. and Pavlovich, K. 2006. Changing Places: Amenity Coastal Communities in Transition, in *Multiple Dwelling and Tourism: Negotiating Place, Home and Identity*, edited by N. McIntyre, D. Williams and K. McHugh. Wallingford, UK: CABI, 239–261.

McIntyre, N., Williams, D.R. and McHugh, K. (eds) 2006. *Multiple Dwelling and Tourism: Negotiating Place, Home and Identity*. Wallingford, UK: CABI.

Milne, B. 2001. The Politics of Development on the Sunshine Coast, in *Writing Off the Rural West: Globalization, Governments, and the Transformation of Rural Communities*, edited by R. Epp and D. Whitson. Edmonton: University of Alberta Press, 185–202.

Mitchell, C.J. 2004. Making sense of counterurbanization. *Journal of Rural Studies*, 20(1), 15–34.

Moss, L.A. (ed.). 2006. *The Amenity Migrants: Seeking and Sustaining Mountain Cultures*. Wallingford UK: CABI.

Müller, D.K., Hall, C.M. and Keen, D. 2004. Second Home Tourism Impact, Planning and Management, in *Tourism, Mobility, and Second Homes: Between Elite Landscape and Common Ground*, edited by C.M. Hall and D.K. Muller. Clevedon, UK: Channel View Publications, 15–32.

Perlik, M. and Messerli, P. 2004. Urban strategies and regional development in the Alps. *Mountain Research and Development*, 24(3), 215–219.

Persson, L.O., Westholm, E. and Fuller, T. 1997. Two contexts, one outcome: the importance of lifestyle choice in creating rural jobs in Canada and Sweden, in *Rural Employment: An International Perspective*, edited by R.D. Bollman and J.M. Bryden. New York: CABI, 136–163.

Ramp, W. and Koc, M. 2001. Global Investment and Local Politics: The Case of Lethbridge, in *Writing Off the Rural West: Globalization, Governments, and the Transformation of Rural Communities*, edited by R. Epp and D. Whitson. Edmonton: University of Alberta Press, 53–70.

Rasker, R. 2006. An exploration into the economic impact of industrial development versus conservation on western public lands. *Society and Natural Resources*, 19(3), 191–207.

Rasker, R., Gude, P.H., Gude, J.A. and van den Noort, J. 2009. The economic importance of air travel in high-amenity rural areas. *Journal of Rural Studies*, 25(3), 343–353.

Roseman, C.C. 1992. Cyclical and Polygonal Migration in a Western Context, in *Community, Society, and Migration*, edited by P.C. Jobes, W.F. Stinner and J.M. Wardwell. Lanham, MD: University Press of America, 33–45.

Satterfield, T. 2002. *Anatomy of a Conflict: Identity, Knowledge, and Emotions in Old Growth Forests*. Vancouver, BC: UBC Publications.

Shaw, G. and Williams, A.M. 2004. From Lifestyle Consumption to Lifestyle Production: Changing Patterns of Tourism Entrepreneurship, in *Small Firms in Tourism: International Perspectives*, edited by R. Thomas. Oxford, UK: Elsevier, 99–113.

Sheller, M. and Urry, J. 2006. The new mobilities paradigm. *Environment and Planning A*, 38(2), 207–226.

Smith, M.D. and Krannich, R.S. 2000. 'Culture Clash' revisited: newcomer and longer-term residents' attitudes toward land-use, development and environmental issues in rural communities in the Rocky Mountains. *Western Rural Sociology*, 65(3), 396–422.

Stedman, R. 2006. Places of Escape: Second-home Meanings in Northern Wisconsin, USA, in *Multiple Dwelling and Tourism: Negotiating Place, Home and Identity*, edited by N. McIntyre, D.R. Williams and K.E. McHugh. Wallingford, UK: CABI, 129–144.

Stefanick, P. 2008. *The Search for Paradise: Amenity Migration and the Growing Pains of Western Canadian Mountain Towns*. Available at: http://www.cpsa-acsp.ca/papers-2008/Stefanick.pdf [accessed 27 February 2011].

Stone, I. and Stubbs, C. 2007. Enterprising expatriates: lifestyle migration and entrepreneurship in rural southern Europe. *Entrepreneurship and Regional Development*, 19(5), 433–450.

Tate-Libby, J. 2010. Places, preservation and mobility: amenity migration and the politics of preservation in the Kau'a District of Hawai'i Island. Unpublished PhD dissertation, University of Otago, Dunedin, New Zealand.

Thompson, S. 2006. Gateway to Glacier: Will Amenity Migrants in North-western Montana Lead the Way for Amenity Conservation?, in *The Amenity Migrants: Seeking and Sustaining Mountains and their Culture*, edited by L.A.G. Moss. Wallingford, UK: CABI, 145–157.

Tuulentie, S. 2006. Tourists Making Themselves at Home: Second Homes as Part of Tourist Careers, in *Multiple Dwelling and Tourism: Negotiating Place, Home and Identity*, edited by N. McIntyre, D. Williams and K. McHugh. Wallingford, UK: CABI, 145–157.

Urry, J. 2000. *Sociology Beyond Societies: Mobilities for the Twenty-First Century*. London: Routledge.

Urry, J. 2004. The New Mobilities Paradigm, in *Mobility and the Cosmopolitan Perspective: Documentation of a Workshop at the Reflexive Modernization Research Centre*, edited by W. Bonss, S. Kesselring and G. Vogl, 25–35. Available at: http://www.cosmobilities.net [accessed: 26 February 2011].

Westerhausen, K. and Macbeth, J. 2003. Backpackers and empowered local communities: natural allies in the struggle for sustainability and local control? *Tourism Geographies*, 5(1), 71–86.

Whitson, D. 2001. Nature as Playground: Recreation and Gentrification in the Mountain West, in *Writing off the Rural West: Globalization, Governments, and the Transformation of Rural Communities*, edited by R. Epp and D. Whitson. Edmonton: University of Alberta Press, 145–164.

Wickham, J. 2008, September. *A skilled migration policy for Europe? Issues and problems.* Available at: http://www.migration-boell.de/web/migration/46_1807.asp [accessed: 27 February 2011].

Williams, A.M. and Hall, C.M. 2002. Tourism, Migration, Circulation and Mobility: the Contingencies of Time and Place, in *Tourism and Migration: New Relationships between Production and Consumption*, edited by C.M. Hall and A.M. Williams. Dordrecht, Netherlands: Kluwer Academic Publishers, 1–60.

Williams, A.M., King, R. and Warnes, A.M. 1997. A place in the sun: international retirement migrationfrom northern to southern Europe. *European Urban and Regional Studies*, 4(2), 15–34.

Williams, A.M., King R., Warnes, R. and Patterson, G. 2000. Tourism and international retirement migration from northern to southern Europe. *Tourism Geographies*, 2(1), 28–49.

Williams, D.R. and McIntyre, N. 2012. Place Affinities, Lifestyle Mobilities and Quality of Life, in *Handbook of Tourism and Quality-of-Life Research: Enhancing the Lives of Tourists and Residents of Host Communities*, edited by M. Uysal, R. Perdue and J.J. Sirgy. London: Springer Publications, 209–232.

Williams, D.R. and Van Patten, S.R. 2006. Home and away? Creating identities and sustaining places in a multi-centred world, in *Multiple Dwelling and Tourism: Negotiating Place, Home and Identity*, edited by N. McIntyre, D.R. Williams and K.E. McHugh. Wallingford, UK: CABI, 32–50.

Chapter 14

Storm Watching: Making Sense of Clayoquot Sound Winter Mobilities

Phillip Vannini

Introduction

From Goa to Bali, from Tuscany to rural and coastal Spain, and from Puerto Vallarta to Palm Springs, one key characteristic of lifestyle migration destinations is clear: warm, sunny climates (for example see Gustafson 2009, Korpela 2009, Trundle 2009, Williams and Hall 2000). Even within a nation not exactly known for its balmy temperatures, Canada, 'the search for a better way of life' (Benson and O'Reilly 2009: 608) is known to concentrate upon its mildest climatic region: southern Vancouver Island and the Southern Gulf Islands. Indeed, as Benson and O'Reilly (2009: 611, emphasis added) simply put it: the most renowned of lifestyle migrants have chosen destinations in coastal resorts or islands in the *sun*'. But as we are about to see, if not all that shines and glitters is gold, then not all that is dark and grey is gloomy either.

Take the case of the western side of Vancouver Island, British Columbia (BC), Canada. In Tofino, the region's best known village, it rains 3306mm[1] per year, on a whopping annual average of 216 days with precipitation. About 100km down the coast the small town of Port Renfrew sees even more rain, topping Vancouver Island's average rain rankings at 3674mm. In between the two is equally damp Ucluelet – which on 6 October 1967 is known to have recorded 489mm of rain in a 24-hour period. And incidentally, nearby Henderson Lake, on the mountains behind, also has two Canadian records: one for greatest annual average precipitation (6655mm), and one for greatest precipitation in one single year: 9749mm. But in spite of all this 'liquid sunshine', this region has recently experienced unprecedented flows of migration – thus presenting us with a challenge to our understanding of the role that climate plays in lifestyle mobilities.

The objective of this writing is to describe and understand lifestyle migration in the geographical context of Clayoquot Sound – a region located on the western side of Vancouver Island encompassing the aforementioned towns of Tofino and Ucluelet. This chapter is primarily driven by the need to make sense of how a uniquely wet and relatively cold climate can draw, rather than repel, short-term tourists, residential tourists and lifestyle migrants. But in broader terms, my aim

---

1 In comparison, London receives 736mm per year, on average.

here is to interpret the significance of climate and weather in the phenomenon of lifestyle mobilities. To this purpose the case of Clayoquot Sound is of great interest because it highlights how lifestyle migrants and short-term and residential tourists alike incorporate climatic characteristics of a region into their own treasured everyday practices, challenging their common values and meanings. As the data show, the redefinition of stormy and rainy weather as a comforting and appealing phenomenon prompts us to focus on the unique meanings of the intersection of different moving forces – such as weather fronts and the flows of short-term tourists and lifestyle migrants – as a complex but relatively harmonious constellation of mobilities.

We draw upon data collected for a broader project focused on the role the weather plays in shaping regional culture (Vannini et al. 2012). Our research included bouts of fieldwork conducted over a year in a variety of locations scattered across the BC coast – including Clayoquot Sound. The main purpose of our data collection was to investigate the sensory experience of weather and the meanings and everyday practices associated with it, and primarily to focus on the mundane significance of the most outstanding climatic feature of the region: the rain.

Rain comes in a variety of forms on the BC coast throughout the year, mostly ranging from long-lasting mist and showers to brief, cold, torrential downpours. On occasion during autumn and winter, especially on the outer coast of Vancouver Island, strong winds accompany wet weather systems creating large swells that crash ashore with notable fury. Such storms acquire particular significance in Clayoquot Sound because they draw out people who eagerly take them in, much like natural spectacles, as part of a loosely organized practice that has come to be known as storm watching.

To understand storm watching my colleagues and I began data collection by inventorying publically available experiences of wet weather and storms, such as narratives and reflections contained in blogs, web-based diaries and other published writings. We then organized a small regional media campaign. During radio show segments and through newspaper editorials focusing on weather as folklore we invited audiences to share with us reflections on the role that the weather plays in everyday life. In response, we received letters and emails containing narratives, poems, and photographs. We then began to conduct interviews with some of the people that contacted us. Throughout this time I also travelled extensively to observe storm watching practices in Tofino and Ucluelet. In all, we interviewed 55 people and observed a handful of storms.

Background

Thanks to blockbuster movies, guide manuals, sensationalist books and novels, popular websites and frequent news coverage the practice of storm *chasing* has become a popular cultural phenomenon, especially in the United States. But whereas storm chasing has arguably reached an apex in popularity, the much less adventurous but equally interesting practice of storm *watching* has only begun to emerge as a recognizable cultural phenomenon very recently. As the name itself suggests, storm watching loosely refers to the witnessing of a storm from a visual spectator's position – something typical of storm chasing as well. But whereas storm chasers pursue hurricanes and other severe weather phenomena often by driving or even flying near their very epicentres and at times even by jeopardizing their own lives, storm watchers take in generally less severe storms from safe positions, and at times even highly comfortable shelters (for example see Figure 14.1), at no obvious risk to them. While official definitions are scarce, it is commonly understood that storm watching refers to a relatively novel phenomenon prevalent especially on the Northwest Pacific Coast of North America, and more precisely on the west coast of Vancouver Island.

Tofino – and in lesser part Ucluelet – offer both the casual storm watcher and the storm watching ethnographer features intense enough to have turned this practice into a trademark institution. Indeed, an Internet search for storm watching yields a vast majority of Tofino-related results, both in terms of journalistic coverage and tourism promotion. For example Travel.bc.ca – a popular BC tourism website – defines storm watching in explicit relation to Tofino's unique climate and links it directly to a handful of hotel accommodations and packages offered by Tofino-based tourist operators. As they write:

> Storm watching season extends from November to March. During the storm watching season there are usually 10–15 good storms each month with the peak months of December-February sure to pack the most whoppers. It is during this season that Tofino receives the majority of it's [sic] nearly five meters of annual rainfall and during storm season this rain often arrives horizontally. Storm watching is a relatively new tourism phenomenon on the West Coast of Vancouver Island, though locals have been watching, bracing against and surviving winter storms here for millennia. Storm watching doesn't really require anything of the observer but stillness and wonder. Storm watching is best advantaged from ocean-fronting hotels and B&B's where a good book, a fireplace and maybe a down duvet across your lap are really all you need to experience the fury and the force of the pounding Pacific Ocean on the other side of your rattling, double paned window. Or for the more adventurous, head out into the storm to experience the power of the wind, to observe the giant waves, and to hear the symphony of the wind and waves.[2]

Three reasons in particular can be identified as key contributing factors in making Tofino a storm watching destination. To begin with, Tofino's luxury hotel, Wickaninnish Inn, is widely credited with having coined storm watching as both an idea in itself – that is, something distinct from merely walking around in a storm – and as a recognizable tourist practice. Secondly, while other accommodation-

---

2   http://tofino.travel.bc.ca/features/storm-watching/.

Figure 14.1   A Tofino storm seen from near the Wickaninnish Inn

Photo courtesy of April Vannini.

providers have now begun to promote storm watching and offer related packages, because the practice was allegedly born in Tofino a great deal of storm watchers now associate 'authentic' storm watching with outings to Tofino's beaches. Thirdly, whereas storm watching in Victoria, Vancouver – or mostly anywhere else – as a way of spending a morning or an afternoon is a relatively unorganized and extemporaneous practice, storm watching in Tofino is a more carefully planned performance for the large number of tourists and tourist operators involved, and consequently for the small village as a whole.

Tofino is a small town of about 1,650 year-round residents. Population swells in the summer, though, to about ten times its size. Situated on the very sparsely populated west coast of Vancouver Island, Tofino lies at the western end of Highway 4. Located about 40km south is the only other sizeable village of the area: Ucluelet – a town of about 1,500 people. Tofino and Ucluelet are not easy to reach. Boat access is limited by very strong currents, so no regularly scheduled ships serve the region. Airplane service is also very limited. A small number of regional carriers serve Tofino with direct flights from the south coast of BC, but a small airport and inclement weather severely restrict access. By car, Tofino and Ucluelet lie about 2½ hours away from the nearest urban hubs situated on the eastern side of Vancouver Island. The car journey itself can be rather treacherous. While over one million visitors a year make it to the Clayoquot Sound, the narrow and winding two-lane road is far from providing easy access. Indeed there is a definite feel that once in Tofino and Ucluelet one has reached the end of the road and thus somewhat of a liminoid space.

The landscape is what draws so many visitors to the area. The road journey itself – which many people describe as a modern-day pilgrimage – meanders through old growth forests, steep mountain cliffs, fast-moving rivers and fresh water lakes. Even before arriving at the coast the journey is a sublime experience for many. Then, when visitors finally reach the Esowista Peninsula, the coastal road wedges inside the Pacific Rim National Park Reserve and the UNESCO-designated Clayoquot Sound Biosphere Reserve. There, a succession of large (up to 200 metres in width) and long (up to 6km) beaches flank the road leading into the two towns. For a coast known for its rugged edges, these sandy beaches are especially unique and work as a magnetic draw for surfers, nature lovers, beachcombers, campers, whale watchers and many other outdoor adventure enthusiasts. While a handful of shops are present in both Tofino and Ucluelet, neither town offers much shopping or related hyper-consumerist escapes. There are no amusements parks, no discos, very few swimming pools and indeed little of the typical flavours of 'triple S' (sun, sand, and sex) tourism. As someone put it to me, 'you don't come here for "triple S" tourism, but mostly for the "triple R" kind: rain, rocks, and rough waters'.

Both Tofino and Ucluelet reinvented themselves as tourist destinations in the 1990s. As fishing and logging became either uneconomical for most operators, or outright outlawed over the last two decades, Clayoquot Sound residents have opened the doors to tourism as a new way of economic sustainment. American, Canadian, Australian, French and especially German and other continental and Northern European tourists 'invade' Tofino and still in lesser part Ucluelet, mostly from June to early September. Given Tofino's rapidly increasing status as a surfing destination, young travellers seeking alternative lifestyles have made Tofino a bit of countercultural heaven. They have joined long-time resident First Nation communities and followed in the footsteps of earlier hippies, environmentalists, artists and hermit-types in forming a laid-back, slow-paced and relatively open-minded community. While many newcomers are eventually pulled back to their points of origin by the necessity of stable employment, a few decide to stay – mostly pursuing jobs in the tourist industry while cultivating more self-authenticating passions and lifestyles after work or as time allows.

With a growing and quite young population, with declining opportunities in the resource extraction industry, and with skyrocketing living costs, the pressure to attract more tourism to Tofino and Ucluelet has been mounting for some time. While far from leaving a light carbon footprint, tourism is viewed by locals as more sustainable than logging – the only other feasible source of employment. But whereas exotic island destinations around the world are better positioned to develop more or larger hotels and fill them with tourists, a strong conservationist mindset combined with strict provincial, federal, and international regulations make it difficult to expand Tofino or Ucluelet in size. Plus there is a logical obstacle to development: Clayoquot Sound tourism is made attractive by the promise of close contact with nature and by the appeal of a slow-paced community living in intimate closeness with the wilderness. So, what could one do to support the local economy? Well, perhaps, rather than attracting more tourists during the short warm season – thus providing more short-term employment for seasonal amenity migrants – it would seem necessary to reinvent what one could do during the long rainy season. Enter the world of storm watching …

The social and cultural geographies of storm watching

What is fascinating about storm watching became obvious to me one day in the fall of 2009. The following words scribbled down in my field journal captures one key essence of it:

> When is the real storm coming? Two hours on the beach and I'm still waiting for the Real McCoy. The dark, menacing clouds I saw coming from the north a while ago have come and gone. They have made way for slightly stronger winds, but the sky seems to have actually cleared a bit. The weather front the TV said should be here by early afternoon should have arrived by now. It must be late. I'm getting cold walking around aimlessly. I don't seem the only one getting cold. The couple I saw walking earlier has gone back into the Wickaninnish. Another couple has come out, though. I am certain I saw them out earlier this morning. And if I have, they are not the only ones coming and going. I feel like doing the same too. Coming out and going back in, over and over. It might just be time again to go to my room, get warm and cozy, watch the waves from there, relax long enough to get bored, and then come out again later for a walk before dinner.

At first I saw nothing important in these words. Then I suddenly realized that I was describing a unique 'ballet' of movements, rest and encounters (Seamon 1980). The beach, the Wickaninnish, Tofino and Clayoquot Sound in general became in my mind the stage of intersecting performances of acts of movement. Winds, clouds, waves, masses of cold air, tourists, locals and I were moving about town, in the performance (see Edensor 2007) of a loosely choreographed 'dance' – coming and going, each moving at different speeds, each lasting different times depending on the pushes and the pulls affecting us (for example see Figure 14.2).

I had come to Tofino for only a weekend this time. It was a carefully planned outing. I had chosen a late autumn date that was likely to feature a good storm. But weather forecasts do not last very long. Meteorologists are rather successful at predicting weather for tomorrow and the day after, but it is much more difficult for them to nail down what the skies will bring five days from now. Weather fronts move rather unpredictably. What is worse is that their movements do not always harmonize with the outings of short-term tourists (and ethnographers) needing to book accommodations and request the necessary travel permissions from work. So, despite a promising outlook, the really nasty weather had taken a turn for the open waters. And instead of a monster storm, I and everyone else in town had to be content with waves, winds and raindrops that were moving pretty fast, but not as fast as everyone hoped. But no one, myself included, seemed to mind. To me, storm watching had started to resemble a mellow encounter: a meeting of people, sea currents and weather fronts moving about a region and coalescing on a fixed mooring, that is, a hotel perched on a rocky bluff.

Figure 14.2   'Dancing' in the rain

Photo courtesy of April Vannini.

To be sure, the Wickaninnish and its adjacent beach is far from being the only place in the Sound where one can practice storm watching. But what the 'Wick' offers in order to lure storm watching tourists captures the essence of this practice very well. The typical 'Wick' storm watching package offers a fireplace-warmed suite with views over the waves crashing ashore on a rocky bluff, a three-hour guided nature walk with a local naturalist, two rain hats, two books on Pacific reef and shore life, and two complimentary coffees to be enjoyed in the lounge. Raincoats are also available for borrowing, gratis. With two nights' accommodation the package starts at $875.85 before taxes, incidentally. During my stay at the 'Wick' – which almost dried up my modest research grant for the entire season – my participant observation yielded the impression that the cosy amenities offered by the hotel were indeed the sources of the guests' inspiration for their activities. Without many exceptions guests took intermittent walks outside at different beaches, then would come back inside for a coffee (or patronized other coffee shops 'in town'), only to peek outside again just to get cold enough to crave retiring back to their warm rooms.

Storm watching from one's rooms – as I understood from practising it myself and talking with others about it – was no less enjoyable than doing it outdoors.

I, and other guests, took marvel in the waves and the fury of the wind and the rain by standing on the small covered balcony of our suites to take pictures, or by sitting on a comfy armchair while cuddling with a book. Storms are clearly visible from the bed too, and if one leaves the balcony door open a bit it is easy to hear a mighty, but strangely relaxing roar. I felt rather guilty the first time I fell asleep in the afternoon to this symphony. When I woke up I felt as though I had missed out on the world outside, but then I realized that the essence of a storm watching getaway allowed – indeed even encouraged – taking comfort in one's shelter and dozing off. Other guests admitted taking long naps after coming out of their warm baths. If storm chasing is about the rush, the risk, and the recklessness, then storm watching is about the sleep, the stillness, and the serenity of it all. Here the triple Rs and triple Ss are inverted.

While the Wickaninnish lodging (and gourmet coffee) prices are prohibitive for most people, storm watching triple Ss do not need to be so luxurious or costly. In fact, while the 'Wick' and other four-star hotels do well at attracting crowds of tired professionals for a mellow weekend or mid-week getaways, the rest of the Sound offers storm watching possibilities that do just as well at attracting others, for longer periods of time even, or for more frequent outings. This exchange with Amelia,[3] a Toronto-born visual artist and waitress who has resided in Tofino year-round for five years, explains the difference and its significance:

> *Amelia:* The marketing department of the Wick and these other luxury hotels are smart. They have turned a bad rainy season into an occasion for pampering, but storm watching is basically free, really. All it takes for a walk on the beach or in the forest is a rain coat and a decent pair of shoes. I suppose it's better if you end it with a $4 latte at the Common Loaf on your way back into town to run errands, but the $1,000 is mostly for the local economy.

> *PV:* Are you saying the tourists are suckers?

> *Amelia:* No, not really. Believe it or not I know locals who once a year or so, if they can afford it, might even stay at the Wick themselves. I've done it a couple of times too. None of us have particularly spectacular ocean views from our homes, or cosy fireplaces, or unbelievably nice [laughs] marble bath tubs. Most of us have modest homes. So, it's kind of nice to indulge for a weekend, you know, even for us locals. All I'm saying is that for someone who doesn't live here that $1,000 is what keeps people like me and most of my friends employed in the winter. And as long as it allows both the tourists and people like me to enjoy life in the area, I don't think there's anything wrong with it. It's better than making a living out of cutting trees, or having to go back East, you know?

---

3   All interviewees' names are fictitious.

Amelia's insightful observation in one of my very first interviews in Tofino came to me like lightning in a thunderstorm. As I followed up on her thought with other local residents I learned that many viewed storm watching as an essential component of the winter economy of Clayoquot Sound. Reframing the value of 'bad weather' allows accommodation industry operators – from hotels, motel, cabin, condo, rental homes, and even campground managers and staff – and ancillary services to stay in business throughout the year. And this prevents many lifestyle migrants from having to move elsewhere for the rainy season. In short, if lifestyle migration is about getting out of the trap of one's former life (see Benson and O'Reilly 2009, 2011), the culture and social organization of storm watching in Clayoquot Sound is about enabling lifestyle migrants to stay away from the 'trap' year-round. The case of Jeff and Patricia highlights this phenomenon very well.

Jeff was born and raised in Vancouver, Patricia in Brisbane, Australia. Both in their late twenties, they have now resided in Tofino full-time for three years. They met in Whistler, where they were both working during the winter. Jeff was a ski instructor and Patricia a waitress and musician. As they got to know each other they learned that they both had a passion for surfing and a deep love for life in Tofino. Both worked in Clayoquot Sound during the summer: Jeff in a surf shop, and Patricia in a number of different jobs in the hospitality industry. During my interview with them I learned that Tofino attracted them for some of the usual reasons that render life more meaningful (for some): for the slow and laid-back lifestyle, for the sublime, idyllic wilderness, for the youthful vibe and feeling of community, and for the calm and quiet atmosphere. In their words:

Patricia: I used to go to Surfers' Paradise a lot when I was younger. I know the surfing world when I see it. And I have a bit of a hard time with it. The scene can get on your nerves after a while, do you know what I mean? You can't live your life in a bikini, going out dancing and drinking every night. It wears out on you. And it feels like it never changes. It feels like it's sunny every day, there is no change. And the thing about Tofino is that you do get that change in the seasons. Summers are great, but it's so nice when the rainy season starts. It's a time to be more introspective, you know? I can take my guitar out on the beach and sing at the top of my lungs and there is no one around to hear me hit bad notes. The rain, the storms, I don't know, it's like they allow you to be dark, moody. It's really the time when I write all my music. I just go out in the storm before work, or sometimes after work, and I can just be alone and be myself.

Jeff: And while she does that we at the surf shop are busy renting out and selling equipment. The whole marketing campaign about storm watching has caught the attention of a lot of people who didn't even know about Tofino and how great surfing is here in the winter.

Patricia: But it's ironic in a way, you know? It's not like the typical surfing scene. It's a very slooooow [voice emphasis] one, despite all the caffeine [laughs].

Weather is an ephemeral, but quintessential component of landscape (Brassley 1998) and regional culture and societies (Vannini et al. 2012). So, not only is the weather 'put to work' to fund the local economy and enable lifestyle migrants to sustain themselves (Madden 1999), but rain appreciation and storm watching lend a distinct flavour to Clayoquot Sound's place temporality. To better understand this phenomenon it seems useful to employ the concept of mobility constellations – to which I now turn.

Constellations of winter mobilities

Cresswell (2010) argues that in order to understand different mobilities we ought to focus on their practices, their experiences and their representations. These different elements ought to allow us to capture different constellations of mobility, that is, different patterns, and different assemblages. Different constellations of mobility characterize different places, different communities and different vectors of movement. Constellations of mobility are related to the concept of constellations of consumption, which refers to the assemblages of products and services sought by consumers to enact and express a lifestyle of choice. Cresswell (2010) argues that in order to capture different constellations of mobility we ought to pay attention to their different characteristics, such as speed, rhythm and feel – as well as others. Speed, rhythm and feel are characteristics of mobility but obviously of lifestyle as well.

With these three characteristics in mind, in my subsequent interviews and observations I tried to capture the unique quality of winter lifestyle mobilities in Clayoquot Sound. What stood as unique, in my mind, was the fact that the practice, experience and representation of wet, cold, stormy weather was a remarkably positive way of capturing the place temporality (Wunderlich 2009) and way of life of Clayoquot Sound. In simpler words, the people I interviewed and observed seemed to enjoy taking in the storms and the rain because it not only helped the local economy, but it also contributed to giving Tofino and Ucluelet a certain slow, mellow feel. This atmosphere gelled well with both one-time and regularly-returning tourists seeking rest from their winter busyness, and with the lifestyle migrants seeking a quiet, contemplative, wilderness idyll. Thus, rather than push people away, the succession of one stormy weather front after another drew people here. These unique mobilities taught me that the sun is not a necessary component of lifestyle mobilities.

Indeed, my interviews showed me quite clearly that many tourists and residents have learned to dwell here in appreciation of the rain. 'What I love about the rain is the growth,' Kathrin reflected, 'there is lushness to the growth on the coast because of the rain and temperate weather. For me, rain is a good thing, part of the cycle of life. If we go for weeks or months without rain, I long for a downpour that will force the green sprouts of life out of the earth to replace the dust and brown of death'. Tofino's moist air is a trademark feature and is unmissable, even by the first time visitor. As Stephen Miller writes on the web for the Canadian Tourism Commission, 'it's not air exactly; it's about one-third water and salt-spray and hovers in a fine mist that is probably really good for your skin, hanging in curtains that remind me of the aurora borealis. If the sun were out, a thousand individual rainbows would be cast by this tactile atmosphere that can't quite decide if it's going to become rain or fog'. The air is so enveloping that the landscape evacuates the background, the place subsumes the body, 'and you realize that all you are is a primate in a rain slicker'.[4] There is a definite poetics to the rain and the storms. Something else is 'in the air' here. Locals integrated the features of the climate into what they call 'Tofino Time': 'the endless waves, the geological timelessness of it all, combine to create a deep inner cleansing' – writes Beni Spieler for the local publication *Tofino Time* – the feeling that you are not just in a different place here, but also in a different time. The rain helps to make this feeling happen, continues Beni, even when one is away from home:

> I love the way it reminds me of being back home in Tofino no matter where I go. I'm always finding myself thinking of home when it begins to rain. A mixture of nostalgia and longing dripping from the sky and into my heart. There may not be an ocean to stare at, or even a beach to sit on, but I do have grey clouds to clear up my day. Every little drop containing a memory, a healing salve for a wandering soul, a thousand little crystals of hope for a wetter tomorrow. When I was stuck at home doing homework, or whatever it was I did instead of finishing my homework, the rain beating against the roof of my home helped me relax. The gentle drumming, or even the heavy symphonic noise over my head always brought a calm to my soul. In that same way, I feel that rain can cleanse my soul when I'm out in it. Removing all those bad vibes, releasing me of any negative energy.[5]

Some people say they can even taste the rain. Adrienne, for example, writes on her blog that 'we have the most fabulous water here ... . Our water comes from the mountains, forests, and streams of Meares Island. ... The forests and soils on Meares hold a fabulous amount of water. They filter and clean it to make some of the best water in the world'.[6] You can directly taste the weather in the water – or in the unique flavours of what temperatures and moist air generate, such as mushrooms, berries and shellfish – but the weather can also indirectly set the stage for unique experiences. It may be difficult to make business out of water itself, but no journey to Tofino is complete without a visit to a few different

---

4   http://mediacentre.canada.travel/content/travel_story_ideas/tofino_short.
5   http://www.tofinotime.com/articles/A-T810-18frm.htm.
6   http://www.theheartoftofino.com/2009/06/wet-coast.html.

coffee places. As Colin observes on his blog: 'From years of casual observation (and much experimentation), I have determined that the West coast rain forest is the perfect breeding ground (or brewing ground) for the caffeine mind-set. ... It is grey outside. The wind is howling at a bracing 70 km/hr and the rain is more horizontal than vertical (which is good, because an umbrella would be useless). The coffee is fabulous. This is the perfect day for it. ... The coffee tastes so good (as does the muffin) because it is so nasty outside'.[7]

On dark, stormy nights the winds often bring Tofino's power lines down and kill the TVs and the computers. Families and friends sit down to play games in the candlelight. With the power still down in the morning schools are closed down, and many high school kids and adults head out surfing, 'laughing' – as Beni Spieler writes for another *Tofino Time* piece – 'at the "Wave Hazard Sign" as it desperately tries to stop you from going out onto the water to spend the day harnessing the turbulent energies of the ocean for some insane surfing'. Or if it is not surfing maybe it will be the perfect morning for just 'standing around on the beach fighting with a lighter, and having a laugh with some friends while you dodge driftwood and get chased by the water' taking in 'the gentle sound of the rain turning into the violent but inspiring sound of the wind fighting with the trees and everything else in its way for that matter'. Or contemplating 'the sight of a wave curling into itself, as if seeking warmth in a vast cold body, before crashing and sending itself further towards its pre-determined destination' or 'walking on the sand the day after, all of it flat and smooth, the texture feeling something not un-like walking on cheese cake'.[8]

Rain storms also perform a unique type of drama in the region. In trying to capture this unique feel of the place Greg Blanchette writes for *Tofino Time*:

> Eight days ago it pounded down a celebration: riotous, wild with corn-kernels of ice. Weather pranced like a girl with her hair out behind, laughing. But that girl hasn't looked back since. Now in the window-glass my face looks gray, trying to remember other kinds of rain. Dreaming of Spring Mist so fine it was darn near holy – stuff you went out special at night to watch floating in streetlight halos. Remembering that practical Water-the-Plants Cloudburst, those friendly Go-In-For-a-Snack Showers. Recalling the October Squall, come to town like travelling German opera, boom, bam, curtain going down on the last act with beams of sunshine, the whole chorus on stage for the finale. But this stuff ... eight unrelenting days of this stuff ...! This is Matador Rain, waving gray capes of water in the air to enrage you. Gumboots, rain pants, slicker all useless as paper bags. Making a mockery of umbrellas, of Gore-Tex ... of slipping, dripping sanity itself. Olé, sucker, and a roar goes up from the whole damn town. Summer showers, those are a punchline, a lark, something to go outside and twirl in. June, July, "Fogust" ... just a bunch of light-fingered, sun-stealing

---

7   http://www.coffeecrew.com/culture/331-the-tofino-blog-1.
8   http://www.tofinotime.com/articles/A-T811-18frm.htm.

punks. Harmless. Bike out to the lake, the little hoodlums won't catch you there. But this! Man, I'm telling you, this is Judge-and-Jury Rain. Hanging Rain. Look at Lone Cone out there, half the cursed mountain gone, beheaded by Attila the Low. The World Wide Weep offering no succour, dishing out satellite pics one big gray smear from here to the gulags of Kamchatka. Hard Time Rain. Cruel and Unusual Rain. Don't-Forget-Who's-Boss Rain. This is burly, bald-headed Bad Cop Rain, sneering as he locks you up. Swallows the key, makes sure you see him doing it. Asylum Rain. Eight days ... think about it: What if it just doesn't stop? Forever Rain. It could happen, you know. Out here, it really could.[9]

The rain brings out emotional drama too. 'One memory,' writes Sarah in an email message to me, 'early in my marriage, when I seemed more prone to emotional breakdowns, the beach in the rain was my solace. I would make my way to some deserted shore and sit on a wave-smoothed log, slick with rain and cry. Here, facing the ocean, the waves would drown out my sobs, the rain would wash away my tears. After a timeless commune here I would be ready to face my life again'. Tourists and amenity migrants elsewhere in the world may seek out the sun to play and have some fun, but here storms afford a different kind of experience, one that allows you to get in touch with sensations and emotions that pour out as intensely as the rain.

Conclusion

As Benson and O'Reilly (2011: 611) suggest, 'the destinations chosen by lifestyle migrants tell us a lot about the lives they wish to lead'. This brief look at the lifestyle mobilities of Clayoquot Sound has shown us that destinations marked by relatively inclement weather attract both short-term tourists and lifestyle migrants who seek what sun-filled destinations could easily give them: a sense of peace, relative solitude, introspective calm, inspiring drama and soporific, therapeutic relaxation. If indeed 'the most renowned lifestyle migrants have chosen destinations in coastal resorts or islands in the sun' (Benson and O'Reilly 2011: 611), and if most research has in fact followed their migration and typical places, this chapter has shown how the health and lifestyle benefits of climate vary in the rain. While the short-term and residential tourists and lifestyle migrants to Clayoquot Sound generally seek out escape, leisure, authenticity, alternative lifestyles, countercultural ideals, relaxation, idyllic connection with landscape, rejuvenation, sense of community, artistic inspiration, simplicity and the good life not unlike their sunny and shiny counterparts do, the wetness and storminess of the local climate show us the value of understanding different lifestyle mobilities as different constellations of practices, experiences and representations – all with different rhythms, speeds and feels, all for different people with different personal and collective identities.

---

9   http://www.tofinotime.com/articles/A-T502-08frm.htm.

References

Benson, M. and O'Reilly, K. 2009. Migration and the search for a better way of life: a critical exploration of lifestyle migration. *The Sociological Review*, 57(4), 608–625.

Benson, M. and O'Reilly, K. (eds) 2011. *Lifestyle Migration: Expectations, Aspirations, and Experiences*. Farnham: Ashgate.

Brassley, P. 1998. On the unrecognized significance of the ephemeral landscape. *Landscape Research*, 23(2), 119–132.

Cresswell, T. 2010. Towards a politics of mobility. *Environment & Planning D*, 28(1), 17–31.

Edensor, T. 2007. Mundane mobilities, performances, and spaces of tourism. *Social & Cultural Geography*, 8(2), 199–215.

Gustafson, P. 2009. Retirement migration and transnational lifestyles. *Ageing and Society*, 21(4), 371–394.

Korpela, M. 2009. When a Trip to Adulthood Becomes a Lifestyle: Western Lifestyle Migrants in Varanasi, India, in *Lifestyle Migration: Expectations, Aspirations, and Experiences*, edited by M. Benson and K. O'Reilly. Farnham: Ashgate, 15–30.

Madden, L. 1999. Making money in the sun: the development of British- and Irish-owned businesses in the Costa del Sol. *Research Papers in Geography*, 36, University of Sussex, Brighton.

Seamon, D. 1980. *A Geography of the Lifeworld: Movement, Rest, and Encounter*. New York: Palgrave.

Trundle, C. 2009. Romance Tourists, Foreign Wives, or Retirement Migrants? Cross-cultural Marriage in Florence, Italy, in *Lifestyle Migration: Expectations, Aspirations, and Experiences*, edited by M. Benson and K. O'Reilly. Farnham: Ashgate, 51–68.

Vannini, P., Waskul, D., Gottschalk, S. and Ellis-Newstead, T. 2012. Making sense of the weather: dwelling and weathering on Canada's rain coast. *Space & Culture*, forthcoming. DOI: 10.1177/1206331211412269.

Williams, A. and Hall, C. 2000. Tourism, Migration, Circulation and Mobility: the Contingencies of Time and Place, in *Tourism and Migration: New Relationships Between Production and Consumption*, edited by A. Williams and C. Hall. London: Kluwer, 1–60.

Wunderlich, F.M. 2009. The Aesthetics of Place-Temporality in Everyday Urban Space: the Case of Fitzroy Square. In *Geographies of Rhythm: Nature, Place, Mobilities, and Bodies*, edited by T. Edensor. Farnham: Ashgate, 45–57.

Chapter 15
Negotiating Tourist Identities: Mobilities in an Age of Climate Change

Stewart Barr and Jan Prillwitz

Introduction: would you stop driving to save fuel for the aeroplanes?

> If you had to give up driving to save the fuel for the aeroplanes would you? Because at some point that choice is going to come isn't it? At some point, you will have to stop driving to save fuel for the aeroplanes. (Tom, Polsloe 1)

This quotation from a participant in a recent focus group discussion led by the authors, which we will return to later in this chapter, presents an intriguing if somewhat extreme example of the potential conflicts and juxtapositions that the seemingly ubiquitous issue of climate change now presents to consumers as they negotiate the landscape of global environmental change alongside the continuing growth in personal mobility. Indeed, although the trade-off highlighted by the participant may seem overly dramatic, in essence this example captures the emerging tensions that are beginning to show between the symbolic values we assign to different forms of mobility in contemporary lifestyles.

This chapter explores these tensions in a number of inter-related ways, drawing on literatures from tourism and transport studies, geography, sociology and psychology. In so doing, we aim to demonstrate the ways in which climate change is altering the ways in which researchers, policy makers and consumers are relating issues of consumption, mobility and practice to the seemingly all-encompassing issue of climate change. We use climate change here as an illustration, rather than seeking to argue that it is a 'special case', because global climate change and its associated discourses is an example of one emergent environmental issue that has the potential to challenge existing understandings of 'sustainable mobility' and wider consumption practices. Another issue that may have similar impacts, albeit with a lower media profile, is the rising concern over 'Peak Oil' (Hopkins 2008) and the consequences for economic and community resilience that could emerge from higher oil prices and increasing levels of resource scarcity.

The chapter will first examine the ways in which climate change has implications for tourism and travel and in particular for *tourists* and *travellers*, progressively viewed by politicians as the appropriate focus for policies aimed at reducing carbon emissions. Accordingly, we will argue that pursuing policies through so-called 'behavioural change' strategies represents a quintessentially neo-liberal framing of the climate change problem, which seeks to drive change through balancing the need to generate consumption with the citizenship responsibilities implied by the need to act collectively. In framing the issue through the notion of 'consumer-citizenship', the chapter will then examine how the focus on behavioural change has been implicated in debates concerning the role of personal mobility. In particular, we will demonstrate the ways in which climate change is re-framing intellectual and policy landscapes surrounding 'sustainable mobility' and providing new insights into the ways in which tourist identities are being framed through space as a result of discourses on climate change. This necessitates the adoption of nuanced and spatially configured approaches by both policy makers and researchers that focus more on the consumption practices of individuals, rather than the specific environmentally-related behaviours often regarded as the primary concern. Accordingly, the chapter ends with a call for greater synergies between research on transport, tourism and mobilities and the wider environmental social sciences.

Climate change, sustainability and mobility

Climate change has rapidly become an over-arching issue that has come to frame considerable academic and public discourse (Whitmarsh et al. 2011). Although notionally framed by many as a scientific issue, dominated by the concerns of climate prediction, modelling and associated impacts, social scientists have rapidly (if sporadically and unsystematically) responded to calls for understanding the socio-economic impacts and causes of global climate change (Whitmarsh et al. 2011). Within the context of transport and tourism, there have been a number of studies which have attempted to appreciate the role of mobility in contributing to global carbon emissions (Becken and Hay 2007, Chapman 2007, Peeters and Shouten 2006) and Chapman (2007) in particular has provided useful examples of the role that different forms of travel mode have on carbon emissions, demonstrating how personal mobility in daily travel contexts is a significant overall contributor to transport's impact on climate change. However, these studies have also illustrated the role of tourism travel modes, notably air travel, as a major contributor to carbon emissions and this has firmly positioned tourism, as well as daily forms of mobility, at the heart of the debate concerning climate change and travel.

Within the context of this chapter, the role of air travel is important in two ways. First, as Scott et al. (2010) have indicated, despite the recent economic downturn, passenger numbers using air travel are expected to rise exponentially over the next 30 years and this clearly has implications for the role of commercial aviation in contributing towards transport's overall carbon emissions. Indeed, although the Conservative-Liberal Democrat coalition government in the UK recently cancelled the construction of a third runway at London's Heathrow Airport, there has been no substantive change in the Department for Transport's (2003) policy that views aviation growth as a key element of the UK's economic strategy.

Second, the growth in air travel and its likely environmental impacts needs to be viewed within the wider context of an underlying shift in the mobility practices of populations in Western nations. As experienced in North America during the 1960s and 1970s, the de-regulation of the European air travel market in the 1990s has led to the emergence of a dynamic 'low-cost' airline sector and has resulted in a significant proliferation of routes and available destinations at very low cost (Graham and Shaw 2008). Indeed, as Ryley and Davison (2008) have illustrated, the proliferation in travel offerings has led to increases in both passenger numbers but also a spread in the socio-economic backgrounds of those utilizing air travel. Most importantly from a mobility perspective, the de-regulation of air travel has fundamentally altered the frequency with which consumers can travel, offering regular, cheap flights to a host of European destinations that permit the emergence of new mobility practices like weekend city breaks, regular visits to second homes and visiting friends and relatives abroad. In essence, the coming of the free market to air travel in Europe, as for many other Western economies, has resulted in nothing short of a mobility boom.

Consumers, citizens and mobilities

Within the context of both a rising media profile concerning the impact of travel on climate change and the rapid rises in personal mobilities associated with changes to the air travel market in Europe, governments have needed to explore ways of tackling these and a whole other host of climate-significant impacts that derive from economic activity. The ways in which states have responded to such environmental dilemmas can be traced back to the emergence of international and national environmental policies from the 1970s (McCormick 1989) in which focus was largely on the role of regulation as a tool for reducing environmental impacts. However, the emergence of a centre-right political philosophy throughout the 1980s in countries like the United Kingdom and United States set in train the development of neo-liberal frameworks for governance that have progressively rolled-back the state (Rose and Miller 2002) in numerous policy arenas, thus placing greater emphasis on the market to fulfil roles previously performed by the state (Clarke et al. 2007). Within this context, environmental policy has progressively been viewed as a 'down-stream' concern, which is related to the ways in which individuals, as citizens, can be persuaded and encouraged to change their consumption habits and thus generate positive change through the marketplace (Scammell 2004). Accordingly, as the Department for the Environment, Food and Rural Affairs' (DEFRA, 2005: 25) Sustainable Development Strategy has highlighted in the UK:

> We all – governments, businesses, families and communities, the public sector, voluntary and community organisations – need to make different choices if we are to achieve the vision of sustainable development.

The notion of choice as a way of protecting consumer sovereignty whilst exercising the necessary responsibilities of a concerned citizen towards the environment has thus become an established mode of governance and pervades much of the literature concerning the role of individuals as consumers (Spaargaren and Mol 2008). Indeed, as Spaargaren and Mol (2008) point out, research from a range of intellectual traditions has focused on the role of individuals as consumers; for example scholarship from economics, psychology and sociology has contributed to understandings of consumption choices and behaviours. Within research on sustainable travel, there has been a particular reliance on the ways in which social-psychological constructs, such as values and attitudes, play a role in framing the responses of individuals to issues like climate change (Barr et al. 2010, Hunecke et al. 2007). Drawing on ideas of segmentation, researchers such as Anable (2005), Dallen (2007) and Götz et al. (2003) have discussed the motion of 'mobility styles' through the social-psychological profiling of different 'lifestyle' groups that share similar attitudes, values and behaviours. Accordingly, such research has attempted to understand the motivations and barriers for the adoption of sustainable travel modes within the context of a much broader intellectual tradition that has developed in travel behaviour studies, which has sought to apply psychological understandings of behaviour drawn from the sub-discipline of social psychology (Ajzen 1991). In so doing, it is closely aligned to research in the environmental social sciences that has explored the notion of 'lifestyle' as a construct for understanding and promoting sustainable practices (Jackson 2005), albeit framing this notion around a narrowly defined and utilitarian construct of lifestyle that is defined by empirical differences between groups of consumers, rather than a broader theoretical framing of the term (Hobson 2002).

Promoting sustainable mobility

The focus in travel behaviour studies on what Hobson (2002) has more broadly termed the social-psychological 'rationalisation of lifestyles' is significant because it is closely aligned to the recent developments in policy for the promotion of environmentally sustainable behaviours that is embedded within the 'citizen-consumer' paradigm. As McKenzie-Mohr (2000) noted more than a decade ago, Western governments are coming to rely more on the techniques of the market for engaging and encouraging citizens to change their consumption habits and in the UK this has been operationalized through the notion of using *social* marketing as a tool for generating behavioural change (Barr et al. 2011). At its core:

> Social marketing ... underscores the importance of strategically delivering programs so that they target specific segments of the public and overcome the barriers to this segment's engaging in the behaviour. (McKenzie-Mohr 2000: 594)

Within the UK context, French et al. (2009) argue that the appeal of social marketing relates to its potential for shifting established behaviours through the use of marketing principles that are commonly applied and experienced daily by consumers, thus it relies on sophisticated marketing mixes and the careful segmentation of the market as a way of targeting particular groups. Applied widely within the health and social services sectors, the UK Government has adopted social marketing as its underlying framework for promoting environmentally responsible behavioural change (DEFRA 2008) and has defined seven broad segments based on their attitudinal, socio-demographic and behavioural characteristics. These segments are designed for use in the promotion of 12 pro-environmental behaviours, which span a range of concerns related to recycling and waste, energy use, water conservation and daily and tourism travel. Indeed, the approach adopted by DEFRA is also the basis for certain travel-based promotional campaigns, the most well-known example being the *TravelSmart* initiative of UK charity Sustrans (Sustrans 2011), which relies on the identification of segments for the promotion of personalized travel planning. Accordingly, at the forefront of policy responses to issues like climate change is the use of techniques that aim to segment the market and explore a range of personal motivations and barriers for adopting different forms of (sustainable) travel. In this way, changing behaviour is regarded as a question of focusing on particular target audiences and behaviours as a way of shifting the practices of individuals within a particular lifestyle group and thus making the group more sustainable.

Practising sustainable mobility: lifestyles, consumption and space

The compelling logic of adopting social marketing and the wider use of 'mobility styles' is that it uses tried and tested techniques from commercial marketing to change behaviour. However, there are a number of important questions that need to be addressed concerning the use of social marketing as a policy tool for changing travel behaviour within the wider context of debates on climate change and the ways in which pro-environmental behaviours are being frequently associated with calls to reduce carbon emissions. Accordingly, we propose that current approaches for promoting environmentally sustainable travel need to be re-examined in three ways. First, researchers need to question the compelling logic underlying the assumptions of scholarship that posits clear, rational relationships between environmental attitudes, knowledge and behaviours. Second, in framing 'behaviour' change, we argue that researchers miss the rich and valuable insights to be gained by focusing instead on practice and the ways in which mobility is entwined with everyday habits, routines and consumption choices. Finally, we question the logic of adopting universal and often totalizing approaches to explore practices across what are often very different and complex sites of consumption. In so doing, we argue that researchers need to distinguish between different spaces of mobility as a way of understanding the conflicts and tensions that an issue like climate change can cause for individuals in their travel choices.

To begin with the notion of behavioural 'rationality', the logic of assuming linear and explicable relationships between different constructs, such as attitudes, values and behaviours, has underlain much of the research in travel behaviour studies, utilizing social-psychological models such as Fishbein and Ajzen's (1975) Theory of Reasoned Action and Ajzen's (1991) Theory of Planned Behaviour. The compelling logic of these models is the relationship between attitudes, intentions and behaviours, and these so-called linear frameworks have sought to establish the combination of factors that are seen to predict changes in behaviour (Owens 2000). Yet as Owens (2000) notes, these rationalistic models make a series of assumptions about personal decision-making, most importantly that behaviour is a clear result of logical, rational decision-making focused on the specific issue of concern (that is environmental behaviour). These models therefore assume that issues such as previous experience, social context and consumption setting are irrelevant and that individuals are able to act upon their attitudes. Indeed, a catalogue of studies (for example Blake 1999, Agyeman and Angus 2003, Hobson 2002, Shove 2010) has questioned the veracity of linear social-psychological frameworks to provide valuable insights into the ways in which individuals behave towards the environment.

One of the main reasons that researchers have questioned the logic of such frameworks is the way in which behaviour is used and framed as a discrete and de-contextualized activity. Accordingly, our second concern with current approaches for studying sustainable travel 'behaviour' is the reliance researchers place on discrete actions rather than exploring the wider role of mobility in the everyday practices of individuals and social groups. Researchers from within the mobilities tradition have recently been arguing for an understanding of the ways in which the whole range of so-called sustainability behaviours are defined and understood within the context of practice, related very much to the assertions of scholars such as Freudendal-Pedersen (2009), Urry (2002, 2007) and Verbeek and Mommaas (2008) that the traditional boundaries between different forms of lifestyle practices (such as 'touristic' and 'daily') are becoming blurred.

Moreover, these assertions have been supported by research on practices within environmental sociology and geography, where authors such as Shove (2003) have theorized the role of practices in demonstrating the ways in which socio-technical systems become embedded into everyday life, thus constituting normality. Indeed, Shove (2003) and Shove et al. (2007) have argued that practices represent the everyday consumption of services associated with maintaining normality; accordingly individuals use energy services (rather than 'energy') for maintaining comfort and cleanliness and so on. In the same way, mobility practices can be seen as a way of living out the routines and expectations of modern consumer societies that are intrinsic to the maintenance of personal identity. In this way, those advancing a practices approach to understanding so-called 'pro-environmental behaviour' argue that it is the very basis for consumption that needs to be the focus, rather than the environment itself (Bulkeley and Gregson 2009). As Shove (2003: 9) states:

> What counts is the big, and in some cases, global swing of ordinary, routinized and taken for granted practice. This requires an upending of the social environmental research agenda as conventionally formulated. Only by setting 'the environment' aside as the main focus of attention will it be possible to follow and analyse processes underpinning the normalisation of consumption and the escalation of demand.

In essence, understanding and moreover promoting sustainable forms of travel requires an appreciation of how mobility practices have developed, what needs these satisfy and the ways in which these are entwined with other routines that constitute normality. Our third concern is therefore an extension of these issues to question the ways in which understandings of mobility practices are reflected in space and the extent to which our appreciation of their relationship with climate change differs between sites of practice. Here we draw on the substantial body of evidence emerging within tourism research that has demonstrated the ways in which tourists respond to climate change. As authors such as Becken (2007), Dickenson and Dickenson (2006) and Gössling and Peeters (2007) have shown, the perceived role of tourism travel in contributing to carbon emissions and climate change is at the very best limited. Indeed, these authors have illustrated a number of discourses emerging that adopt strategies of 'denial' (Stoll-Kleemann et al. 2001) that appear to demonstrate an unwillingness to accept the scientific evidence for the contributions made to carbon emissions by activities such as air travel.

This apparent 'denial' of climate change in spaces of tourism consumption raises questions about the extent to which such individuals are unwilling to engage in environmentally conscious practices within daily travel and domestic contexts. Yet, as Barr et al. (2010) have shown, it can often be those with the highest levels of environmental awareness and commitments to environmentally responsible behaviours in a domestic context who are the most likely to fly frequently, despite the high carbon-impact of air travel. In this way researchers need to be attentive to the ways in which sites of consumption interact through practices with an issue like climate change and sustainability. In the case of mobility, there are questions concerning the ways in which perceptions of 'sustainable' mobility are framed at different sites of practice and the extent to which climate change, as an issue that appears to demand substantial changes in consumption when it comes to tourism travel, may be challenging normalized forms of consumption and identity. In turn, this raises questions concerning the ability of 'mobility styles' and segmentation research to accurately plot the ways in which individuals respond to environmental issues and thus highlights the potential problems that may be encountered when policy makers attempt to market reduced consumption to combat climate change.

The climate 'problem' for sustainable mobility

The three concerns we have outlined in the previous section form the basis for a brief exploration of empirical material gathered as part of an Economic and Social Research Council (ESRC) funded project exploring the promotion of sustainable travel using social marketing. The research was undertaken from 2008 to 2010 and involved a three-stage strategy that was based on exploring the travel practices of individuals in five study areas in and around the city of Exeter in the South West of the UK, each location being selected to represent a different form of residential built environment (Polsloe Ward: inner-city densely populated; Pennsylvania Ward: inner-city medium-density; St. Loyes Ward: sub-urban low density; Cullompton North Ward: low-density commuter settlement; Crediton St. Lawrence Ward medium-density rural centre). First, the authors held a series of focus group discussions in each study location to explore the ways in which individuals framed 'sustainable travel' and described their travel practices, both within and beyond a daily context. On the basis of these discussions and a stakeholder panel meeting, a questionnaire survey was developed to test and simulate research that uses social marketing and segmentation methods. This was administered to 2000 households across the five study areas and on the basis of the results from this survey five further focus groups were convened to discuss the quantitative findings across the study areas.

The material presented in this chapter focuses on the qualitative data collected from both sets of focus group discussions (15 in total) and therefore centres on the ways in which participants framed their travel practices and discussed these within the context of sustainability through both daily and tourism mobility. As such, in the following sections we initially show how participants defined sustainable travel in a daily setting as an unproblematic and locally-defined issue, connected to problems like congestion and air pollution. We then demonstrate how sustainable travel becomes contested as a concept when considered in tourism contexts and framed around issues of climate change and personal carbon emissions. In so doing, we aim to show the importance of understanding the wider consumption settings for travel practices, along with the importance of exploring practices and their spatial configuration as ways of exploring tourist identities.

'Sustainable' mobility as embedded practice

In understanding the ways in which travel practices are framed in different consumption settings, we focus initially on the ways in which sustainability has become a normalized and unproblematic concept within daily travel contexts. In this way, participants in the focus groups we convened largely framed the challenge of sustainable travel through localized notions of traffic congestion and its associated problems:

> I was talking about how life has changed so much from when I was a child to what it is here. We can't go on can we? Having more cars and more ... The whole town is chaos ... (Dick, Pennsylvania 1)

Indeed, problems of unsustainable travel were often related to concerns directly aligned with quality of life, such as congestion, air pollution and traffic noise, and thus there was an (unquestioned) assumption about the negative role of private car use. Accordingly, given the perceived social undesirability associated with car travel, participants were keen to justify their own behaviour through explanations of their personal circumstances:

> ... well I feel guilty about the pollution of the car but I just have to [use the car] ... with the nature of my work, because I am self employed I can work anything between 80 and 60 hours a week and very flexible hours. So you know I might need to pop into [town for] 2 hours, I might need to come back later, I might need to have a passenger, I might need to go onto hospital. It's just absolutely impossible to do by bus. (Cheryl, Crediton 1)

Consequently, there were prescribed norms that emerged through the discussions concerning the role of sustainable mobility and its social acceptability. To this extent, participants were frequently at pains to illustrate their sustainability credentials:

> I cycle everywhere really and years ago I made a decision not to use a car again, about fifteen years ago, and so far I haven't. (Albert, Polsloe 1)

Indeed, those with less sustainable travel practices often sought to highlight the ways in which barriers emerged to the (logical) adoption of sustainable travel practices in their daily routines:

> ... buses are extremely expensive. I mean they are fairly regular but they are ludicrously expensive. (Tim, Crediton 1)

> If you go with two people and you pay for it, for that money you can pay the car parking and the petrol and it's still cheaper. (Becky, Crediton 1)

Clearly these discussions were undertaken in an environment where there was possibly an unspoken social norm to confirm to a sustainability ethic, yet despite this concern, there were few who challenged the notion that sustainable travel was socially and environmentally responsible, helping to reduce congestion and noise pollution. In other words, sustainable travel was uncontested and largely supported as something which was a social and environmental 'good', even if personal circumstances made adoption of certain travel modes problematic.

Climate change, mobility and tourism: conflicting identities?

In contrast to the ways in which participants were able to comfortably discuss their mobility related to daily travel and sustainability, discussions of sustainable tourist travel were more conflictual in nature and began to demonstrate the ways in which participants had to start negotiating their identities as supporters of sustainable travel in a daily setting, but not necessarily in touristic sites of practice. As a way of generating discussion on the ways in which holiday travel was viewed by participants, the focus group moderator asked respondents about the influence of new forms of tourist mobility that had been enabled by the emergence of low-cost flights. The following quotation illustrates the ways in which individuals in the groups discussed their mobility in this context:

> It's just fun, you get nice places. I went to Morocco at Christmas, I went to the South of France last summer; I'm going to the south of France again, yeah going to Lanzarote at Christmas. (Simon, Polsloe 1)

The enthusiasm with which participants discussed what appeared to be a revolution in their mobility practices is indicative of the ways in which the de-regulation of the air travel market in Europe has introduced both a proliferation in routes and stiff competition between large carriers, driving down prices and enabling consumers to search and book low cost travel through the Internet (Graham and Shaw 2008). Indeed, what was striking about the discussion in the groups was the way in which low cost air travel had enabled a diversification in mobility. Accordingly, as Urry (2007) has suggested, the boundaries between tourism, leisure and the everyday have become blurred by the ability of people to have cheap and fast mobility that is often more than just about leisure and tourism, but which is entwined with 'everyday' relationships and social ties.

As a way of exploring how notions of sustainability related to tourism and mobility, participants were asked about what they considered to be sustainable tourism travel. Respondents were quick to highlight global climate change as a major issue, covered at length by popular media and high in the public's consciousness at the time the research was undertaken. Yet discussions of climate change immediately focused on the very basis of the science underpinning predictions of global warming rather than how to address the issue through policy or practice:

> ... you hear so many conflicting suggestions, and you know, sort of ideas which don't add up, somebody else says oh that's wrong, and you know, don't believe that. (Loveday, St. Loyes 3)

> Like I said I think it's beyond repair and until something happens I'm going to carry on enjoying myself and why not, there's nothing I can do to stop this so I'm just going to fly and drive until ... (Simon, Polsloe 1)

The sense of fatalism displayed in this quotation reveals a feeling that climate change as an issue was too large to deal with on a personal basis and that the 'damage had been done', justifying the maintenance of current practices before an inevitable crisis occurs. Indeed, alongside a feeling of fatalism, participants also argued that tourism was a special case:

> Holidays are holidays, you know ... although it's a catch 22 because flying is the worst form of, you know, pollution that there is. But, it's also the thing that you've looked forward to most of the year and you don't really get to do that often. So, it's quite hard. (Matt, Pennsylvania 2)

Here tourist mobility is characterized as a differentiated and special type of consumption that has additional value and which takes precedence over the need to reduce environmental impacts. Indeed, as the following participant revealed, there was animosity towards the suggestion put to respondents that policies could and should in some way attempt to restrict highly polluting forms of travel:

> That's not going to work, is it! That's like it's too much dictatorial ... I think, anyway. [influencing people's holiday choices] (Thomas, Pennsylvania 2)

Overall, the discussions concerning sustainable tourism travel and climate change, when compared to the ways in which sustainable travel in daily settings was framed, illustrate how participants were brought into a zone of potential conflict when climate change was discussed. We argue that such conflicts are fundamentally related to the identities which individuals represent through their practices and as such we argue that tourism mobility holds a particularly important symbolism in conveying identity in an age of low-cost and readily available air travel. In this sense, despite the potential conflicts between daily and tourist travel, many individuals were able to cross a boundary between being an 'environmentalist' (or at least an environmental supporter) in a daily travel setting and a profligate user of highly-polluting but symbolically critical modes of travel in other sites of practice:

> ... I called myself formally environmental ... but from Bournemouth airport, they do these flights for basically free to Glasgow Prestwick. I think the maximum my family has ever paid is £30 for a ticket but more often you can find them for £10, £5 ... I think my sister has come down for £0.99 a couple of times with the kids. That is just convenience. (Simon, Polsloe 1)

Conclusion: negotiated identities for climate change and mobility

The evidence in this chapter and from a host of emerging research in the environmental social sciences suggests that climate change poses a significant challenge for both researchers and policy makers as they attempt to understand the ways in which 'citizen-consumers' can become agents for and of change. In the following paragraphs we offer some initial conclusions on the ways in which current epistemological and political framings of climate change, individuals and mobility need to be critically evaluated as a way of responding to the increasing evidence showing that the challenge of climate change is seemingly irreconcilable with current demands for mobility in the twenty-first century.

In the first instance, we argue that by driving down the agenda for resolving many of the challenges associated with climate change to the level of the individual, as both consumer and citizen, presents a significant challenge for marrying-up these two distinct and potentially opposing concepts. Our research demonstrates that small-scale adjustments in travel behaviour within the setting of daily practices are largely uncontested because such alterations to practice are connected to the everyday lives of individuals (with concerns of noise and congestion) that support ascriptions of responsibility. Accordingly, there is at least the possibility as a consumer and a citizen to choose more or less environmentally polluting modes of travel and to be content that this does have an impact. Conversely, when tourism travel is considered, the predominant environmental concern becomes climate change, particularly when flying is discussed. In this context, the 'choice' for consumers is often between taking a cheap flight to access their holiday experience or not travelling at all. Indeed, because of the contested nature of climate change as an issue, there is no embedded sense of responsibility for acting as an individual. Accordingly, the two primary functions of the 'citizen-consumer' are rendered incapable of dealing with an issue like climate change, which necessitates major changes in consumption and a global sense of responsibility. Indeed, as critics of the citizen-consumer construct have noted (Johnson 2008), the fusing of consumption and citizenship necessarily results in a deterioration of critical politics and a sense of collective identity that are both likely to be requirements for the major social changes the threat of climate change necessitates.

A second theme we wish to highlight is the need for researchers and policy makers to explore ideas of practice. Although research on mobility styles and the adoption of this approach in segmentation studies and resultant social marketing policies has provided valuable insights into discrete travel behaviours and environmental motivations for adopting sustainable transport modes, the research in this chapter and from other areas of environmental social science suggest that researchers and policy makers need to look at the underlying drivers for consumption practices and the implications of these for mobility. As authors such as Shove (2003) have highlighted, the key to changing unsustainable practices lies in the appreciation of what underlies the construction of normal, everyday routines and habits that are less about transport, energy, water or other commodities, but rather concern the ways in which these services maintain the needs of everyday life – comfort, convenience, and of course mobility.

Finally, as geographers we make a particular call for researchers and policy makers to consider space as a key framing device for understanding the ways in which consumers are able to cross the boundaries between different sites of consumption and thus adopt apparently different identities when issues like sustainability and climate change are considered. Our research demonstrates that whilst these potential conflicts are acknowledged by individuals, they are rationalized by the different meanings associated with 'sustainable mobility' across space and the ways in which consumption mobility is valued at alternative sites of practice (from the daily to the holiday). Accordingly, understanding the symbolic value of consumption at these different sites and the ways in which issues like climate change are creating more fluid and negotiated identities between these spaces is critical.

Acknowledgement

The authors would like to thank the Economic and Social Research Council for financial support to undertake the research reported in this chapter (Grant No. RES-061-25-0158).

References

Agyeman, J. and Angus, B. 2003. The role of civic environmentalism in the pursuit of sustainable communities. *Journal of Environmental Planning and Management*, 46(3), 345–363.

Ajzen, I. 1991. The theory of planned behavior. *Organizational Behavior and Human Decision Processes*, 50(2), 179–211.

Anable, J. 2005. 'Complacent car addicts' or 'aspiring environmentalists'? Identifying travel behaviour segments using attitude theory. *Transport Policy*, 12(1), 65–78.

Barr, S., Gilg, A.W. and Shaw, G. 2011. 'Helping people make better choices': exploring the behaviour change agenda for environmental sustainability. *Applied Geography*, 31(2), 712–720.

Barr, S., Shaw, G., Coles, T.E. and Prillwitz, J. 2010. 'A holiday is a holiday': practicing sustainability home and away. *Journal of Transport Geography*, 18(3), 474–481.

Becken, S. 2007. Tourists' perception of international air travel's impact on the global climate and potential climate change policies. *Journal of Sustainable Tourism*, 15(4), 351–368.

Becken S. and Hay, J.E. 2007. *Tourism and Climate Change: Risks and Opportunities*. Clevedon: Channel View.

Blake, J. 1999. Overcoming the 'Value-Action Gap' in environmental policy: tensions between national policy and local experience. *Local Environment*, 4(3), 257–278.

Bulkeley, H. and Gregson, N. 2009. Crossing the threshold: municipal waste policy and household waste generation. *Environment and Planning A*, 41(4), 929–945.

Chapman, L. 2007. Transport and climate change: a review. *Journal of Transport Geography*, 15(5), 354–367.

Clarke, J., Newman, J., Smith, N., Vidler, E. and Westmarland, L. 2007. *Creating Citizen – Consumers: Changing Publics and Changing Public Services*. London: Sage.

Dallen, J. 2007. Sustainable transport market segmentation and tourism: the Looe Valley branch line railway Cornwall UK. *Journal of Sustainable Tourism*, 15(2), 180–199.

Department of the Environment Food and Rural Affairs (DEFRA). 2005. *Securing the Future*. London: DEFRA.

Department of the Environment Food and Rural Affairs (DEFRA). 2008. *Framework for Environmental Behaviours*. London: DEFRA.

Department for Transport (DfT) 2003. *The Future of Air Transport*. London: DfT.

Dickinson. J.E. and Dickinson, J.A. 2006. Local transport and social representations: challenging the assumptions for sustainable tourism. *Journal of Sustainable Tourism*, 14(2), 192–208.

Fishbein, M. and Ajzen, I. 1975. *Belief, Attitude, Intention and Behavior: An Introduction to Theory and Research*. Reading, MA: Addison-Wesley.

French, J., Blair-Stevens, C., McVey, D. and Merritt, R. 2009. *Social Marketing and Public Health: Theory and Practice*. Oxford: Oxford University Press.

Freudendal-Pedersen, M. 2009. *Mobility in Daily Life*. Farnham: Ashgate.

Gössling, S. and Peeters, P. 2007. 'It does not harm the environment!' An analysis of industry discourses on tourism, air travel and the environment. *Journal of Sustainable Tourism*, 15(4), 402–417.

Götz, K., Loose, W., Schmied, M. and Schubert, S. 2003. *Mobility Styles in Leisure Time: Proceedings of the 10th International Conference on Travel Behaviour Research* (Lucerne: International Conference on Travel Behavior Research).

Graham, B. and Shaw, J. 2008. Low-cost airlines in Europe: reconciling liberalization and sustainability. *Geoforum*, 39(3), 1439–1451.

Gregson, N. 2006. *Living with Things: Ridding, Accommodation, Dwelling*. Oxford: Sean Kingston Publishing.

Gregson, N. and Crewe, L. 2003. *Second-hand Cultures*. Oxford: Berg.

Gregson, N., Metcalfe, A. and Crewe, L. 2007. Identity mobility and the throwaway society. *Environment and Planning D: Society and Space*, 25(4), 682–700.

Hobson, K. 2002. Competing discourses of sustainable consumption: does the 'rationalisation of lifestyles' make sense? *Environmental Politics*, 11(2), 95–120.

Hopkins, R. 2008. *The Transition Handbook: From Oil Dependency to Local Resilience*. Dartington: Green Books.

Hunecke, M., Haustein, S., Grischkat, S. and Böhler, S. 2007. Psychological sociodemographic and infrastructural determinants of ecological impact caused by mobility behaviour. *Journal of Environmental Psychology*, 27(4), 277–292.

Jackson, T. 2005. *Motivating Sustainable Consumption: A Review of Evidence on Consumer Behaviour and Behavioural Change*. London: Sustainable Development Research Network / RESOLVE.

Johnson, J. 2008. The citizen-consumer hybrid: ideological tensions and the case of Whole Foods Market. *Theory and Society*, 37(3), 229–270.

McCormick, J. 1989. *The Global Environmental Movement*. 2nd edition. London: Belhaven.

McKenzie-Mohr, D. 2000. New ways to promote proenvironmental behaviour: promoting sustainable behaviour: an introduction to community-based social marketing. *Journal of Social Issues*, 56(3), 543–554.

Owens, S. 2000. Engaging the public: information and deliberation in environmental policy. *Environment and Planning A*, 32(7), 1141–1148.

Peeters, P. and Schouten, F. 2006. Reducing the ecological footprint of inbound tourism and transport to Amsterdam. *Journal of Sustainable Tourism*, 14(2), 157–171.

Rose, N. and Miller, P. 1992. Political power and the state: problematics of government. *British Journal of Sociology*, 43(2), 173–205.

Ryley, T. and Davison, L. 2008. UK air travel preferences: evidence from an East Midlands household survey. *Journal of Air Transport Management*, 14(1), 43–46.

Scott, D., Peeters, P. and Gössling, S. 2010. Can tourism deliver its 'aspirational' greenhouse gas emission reduction targets? *Journal of Sustainable Tourism*, 18(3), 393–408.

Shove, E. 2003. *Comfort Cleanliness and Convenience: The Social Organization of Normality*. Oxford: Berg.

Shove, E. 2010. Beyond the ABC: climate change policy and theories of social change. *Environment and Planning A*, 42(6), 1273–1285.

Shove, E., Watson, M., Hand, M. and Ingram, J. 2007. *The Design of Everyday Life*. Oxford: Berg.

Slocum, R. 2004. Consumer citizens and the Cities for Climate Protection campaign. *Environment and Planning A*, 36(5), 763–782.

Spaargaren, G. and Mol, A.P.J. 2008. Greening global consumption: redefining politics and authority. *Global Environmental Change*, 18(3), 350–359.

Stoll-Kleemann, S., O'Riordan, T. and Jaeger, C.C. 2001. The psychology of denial concerning climate mitigation measures: evidence from Swiss focus groups. *Global Environmental Change*, 11(2), 107–117.

Sustrans 2011. *TravelSmart Initiative*. Available at: www.sustrans.org.uk/what-we-do/travelsmart [accessed 28th July 2011].

Urry, J. 2002. *The Tourist Gaze*. London: Sage.

Urry, J. 2007. *Mobilities*. Cambridge: Polity Press.

Verbeek, D. and Mommaas, H. 2008. Transitions to sustainable tourism mobility: the social practices approach. *Journal of Sustainable Tourism*, 16(6), 629–644.

Whitmarsh, L., O'Neill, S. and Lorenzoni, I. (eds) 2011. *Engaging the Public with Climate Change: Behaviour Change and Communication*. London: Earthscan.

Chapter 16

Respect for Nature at 200 km/h?
Exploring the Role of Lifestyle Mobilities
in Environmental Responsibility

Leslie Mabon

Introduction

This chapter explores the potential of the idea of lifestyle mobilities in rising to some of the environmental challenges posed by contemporary mobility choices. I argue that developing a nuanced, contextualized understanding of how mobilities fit into people's lifestyles can play a pivotal role in imagining more sustainable mobility futures. What this means is that – particularly with more destructive means of mobility such as air travel and automobility – getting under how particular kinds of mobility fit into broader life narratives might help to explain why people continue with seemingly environmentally damaging practices.

I consider this idea of lifestyle mobilities in practice through empirical work carried out with rally drivers in Scotland. Rally driving is a form of motor sport in which two crew members – a driver and a navigator – attempt to drive their car in the fastest possible time between two points along a pre-defined set of courses. Rally driving takes place on courses closed to public vehicles, typically forest tracks or closed asphalt roads. Drawing on data constructed through ethnographic participant observation, in-depth interviewing, field notes and participatory action research, this chapter considers the role life narratives play in shaping rally competitors' continuation of an arguably environmentally damaging practice. The focus is on the physical nature of movement, the representation of rallying and the practice of rallying in order to consider how exactly rallying affects the environment, and what moves people to continue doing it.

I contend that thinking about environmentally damaging mobilities as part of people's broader lifestyles can help to illuminate what precisely is valued in different mobilities. In turn, it might be possible to imagine more sustainable futures that preserve the aspects stakeholders' value whilst mitigating some of the more environmentally harmful aspects. Furthermore, I also suggest that thinking through the ways in which lifestyle mobilities fit into stakeholders' world views can aid understanding of why some stakeholders may be hostile to critical reflection on the environmental effects of their mobility, and can give pointers as to the kind of engagement or information to which such stakeholders are more likely to be amenable.

The project

The data and ideas upon which this chapter is based comes from a larger project on environmental issues and the role of environmental philosophy in engaging stakeholders perhaps more sceptical, cynical and/or outright hostile towards ideas of environmental responsibility. These issues are explored through the case study of rally driving in Scotland, looking at how rally participants speak about the natural environments through which they drive, how they explain their continued fascination with a somewhat opaque and small-scale form of motor sport, and how they feel about environmental issues. The research does not start from the premise that rallying is necessarily *bad* for the environment, rather that there are some physical effects of driving vehicles at speed through the landscape, and that these effects potentially have negative consequences for biodiversity or other human users of the environment in question. Furthermore, there is also a *perception* within motor sport circles that the sport is under constant threat from an amorphous 'green lobby' (Collins 2009, Saward 2010) seeking to 'stop' motor sport on environmental grounds. In Scotland at least, however, there is no sustained and organized opposition to motor sport like the kind that may exist for, say, air travel (Lynes and Dredge (2006) note that air travel is associated with some of the most significant environmental impacts of tourism and comes under pressure from environmental groups to take action, and Mayer et al. (2012) discuss increasing passenger interest in airlines' environmental credentials).

Empirical research takes the form of observation and participant observation of rally crews competing on events (video recorded where possible, written up as field notes when not), in-depth interviews with rally participants and organizers, and two small participatory projects with rally events aiming to reduce what the organizers think the environmental impacts (if any) of rallying are. Other users of the natural environments (mainly forests) in which Scottish rallying takes place are also observed and interviewed in order to identify any potential areas of conflict or difference in lifestyle, however data pertaining to other users is not discussed in this chapter. The aim of this multi-method approach is to consider how the environment is experienced by rally participants in the first instance, how rallying is spoken about as a 'lifestyle' and something relating to broader life contexts, and to look at how environmental responsibility might be enacted in practice.

A question I am frequently asked when discussing my work is: why rallying? For much of my postgraduate years I attempted to come up with some kind of answer about rallying as a unique and extreme case study; however the actual reason for my interest in rallying lies much closer to home. Namely, it is a kind of lifestyle mobility about which I am very enthusiastic (I have written a number of media articles on rallying). Whilst it may seem a little odd for someone with an academic interest in environmental issues to be also so passionate about something like motor sports, this is not something I see as being overly problematic. After all, Mary Midgley (1989: 23) reminds us when talking about academic work more broadly; we must situate ourselves within existing debates and not 'sneer from the sidelines'. When we think about the environmental effects (or, indeed, social effects more broadly) associated with lifestyle mobilities, then, there is perhaps a moral imperative to reflect critically on our own mobilities and to consider why we might continue with these more environmentally damaging forms. Working in a field with which I am familiar and interested therefore serves only to bring questions of the researcher's personal relationship to the fore, and indeed can be a force for good in offering additional explanatory purchase if reflected upon appropriately.

Additionally, I do genuinely believe a case study such as rallying can offer much in ensuring the continued applicability of lifestyle mobilities research. The environmental challenges that are likely to arise over the coming decades will affect all areas of society, not only those who wish to take action now to mitigate their environmental impacts, hence it is useful to build up experience in working with stakeholders perhaps more cynical, sceptical or outright hostile towards environmentalist thinking. Spending a little time thinking about why some stakeholders may continue to practice lifestyle-related mobilities likely to cause harm to natural environments can help us to be prepared for some of the difficult decisions that lie ahead (see McShane 2008). Illuminating what precisely is valued in these kinds of mobilities can perhaps allow some of the more environmentally damaging elements to be eliminated whilst the things that are really valued are retained.

Theoretical context

This kind of research has links to the burgeoning field of automobility literature in geography and the social sciences more broadly, in particular some of the more recent research that looks at the emotional and relational aspects of car driving and car ownership. Sheller's (2004) work on automotive emotions in particular is a touchstone for my research, especially her assertion that because many people find cars enthralling, exhilarating or exciting, vehicles will not be given up easily in spite of apparent ethical or environmental criticisms. To help understand why exactly some people find the process of driving so attractive, it is also useful to draw on the work of Peter Merriman (2004, 2006) on the relationship of car drivers/occupants to the environments through which they travel. Going beyond the idea of the landscape through which the car travels as being a flat, two-dimensional 'backdrop' – Augé (1995) even goes as far as to term motorways non-places – and instead considering the ways in which car drivers can form relationships with the environment is a useful step in understanding what moves people to continue driving. As well as the relationship with the vehicle itself, then, the emotions and feelings generated from the relationship with the environment through which the car travels may lead people to continue driving for pleasure.

It is important to register that much of the automobility work to date focuses on driving as an 'everyday', mundane activity. That is, driving for the purpose of travelling to somewhere or doing some other kind of activity which is dependent on driving for access. Bull's (2004) consideration of the soundscapes of automobility, and Laurier's (2005) ethnomethodological work on looking for parking spaces stand as fine examples of this very interesting and thought-provoking work on everyday automobilities. Rallying is perhaps somewhat different in that it is the process of driving itself that is the main source of value. What rally participants actually seem to value is the embodied experience of driving and the participation in this driving experience, rather than the wider freedoms that driving affords. Nonetheless, I believe the key ideas in much of the automobility work, especially the role of emotion and feeling in leading people to continue driving and the complicated relationship with the surroundings, still hold for a case study of 'driving for pleasure' – as the coming sections illustrate.

What I am primarily interested in is the embodied experience of rally driving, and how this experience is interpreted and re-interpreted as something its participants wish to continue doing in the face of mounting ethical criticisms (British organization 'Save Motorsport' has a comprehensive database of conflicts on their website, www.savemotorsport.com). Nevertheless, the concept of lifestyle mobilities (this volume) is extremely useful in getting analytical purchase on what precisely is valued in the rally experience. Although the kind of lifestyle mobility in this study is perhaps slightly different in that rally participants are not 'migrating' as such and end up back at their homes after a very short period of time away following an event, I believe the emphasis on the context in which movement takes place is vital in understanding why people continue with perhaps more environmentally damaging mobilities. That is, the ways in which people reason round and justify their mobility choices may well be bound up with much broader life contexts. Having said that, given the interest in the environmental effects of lifestyle mobility choices and Crouch's (2001) assertion that it is at the scale of the body that wider contexts are enacted, my focus here will be in the embodied experience of rallying and how this embodied experience of driving at speed is made sense of in relation to the idea of participating in a rally driving 'lifestyle'.

In order to consider these themes in relation to my case study, Cresswell's (2010) three key themes of mobility – movement, representation and practice – are considered in turn. Just as Cresswell is careful to note that his disentangling of these three elements is to aid theory building, I would say my disentangling is to aid analytical purchase and the application of theory. In other words, attempting to disentangle movement, representation and practice is a temporary and partial move in order to get a handle on what is going on here, and some overlap is perhaps inevitable.

Movement

First of all I want to spend a little time reflecting on what Cresswell (2010) calls 'movement'. Cresswell suggests that this physical movement is the 'raw material' for mobility, movement that can be measured and mapped. Cresswell (2010: 19) notes, however, that understanding physical movement tells us 'next to nothing about what these mobilities are made to mean or how they are practiced'. Nonetheless, if one is trying to understand the environmental effects of particular lifestyle mobilities, then it is in some ways important to pay at least a little attention to the physical nature of movement – because it is very often this physical movement that actually causes harm to the environment.

This is something that comes across very clearly in rally driving. Smoke and flames blast out of exhausts, clouds of dust rise up, rocks go flying, the occasional deer gets hit. How this then becomes construed as 'environmental damage' is a question bound up with representations and practices of mobility, but it is certainly true that rally cars change the physical nature of the environment as they speed along within it.

Let me briefly illustrate this with a couple of examples. First of all, rally cars can disrupt the forest ground (see Figure 16.1). Forest engineers suggested to me that gravel sent flying by rally cars driving at speed along forest racks may in turn get into water courses and can take a considerable amount of time and money to rectify. Specialist machinery needs to be brought into the forest to replace and re-level the disrupted gravel, and the ditches at the roadside sometimes need to be re-constructed after rally cars have driven into them. Secondly, materials such as tape and signage are used to change the physical nature of the forest on the days when rallies take place, in order to ensure public safety by limiting non-rally access. Signs stating that 'Motor Sport Can Be Dangerous' are placed at forest entrances, whereas more detailed notices explain that the right of free public access to the forest has been suspended for the day of the rally.

These physical manifestations of rally activity, the 'stuff' that is needed for rallying to happen and the 'evidence' of a car rally having taken place, can give useful initial insights into how other stakeholders might come to see rallying as objectionable. Affording a little time to the nature of physical movement can help to give an indication of how particular practices may be viewed and how claims over environmental damage by some kinds of lifestyle mobilities might be formed.

When lifestyle mobilities and environmental issues are at stake, it is also important to get clear in the first instance what 'the environment' actually means to the different stakeholders involved. Again, this cannot be separated from the ways in which this 'environment' is represented and practiced, but paying heed to the ways people physically move within the environment is an important first step in getting analytical purchase on how people come to engage with the environment and form environmental values.

Figure 16.1   'Rutting' of forest track caused by passing rally cars

Source: Leslie Mabon.

This is something that comes across quite clearly when we look at the rally course. The movement of rally cars and their occupants over the whole day of an event is very tightly regulated, with crews having to follow very strict time schedules and stick to the correct route in-between sections. On the competitive 'stages', a series of numerical and directional instructions read out by the navigator tells the driver exactly where to go and at what speed to drive for each particular corner. Roads not being used for the rally are blocked off with tape and cones. Orange arrows indicate sharp-angled corners. Yellow and red boards tell the crew when the competitive action is at an end and when to come to a stop.

Looking at how the physical movement of participants in a car rally is shaped can thus give useful insights into the kind of experience the crew might have. The positioning of signs, the placing of hay bales and the reading of danger warnings by the co-driver all help to instil the sense of some parts of the environment being more hazardous to the humans driving quickly through it. Moving in the natural environment as a rally competitor, as a participant in the rallying way of moving within the natural environment, shapes a particular way of evaluating the environment – hardly an earth-shattering revelation, but one that is nonetheless reinforced by spending some time exploring how the physical movement of the rally crew pans out. Further enquiry is, of course, needed into how this mobility is then represented and practiced and the work that this does, but in terms of getting a handle on a somewhat opaque kind of mobility it is a significant initial step.

Lastly, it is also important to acknowledge the energy usage of the rally cars themselves. Rally cars almost exclusively run on petrol, a fossil fuel whose burning is generally acknowledged to contribute to climate change through carbon dioxide emissions. Further, due to the high speeds and rapid accelerations involved, rally cars also use far more fuel with far less efficiency than ordinary road-going vehicles. Whilst some rally participants involved in my study argued that the very small numbers of rally cars globally meant these emissions were negligible, it is still worth bearing in mind that these kinds of vehicles do burn fossil fuels at a very high rate in the name of sporting endeavour.

I do agree with Cresswell (2010), then, about the limitations of more positivist studies in shaping an understanding of what different mobilities mean and how they are practiced. But I would also suggest that it is important not to lose sight of the materialities of lifestyle mobilities, for it is through physical movement that conflicts over mobilities often arise and play out. Above all else, we need to keep in check what is actually at stake and what is actually being damaged when we talk about the environmental effects of lifestyle mobilities.

Representation

The chapter will now turn to the notion of representation. This is where the idea of rally driving as a particular kind of lifestyle mobility really comes to the fore. It is through looking at how rallying is represented that I feel we can really start to develop an understanding of how people can be moved to continue such a practice in spite of clear ethical criticisms. Alternative representations of motor sport can also reveal much about what precisely those opposed to motor sport find ethically objectionable.

This is particularly relevant when we think about why rallying goes on in largely natural landscapes such as forests, countryside or deserts as opposed to other forms of motor sport that take place on almost completely human-made race tracks. Whilst it is certainly possible to host a car rally in a more obviously human-made environment such as a disused airfield or a run-down army base, the vast majority of competitors prefer to get out into the forests and rally through the trees.

The Glentrool forest complex in south-west Scotland stands as a fine example of how a forest environment can come to be seen – and continue to be seen – as the 'right' kind of location in which rallying should take place. In the in-depth interviews, ethnography and document analysis I carried out over the course of my fieldwork, Glentrool was frequently referred to as a special location for Scottish rallying, a section of forest where the most skilled drivers would stand out, and where talent and a lack of fear were crucial to success. Doing well in Glentrool – or at the very least not crashing – seemed to be central to being part of the Scottish rallying lifestyle. As well-known rally journalist John Fife (2009) wrote when reporting on a rally taking place in Glentrool:

> If you want to find out if your heart is in good shape, forget the hospital heart rate monitors, they're kids stuff compared to strapping yourself into a rally car and going rallying in Glentrool in the rain! ... (i)n my book anyone doing this one in under 13 minutes is a hero. And there were 8 of them today. It's the crests you see. You either commit to them and go fast, or you chicken out and stay safe ... one of (my) original heroes, Drew Gallacher, had his ashes scattered over a certain stretch of road in Glentrool, and I reckon the big man would have been taking an interest.

Particularly interesting here is the way the roads of the forest come to take on so much significance for rally participants. Such roads were originally designed for the purely utilitarian purpose of allowing timber lorries to enter and exit the forest as quickly and efficiently as possible, commercial forestry and logging itself being a practice that is not without potential negative environmental impacts. In the above extract, the natural landscape of Glentrool is portrayed as being more than up to the challenge of hosting a rally, to the extent that setting a certain time through the forest and driving with a certain level of confidence becomes almost a rite of passage. Responding to the challenges of undulating topography, unpredictable gravel and adverse weather can therefore be seen to be an important part of participating fully in the rallying lifestyle. Looking at the contexts within which the natural environments of rallying sit, it becomes clear that paying attention to the rallying 'lifestyle' – driving through famous locations, shaping one's own heroic tales, contending with the physical challenges of the terrain – can give insight into why some forests are so revered by rally participants, and thus why these groups may continue to rally in more sensitive environments.

On the other hand, the concept of representation can also help to explain the reasoning behind opposition to motor sports. The edited collection *Thrillcraft* explores the environmental consequences of motorized recreation in some depth. Although the collection's main focus is on off-road vehicle (ORV) use in the USA (motorized recreation rather than motor *sport* per se), it nonetheless raises points valid and pertinent to rally driving. As Williams (2007: 81) puts it:

In the end, the problem comes down not so much to the nature of ORV users as to the nature of ORVs. ORVs are designed to go "off road," where motorised vehicles don't belong. Their noise is undemocratic, much like second-hand smoke. They need to be removed from our wildest and best public land ... because they intrude and usurp.

Key to Williams' (2007) concerns here seems to be the notion that a natural wild environment is not the 'right' place for a motorized vehicle. The use of words such as 'intrude' and 'usurp' illustrates very clearly the view that motorized vehicles are somehow out of place in a natural environment. The allusion to democracy is more interesting still, for it implies that motorized vehicles are also at odds with the kinds of values implicit in natural environments. This is clearly in stark contrast to the rallying view of Glentrool above – in the rallying narrative, Glentrool comes across as a place where the weather and the physical landscape are set as a challenge or even an invitation for the rally car and its crew, whereas in Williams' narrative, vehicles should not even be in such environments in the first place. Instead of representing vehicles as being 'in place', Williams (2007) very much represents them as being 'out of place' in nature.

How particular environments come to be seen as the right – or wrong – kinds of environments for particular mobilities, then, seems to be bound up with the lifestyle context in which the mobility sits. In particular, the way that mobility is presented and re-presented to participants of that kind of mobility can help to reinforce the idea of a certain kind of environment being the appropriate manifestation of the lifestyle associated with that kind of mobility – as with the telling of tales in which twisty, fast forest tracks serve as the setting for heroic deeds of past rally drivers. Nonetheless, when the same natural environment is drawn on by a different lifestyle as representing very different characteristics and values, then the potential for conflict arises. Similarly, when the environment seen as appropriate or meaningful also happens to be a natural environment sensitive to the effects of excessive human activity, then it becomes important to forge an understanding of why stakeholders may continue to move in a way that damages that environment.

Practice

Finally, the empirical data will be explored in relation to the notion of practice. If we are to understand why participants might continue with an activity such as rallying in spite of ethical criticisms, I believe it is crucial to look at the experience of rallying as sensed through the body. After all, as Cresswell (2010: 20) notes, 'it is at the level of the body that human mobility is produced, reproduced and, occasionally, transformed'. If it is indeed at the level of the body that mobility is produced and reproduced, then it follows that enquiry into the embodied experience of rallying will give us clues as to what the sensations, emotions and feelings are that make people want to belong to and participate in this lifestyle-related mobility.

Just as the landscapes of rallying are represented, so they are also practiced when crews drive over them over the course of a rally. The physical features of the natural environment within which the rally car moves – steep hills, sharp drops, tight corners – can provoke strong reactions from drivers and navigators. These feelings in turn lead competitors to see some environments as more meaningful for rallying. For instance, when asked to talk about his favourite forests in which to go rallying, international-licenced co-driver Martin was quick to mention those with challenging topography:

> I think one of the most exciting stages is Drummond Hill, because it's, it's a complex stage, it's a very, very complex stage with some very, very hairy moments and big drops depending on which way you're going round. And it's always amusing as a co-driver to see the difference in commitment between if it's on the driver's side or on the co-driver's side between the driver. I mean some of the stages in Argyll where there's huge big drops, very often I, I just used to put something at the side window there so that I couldn't see it, honestly because it does, it intimidates you and again if it's on the driver's side of the window it slows them down as well.

What makes the locations of Drummond Hill (in Perthshire, central Scotland) and Argyll (west coast of Scotland) so memorable for Martin is the topography of the land over which the car travels. The drops are not necessarily described as being positive features, for language such as 'hairy moments' and 'it intimidates you' suggests such landscapes can instil an element of fear in the competitors, perhaps through the potential for a serious accident to occur. Nonetheless, the forests in question are subsequently recounted as being the 'best' for rallying, with Martin foregrounding the topography as his justification for saying this.

Askins (2009) claims that it is the way physical sensations are translated by the body that gives rise to emotions and feelings, and in the case of Martin (and many other competitors like him), I would argue that it is the way the undulations of the forest tracks and the movement of the car to dodge rocks and other natural hazards are processed by the body that leads to some environments being seen as being 'right' for rallying. In other words, it is the sensation of moving within a natural landscape that becomes meaningful to rally competitors, not just the feeling of being in a car that is driving quickly.

The sensations that are felt by the body, and processed and later reflected upon to mark the rallying experience as worthwhile and meaningful, are generated in the first instance by the interplay between the human body, the car and the natural environment. Participants describe the 'feeling' of rallying as being multi-sensual. It involves, among many other things, the physical forces exerted on the body as the car jumps on elevation changes, stops suddenly and turns corners, the sounds of rocks hitting the underside of the car, the sights of trees flashing past, and even tactile cues from the vehicle to detect the effect of changing weather on driving conditions. Understanding why people rally, then, perhaps necessitates looking at how rallying feels in practice, and getting under the emotions and feelings that this shapes.

Linking back to questions of representation, it is also important to note that these embodied experiences and attendant feelings then feed back into the broader rallying 'lifestyle' narrative, thus reinforcing the idea of what the right kind of landscape for rallying is. What I mean by this is that tales of exciting experiences are recounted by drivers and navigators, thereby continuing the narratives of rallying's places, and those who manage to keep the sensations and emotions generated by this topography in check are fêted and viewed as the most heroic drivers – as witnessed through Martin's observation of how committed his driver can be in spite of the intimidating nature of the landscape. A good example of the kind of recounting I am getting at here could be viewed in the blog of former rally driver James Stewart (2005), who provided reports similar to this for all events on which he competed:

> ... through a 50° left into 50° right. It was quite interesting overtaking between a car and a ditch, round a bend while sliding on gravel! We pushed on, cutting corners and running through the ruts, bouncing and dragging the bottom of the car along the ground. After a blind right-hander over a crest into a 50° left we found a Mk1 Escort stuck on the inside of the left bend. We slid through the left bend with the tail out ...

As with Martin's account, it seems here to be the way the features of the natural landscape, mediated of course by the car, are sensed by the human body that gives rise to the idea of rallying as a positive experience upon reflection. What makes this the mark of a particular 'lifestyle' mobility, however, is the way in which this tale is recounted and shared with other competitors and interested parties through a publicly available website. It is participation in a particular kind of driving – namely, using the gravel to skid round corners, pushing the car so hard that its floor bounces off the ground, and flying over unsighted crests. As well as participation in a particular kind of *driving*, however, it is also participation in a particular kind of *mobility*, participation in the lifestyle of a rally driver. Through the recounting of and reflection on embodied experience of driving at speed in particular places, orally as well as verbally, the idea of the rallying lifestyle as being best lived by driving in particular kinds of natural environments is reinforced.

Whilst this idea of recounting tales of participation in the rallying 'way of life' suggests that representations of mobility and practices of mobility are far from separate, critically disentangling representation and practice can give a certain degree of analytical purchase on different lifestyle mobilities. In particular, what is of interest here is to look at how different mobilities *feel* in practice, especially how the physical sensations of mobility translate into emotions and feelings. It is then interesting to consider how these emotions and feelings – which stem from the physical practice of different mobilities – come to shape sensibilities that situate the practitioner within a particular kind of lifestyle mobility. In other words, how does the embodied sensation of a certain kind of mobility, in this case rally driving, come to shape the notion of participating in a particular lifestyle? And, in light of that, how does the notion of belonging to a particular lifestyle mobility shape the way one then interprets the physical sensations inferred during conditions of mobility?

Discussion and conclusions

This chapter has tried to sketch out some of the ways in which thinking of mobilities as being situated within broader lifestyles can help us to understand why people choose to move in the ways they do. It has also attempted to show – with reference to environmental issues and a mobility choice that can be seen to be damaging to the natural environment – that thinking in this way can help to open up very pressing 'real world' issues to critical scrutiny. Particularly when mobilities with potentially significant environmental impacts are at stake, I believe it is important to spend some time getting under the values and contexts bound up with that kind of mobility, in order to understand why that kind of mobility *matters* to the individual or group in question and why they might continue with it in spite of ethical criticisms.

I have suggested here that Cresswell's (2010) three facets of mobility – movement, representation and practice – can be temporarily disentangled in order to help us understand how the desire for certain kinds of mobility and the effects of this mobility play out. As far as *movement* is concerned, whilst I do take on board Cresswell's concerns about the positivist approach to which such a line of enquiry lends itself, I also think it is crucial to acknowledge the materiality of mobilities – particularly those that might cause notable physical damage to the natural environment. This can also help to identify areas over which conflict between mobilities may occur. This chapter's treatment of *representation* explored how particular representations of a lifestyle, in this case rallying, can help to shape the notion of certain kinds of environment being the 'right' place in which to undertake mobility for pleasure. This becomes interesting when the image of an 'appropriate' location also happens to be a sensitive natural environment, for it can illuminate what kinds of qualities draw participants to the landscape, and in turn help to suggest alternative locations where the same landscape qualities may still be present. Such locations could include, for example, carefully designated and restricted sections of commercial forestry, or post-industrial landscapes such as quarries or spoil tips formed as a legacy of coal mining. Finally, in *practice*, the physical feeling of being involved in a kind of mobility like rallying was discussed. I explored the physical sensation of driving through the landscape, how the way the body – mediated by the car – sensed movement through the natural landscape, and how this in turn might be translated into positive feelings about the rallying technique of movement. This in turn involved reflecting on how re-telling or representing these feelings might reinforce the feeling among participants that they were really participating in the rallying lifestyle, that what they felt was a 'rally' experience in the natural environment.

It is important to register here that I do recognize the difference between rally driving and many other movements that could be termed 'lifestyle' mobilities such as air travel or migration for employment reasons. Although the participants in these kinds of movement generally have a certain amount of choice in the nature of their movements, rallying is perhaps slightly different in that it is the journey itself that is of value, and also in the sense that participants end up back in their own homes at the end of the event! Nonetheless, I would contend that my focus here on materiality, context and embodied experience as a way of understanding *why* people might *choose* to move in the way they do is applicable also to lifestyle mobilities where the main physical movement phase is not necessarily the most important element. Further, I would also hope that this study has illustrated the importance for us, as researchers interested in mobilities, to situate ourselves within debates and consider the mobilities and mobility choices associated with our own lifestyles. If we open our own mobilities up to the same critical scrutiny that we afford to those of the groups we study, then perhaps we will be better placed to understand and account for the apparent incoherencies and inconsistencies in the lifestyle mobility stories of others.

References

Askins, K. 2009. 'That's just what I do': placing emotion in academic activism. *Emotion, Space and Society*, 2, 4–13.

Augé, M. 1995. *Non-Places: Introduction to an Anthology of Supermodernity*. London: Verso.

Bull, M. 2004. Automobility and the power of sound. *Theory, Culture and Society*, 21(4–5), 243–259.

Collins, P. 2009. Phil Collins enters the debate on perfectly legal road rallies. *Herefordshire Times*, 27 November, 28.

Cresswell, T. 2010. Towards a politics of mobility. *Environment and Planning D: Society and Space*, 28(1), 17–31.

Crouch, D. 2001. Spatialities and the feeling of doing. *Social and Cultural Geography*, 2(1), 61–75.

Duncan, T., Cohen, S. and Thulemark, M. 2013. *Lifestyle Mobilities: Intersections of Travel, Leisure and Migration*. Farnham: Ashgate.

Fife, J. 2009. Rally Report – 8th September 2009. *Jaggy Bunnet* [Online]. Available at http://jaggybunnet.co.uk/RRPage13.html [accessed: 25 January 2011].

Laurier, E. 2005. Searcing for a parking space. *Intellectia*, 2–3(41–42), 101–116.

Lynes, J.K. and Dredge, D. 2006. Going green: motivations for environmental commitment in the airline industry. A case study of Scandinavian Airlines. *Journal of Sustainable Tourism*, 14(2), 116–138.

McShane, K. 2008. *Environmental ethics: problems and prospects*, American Philosophical Association Pacific Division Meetings, Pasadena, CA, USA, 18–23 March 2008.

Mayer, R., Ryley, T. and Gillingwater, D. 2012. Passenger perceptions of the green image associated with airlines. *Journal of Transport Geography*, 22, 179–186.

Merriman, P. 2004. Driving places: Marc Augé, non-places, and the geographies of England's M1 motorway. *Theory, Culture and Society*, 21(4–5), 145–167.

Merriman, P. 2006. 'A new look at the English landscape': landscape architecture, movement and the aesthetics of motorways in early postwar Britain. *Cultural Geographies*, 13(1), 78–105.

Midgley, M. 1989. *Wisdom, Information and Wonder: What is Knowledge For?* London: Routledge.

Save Motorsport 2011. *Circuit Case Histories* [Online: Save Motorsport]. Available at: http://www.savemotorsport.com/histories.php [accessed: 19 February 2011].

Saward, J. 2010. *Why France is colour blind ...* [Online: Joe Saward's Grand Prix Blog]. Available at: http://joesaward.wordpress.com/2010/05/25/why-france-is-colour-blind/ [accessed: 13 July 2010].

Sheller, M. 2004. Automotive emotions; feeling the car. *Theory, Culture and Society*, 21(4–5), 221–242.

Stewart, J.D. 2005. *Colin McRae Forest Stages Rally Report* [Online: JSRallying]. Available at: http://www.jsrallying.co.uk [accessed: 18 April 2008].

Williams, T. 2007. Undemocratic Din: The Commandeering of Public Lands by Off-road Vehicles, in *Thrillcraft: The Environmental Consequences of Motorised Recreation*, edited by G. Wuerthner. White River Junction, VT: Chelsea Green, 79–81.

Chapter 17
Lifestyle Mobilities:
Conclusions and Future Research

Maria Thulemark, Tara Duncan and Scott A. Cohen

Through the chapters in this book we have demonstrated that the complex intersections of mobility and lifestyle, two areas in their own right of increasing importance in the social sciences, have not been subject to a sufficient sustained examination. Using the lens of lifestyle mobilities, we have begun to redress the limitations of current knowledge between mobilities, travel, leisure and migration (Cohen, Duncan and Thulemark 2013; see also McIntyre 2009). In progressing the concept of lifestyle mobilities, we have illustrated how it can offer a broader perspective through which to view those whose mobile lifestyles cannot be easily 'pigeon-holed'.

As an example, King (Chapter 6) argues that research on young people is underrepresented within the mobilities field. Through using lifestyle (mobility) as a conceptual tool, the complexities of young people's everyday negotiations with their surroundings are fruitfully explored, and as such, our understanding of youth lifestyles and mobility is enriched. Hence, we suggest that, instead of researching young people and children by considering the spaces they move between, lifestyle mobilities offers a way to value how, where and with who they move, and so allows for a wider appreciation of their relationships with space.

This highlights one of the themes running through the book. As Erskine and Anderson (Chapter 9) point out, the mobility *within* place is equally important to lifestyle travellers as the movement *between* places as it allows them to 'discover' themselves. O'Regan (Chapter 3) also examines this idea when he suggests that it is through the bodily mobility of hitchhikers – with their fragmented journeys – that they find perceived 'authentic' experiences and demonstrate belonging. With hitchhiking it would be impossible to consider mobility without considering the moving 'with' that King alludes to in her chapter. In a very literal sense, Sideri's experiences of commuting in Tbilisi (Chapter 8) also highlight how subtleties of our movement become important. Her simultaneous sigh with another passenger created a sense of togetherness that, as she suggests in her conclusions, allows us to see the sensory, corporeal and emotional elements of mobility (Vannini 2009). Thus, her examples provide us with the opportunity to observe the different performances and meanings attached to different lifestyles and different mobilities and so reconsider the relations produced. Rickly-Boyd (Chapter 4) takes this a slightly different way by suggesting that mobility for her 'dirtbags' (rock climbers) can be both horizontal (as in place to place) and vertical (as in up a cliff face). Yet in suggesting these differences, so she is also highlighting the complexities of lifestyle and mobility for this diverse community, stressing that this is a highly mobile community *because* of ability for them to have such multiplicity of mobility.

A second theme in the book utilizes the existing work around lifestyle migration. As a concept, lifestyle migration has allowed for the exploration of the social and cultural within current conceptions of wider (often) across-border movement. However, as we argue (see Cohen et al. 2013), compared to lifestyle migration, lifestyle mobility allows a broader account of the networks, scapes and flows involved (McIntyre, Chapter 13). Hence, the fluidity in the temporal and spatial aspects of mobility comes to the fore. Using lifestyle mobility rather than lifestyle migration allows for periods of immobility (or perhaps stillness) within the lives of those who are mobile rather than just one movement to another place as lifestyle migration often seems to suggest (Benson and O'Reilly 2009). Koth's (Chapter 10) bluewater sailors exemplify this mobility. She found that periods of being very mobile were balanced with other periods that were purposely immobile (due to cyclone/hurricane seasons for example). As such, her bluewater sailors' negotiations of leisure, work, sailing, being a tourist and living in a port distinguish them from lifestyle migrants and show how they practise lifestyle mobility.

McIntyre (Chapter 13) suggests that lifestyle migration is often characterized by movement to more rural areas – or as one of Vannini's respondents (Chapter 14) put it, to areas epitomizing the triple 'S' (sun, sea, sand). He argues that this neglects much movement within this type of migration and proposes a more fluid and dynamic conception of lifestyle mobilities that takes into account the wider networks, scapes and flows involved with lifestyle migration. A final chapter that considers lifestyle migration is Vannini's (Chapter 14) study of weather in the Clayoquot area of Vancouver Island, British Columbia, Canada. Here there is a more implicit use of lifestyle migrants as one of a number of groups whose lives, movements and identities are intimately bound up with the 'dance' of the storms that bring people to this area. Thus, for Vannini, the different lifestyle mobilities are constituted of constellations of practices, experiences and representations, all with their own rhythm, speeds and feel.

A third key theme that emerges relates back to Cresswell and Merriman's (2011) contention that it is necessary to study mobilities of the past in order to appreciate and value mobilities today and in the future. Dunkin and Grimwood's chapter (11) considers a historical case study and a contemporary one. They suggest that their examples highlight that interpolations of mobility are not transhistorical, but rather are contextual, reflecting place and time. Their conclusions highlight that mobility is deeply embedded within everyday life and that these canoeists, whether past or present, can provide us with more nuanced understanding of movement and practice as social phenomena. Ntaousani's (Chapter 12) example of Isamu Noguchi as a 'global citizen' draws attention to the ways that the recent past can shed light on current conceptions of mobility. Her exploration of Noguchi's tension with his self-awareness and sense of belonging resonate with many today (think, for instance, of 'third culture kids', Pollock and Van Reken 2009) and we could further relate his experiences of being at home everywhere back to Germann Molz's (2008) more recent ideas of being at home in the world.

A final theme that emerges is introduced in Chapter 2 by Claudia Bell. She suggests that the artists she was travelling with collect 'mobility capital' where recognition has little to do with fiscal wealth or social classification and much more to do with the evidence of global achievements. In suggesting this term she is responding to Cresswell's (2010: 29) call for a 'fine-tuning' of the mobility paradigm. The term 'mobility capital' strikes us as immensely important here. If we consider Erskine and Anderson's lifestyle travellers (Chapter 9), O'Regan's hitchhikers (Chapter 3) or Rickly-Boyd's 'dirtbags' (Chapter 4), their lifestyle *and* their mobility are what is important. Mobility capital can perhaps therefore be viewed as the 'new' cultural capital. For these groups, money has much less importance in terms of their identity and sense of belonging than their ability to be mobile. We can see Koth's (Chapter 10) bluewater sailors as another group that could claim mobility capital. Even Tzanelli's (Chapter 5) bellydancing women use their lifestyle and mobility as the medium through which to both define their own selves and to convey to others how they too can have this lifestyle. Her work highlights that the experiences within this type of tourism are what can define a lifestyle. Therefore, it is more than cultural capital and moves closer to Bell's idea of mobility capital.

The chapters within this book, and these four main themes, suggest avenues for the further study of lifestyle mobilities. We believe that the authors in this volume have given us room to (re)consider our understandings of different mobilities and, as we stated in the Introduction, and as Cresswell argues (2010), encourage us to pay closer attention to (im)mobile practices, experiences and their representation. The final two sections of this book further expand on areas we see of particular importance for lifestyle mobility. The first relates back to the growing use of and innovation within mobile methods and the second asks questions of lifestyle mobility particularly around who is able to travel for lifestyle and what will happen as travel patterns change and shift due to changing economic, environmental and political factors.

The mobile research(er)

The blurrings, disjunctions and interdependencies inherent within the mobilities paradigm highlight the ways in which movement – whether it is voluntary, enforced; whether there is a lack of movement or whether this movement is fleeting – merges, digresses, intersects across time and space and involves more than just the human body (Latour 1993). As Laurier (2011) argues, mobility is not one thing. Rather, it is a collection of questions, ideas, perspectives that consider more than the sedentary and can include time, space, performance, the sensuous, the haptic and the affective. Whilst current methods may focus or prioritize one kind of mobility over another, this belies the complexity of such movement (see Büscher and Urry 2009). As Law and Urry (2004: 403–404) suggest, conventional methods tend to be inadequate for the fleeting, the distributed, the multiple, the non-causal and complex. They go on to say that current methods tend not to deal well with the sensory, the emotional, the spiritual and the kinaesthetic. Thus, the challenge for researchers is not what methods to use but how those methods engage with their respondents and their surrounds. How is their movement, and their stasis encountered, 'captured' and analysed and shared with a wider audience?

Büscher and Urry (2009) suggest two ways to engage with these questions. The first is to follow – or be 'with' – the research participants. The second, they suggest, is that by being involved in this movement (or lack of movement), so the researcher becomes embedded in the 'social organisation of "moves"' (Büscher and Urry 2009: 103). Thus, mobile methods allow researchers to move away from an intense or deep engagement with a single site, person or 'thing' and instead allows us to analyse 'several sites at once (multisite ethnography)' or to undertake 'ethnography that moves along with, or besides, the object of research (mobile ethnography)' (Cresswell 2012: 647). The need for doing research 'with' rather than 'on' people is addressed within King's research (Chapter 6). Within her study mobile methods make an important contribution as it acknowledges young people's ability to be active agents in their own right and by doing so it increases our understanding of the complexities of their everyday lives (King, Chapter 6). The case of Bell's (Chapter 2) participation in gatherings of travelling artists or Terranova-Webb's (2010) participation in a travelling circus constitute other examples of taking on research 'with' rather than 'on' respondents. The importance of being a part of the community that you are studying is highlighted within Lean's (Chapter 7) use of a webpage to attract respondents. Through photos from his own travels, he was able to show that he was a part of the 'travel community' and so he and his research was someone/something to 'trust' rather than being considered a scam.

Sideri's (Chapter 8: 116) ethnographical research is also an experience within the field as she argues that '[we] do not follow the sites, but space-time lived experiences and how our mobility takes part in or generates them'. She suggests that as researcher, we do not stand on the outside and simply study different lifestyles, but instead we should participate, perform and so merge into these lifestyles. She is not just reporting information about mobile life, she also generates imaginative journeys (through her photos, videos, information and memorabilia), for those who cannot be mobile. Through her three examples she forms an ethnography of lifestyle mobilities. Therefore, in this instance, the researcher, through ethnographical techniques, illustrates a wider sense of lifestyle and (im)mobility that can incorporate the past, and combine it with the present and the imagined future.

The future of lifestyle mobility?

Nonetheless, even as this volume suggests the need to further contextualize lifestyle mobilities, so we also need to ask questions that recognize that lifestyles of mobility are situated in changing socio-cultural, economic, technological and environmental contexts. As the economic crises in some Western countries continue, so questions begin to surface as to whether such crises will impact and disrupt the fluidity of forms of lifestyle mobility. At the same time, when or how will emergent forms of lifestyle mobility be created in the rise in power of other nations and populaces? Moreover, much of what we now see as mobility relies on carbon-dependent fuel. How will these forms of lifestyle mobility change and react as the world begins to deal with shortages in these types of fuel and so as society begins to deal with issues of 'peak oil' (see Urry 2010)? In what ways will our carbon-dependent (and often privileged) mobilities be impacted by future alternative transport systems that mean less mobility – or slower mobility? Already, there is literature on slower forms of travel – such as the use of container ships (Symes 2012; Szarycz 2008); can we expect more of this type of travel? Or, as O'Regan's chapter (3) suggests, will hitchhiking (again) gain social acceptance and allow us to practice an alternative, if sometimes more fractured, form of mobility? We can ask these questions, but as Barr and Prillwitz (Chapter 15) suggest, perceptions may first need to change. As they argue, whilst air travel increasingly features in current debates about climate change, people's behaviour towards travel has not necessarily changed. Whilst they may perform 'environmentally friendly' behaviours at home, their travel and mobility behaviours (whether for work, leisure or lifestyle) may reflect a different set of values or they may find reasons why they no longer have to adhere to the same environmental values they adopt in their day to day lives (see also Cohen, Higham and Reis 2013). Thus we need to consider if other/different types of sustainable lifestyle mobilities will surface to allow the seemingly growing numbers of global, transnational peoples to continue their ways of life and so their lifestyles? These concerns also resonate within Mabon's research (Chapter 16). He recommends we look at sports such as rally driving where participants and audiences may be more cynical or resistant to environmental/sustainable thinking. Through his research, he suggests that in understanding how mobility fits within people's lifestyles, so we may be able to shift perceptions and play a crucial role in moving towards a more sustainable mobility future for such sports.

With patterns of lifestyle mobility often only accessible to the relatively privileged, further questions emerge as to whether the power asymmetries within lifestyle mobility warrant further inquiry. Future research may thus adopt a social class perspective and take the question further of 'who' is able to access lifestyle mobilities. Linked to this issue of exclusion, is the question of how the characteristics of lifestyle mobility will change as available technologies continue to advance. Already Macheroni's (2007) work has suggested that communities are now mobile and existing on- and off-line with the significance of time and space being, necessarily, reconfigured. Will reconfigurations make lifestyle mobility more accessible to wider populations and contribute further to the deterritorialization of place?

In asking these questions and in aiming to find a space/place in which to problematize the intersections of travel, leisure and migration through the lens of lifestyle mobilities, so we hope to have opened a fresh interdisciplinary route with which to further interrogate the grey zone between temporary mobility and permanent migration, where a range of social phenomena are challenging and circumventing conventional understandings of travel and migration and subsuming binaries of home/away, here/there and work/leisure.

References

Büscher, M. and Urry, J. 2009. Mobile methods and the empirical. *European Journal of Social Theory*, 12(1), 99–116.

Cohen, S.A., Duncan, T. and Thulemark, M. 2013. Lifestyle mobilities: the crossroads of travel, leisure and migration. *Mobilities*, DOI: 10.1080/17450 101.2013.826481.

Cohen, S.A., Higham, J.E.S. and Reis, C.T. 2013. Sociological barriers to developing sustainable discretionary air travel behaviour. *Journal of Sustainable Tourism*, DOI: 10.1080/09669582.2013.809092.

Cresswell, T. 2010. Towards a politics of mobility. *Environment and Planning D: Society and Space*, 28(1), 17–31.

Cresswell, T. 2012. Mobilities II: Still. *Progress in Human Geography*, 36(5), 645–653.

Cresswell, T. and Merriman, P. 2011. Introduction: Geographies of Mobilities – Practices, Spaces, Subjects, in *Geographies of Mobilities – Practices, Spaces, Subjects*, edited by T. Cresswell and P. Merriman. Farnham: Ashgate, 1–19.

Germann Molz, J. 2008. Global abode: home and mobility in narratives of round-the-world travel. *Space and Culture*, 11(4), 325–342.

Latour, B. 1993. *We Have Never Been Modern.* Harlow: Prentice Hall/Harvester Wheatsheaf.

Laurier. E. 2001. Why people say where they are during mobile phone calls. *Environment and Planning D: Society and Space*, 19(4), 485–594.

Law, J. and Urry, J. 2004. Enacting the social. *Economy and Society*, 33(3), 390–410.

McIntyre, N. 2009. Re-thinking amenity migration: integrating mobility, lifestyle and social-ecological systems. *Die Erde*, 140(3), 229–250.

Pollock, D.C. and Van Reken, R.E. 2009. *Third Culture Kids: Growing Up Among Worlds*. Boston: Nicholas Brearley Publishing.

Symes, C. 2012. All at sea: an auto-ethnography of a slowed community, on a container ship. *Annals of Leisure Research*, 15(1), 55–68.

Szarycz, G., 2008. Cruising, freighter-style: a phenomological exploration of tourist recollections of a passenger freighter travel experience. *International Journal of Tourism Research*, 10(3), 259–269.

Terranova-Webb, A. 2010. Getting Down the Road: Understanding Stable Mobility in an American Circus. Unpublished PhD Thesis, Milton Keynes: Open University.

Urry, J. 2010. Consuming the planet to excess. *Theory, Culture and Society*, 27(2–3), 191–212.

Vannini, P. 2009. *The Cultures of Alternative Mobilities. Routes Less Travelled.* Farnham: Ashgate.

Index

For Product Safety Concerns and Information please contact our
EU representative GPSR@taylorandfrancis.com Taylor & Francis
Verlag GmbH, Kaufingerstraße 24, 80331 München, Germany